A SHORT HISTORY OF TOMB-RAIDING

Come to me, that I might take you to the place where this scroll is, since it was Thoth who wrote it with his own hand . . . and if you read it, you will enchant heaven, the earth, the underworld, the mountains and the seas.

– 'THE ROMANCE OF SETNA AND THE MUMMIES', *c.* 300 BC

A SHORT HISTORY OF TOMB-RAIDING

The Epic Hunt for Egypt's Treasures

MARIA GOLIA

REAKTION BOOKS

*To the treasured memory of my aunts
Sophie Rafalowska Rusnak (5 August 1908–28 November 1992)
and Loretta Rafalowska Pogorzelski (12 February 1913–6 October 1996).*

Published by
Reaktion Books Ltd
Unit 32, Waterside
44–48 Wharf Road
London N1 7UX, UK

www.reaktionbooks.co.uk

First published 2022
Copyright © Maria Golia 2022

All rights reserved

No part of this publication may be reproduced, stored in a retrieval system or transmitted, in any form or by any means, electronic, mechanical, photocopying, recording or otherwise, without the prior permission of the publishers

Printed and bound in Great Britain by TJ Books Ltd, Padstow, Cornwall

A catalogue record for this book is available from the British Library

ISBN 978 1 78914 629 5

CONTENTS

INTRODUCTION *7*

ONE NEVER SAY DIE *13*

TWO GRAVE MATTERS *49*

THREE THE SEEKERS *105*

FOUR DEN OF THEBES *161*

FIVE A HOUSE OF MANY STORIES *227*

EPILOGUE: WONDERING *263*

CHRONOLOGY *267*
REFERENCES *269*
BIBLIOGRAPHY *297*
ACKNOWLEDGEMENTS *298*
PHOTO ACKNOWLEDGEMENTS *299*
INDEX *301*

Map of Egypt and Arabia Petraea by J. Rapkin, 1851, with vignettes by J. Marchant showing the Mosque of the Sultan Hassan, Alexandria, the Temple of Karnac and the Great Sphinx and Pyramids at Giza.

INTRODUCTION

Egyptologists warn against the tendency to compare the ancients with ourselves; their mindsets and perspectives, some say, are alien. Whatever resemblance we may find between past and present societies is deceptive, and only by 'thinking away modernity', suggests one historian, might we see them clearly.[1] Even supposing it were possible to subtract context from the way one thinks, didn't every era consider itself 'modern', the latest, greatest iteration of humanity, looking down on the past, even while standing on its shoulders? It has been said that when it comes to comprehending distant ancestors, contrast matters more than comparison, because differences are what define us; yet they only exist in relation to similarity. Yes, societies are different now from how they were 3,000 or three hundred years ago, thanks to industrialization, urbanization, transport and communication technologies that have divorced us from nature and each other. But are we so very different in terms of our desires and manoeuvres to fulfil them?

When it comes to tomb-raiding, or treasure hunting as a more general term, the motivations are the same today as they were in yesteryear. If several millennia's worth of history is anything to go by, need and greed are human constants, along with the twin urges to establish order and overturn it, all illumined by that ineluctable mover called hope. The Egyptologist Barry Kemp remarked that 'the ways of thinking we encounter in ancient sources are still with us . . . collectively we may call them "basic thought".'[2] This brief survey of treasure hunting in Egypt describes the varied social contexts and striking continuities surrounding the practice throughout time.

With 7,000 years of documented history, Egypt offers a long view of the human endeavour; the entire Christian era could be swallowed up in its pre-dynastic period (5000–3000 BC). In the fourteenth century BC, when Thutmosis IV decided to free the Sphinx from encroaching sands, it had been around for a millennium; monuments we consider ancient were already old back then. The most characteristic monument the ancients left us, aside from temples, were the tombs built by the elite since the start of recorded Egyptian history. Their architecture evolved along with their costly contents, including the deceased's mummy, all necessary for transiting to the afterlife. Royal tombs were essentially defence structures designed to shield wealth and advertise status, a contradictory conceit that (un)sealed their fate. Chapter One, 'Never Say Die', explains why so much wealth was buried in the first place, the ingenious precautions taken to secure it and the raiders' perseverance in overcoming them.

Tomb-raiding was a heinous crime, a violation of societal and sacred norms, but not everyone felt that way. 'This sarcophagus is ours; it belonged to our great men,' claimed a convicted raider in a court deposition in 1100 BC: 'we were hungry [and] set out . . . to search for this piece of bread so as to profit from it.' More than mere theft, raiding was rebellion. During the periodic turmoil resulting from famine, civil war or invasion, tombs were more vulnerable, the people needier and raiders more audacious. Royal burials were plundered throughout antiquity's hard times, not just by the poor but by the men in charge of protecting them. Priests, generals and pharaohs despoiled ancestral graves to pad their coffers, in cahoots with necropolis police and the royal tomb builders. Against a backdrop of institutionalized theft, the spectacle of power emanating from the temples and palaces of Memphis and Thebes was reduced to empty theatrics. Chapter Two, 'Grave Matters', describes the fallout of a belief system based on the accumulation of dead capital, and how the New Kingdom, the apex of pharaonic civilization, was laid low by systemic corruption.

Egypt's buried treasures multiplied throughout later antiquity as the occupying Greeks and Romans followed traditions involving elaborate funerary equipment. When the Arabs took Egypt in the seventh century AD, they hit the jackpot. Aside from fertile Nile-fed land farmed to nourish their expanding empire, the earth surrendered pots of gold. The past was mined like a mineral resource by rugged professionals called 'seekers', who paid a tax in exchange for the licence to dig. Like wildcatting (the search for oil in unproven areas), treasure hunting was a contest with the dumb ground, involving blood, sweat, luck and risks both physical and financial, odds that were weighed against the potential rewards and considered beatable. But what distinguished the seeker's profession from similar profit-driven activities was its occult dimension. Legend held that tombs were protected by lethal spells and supernatural entities installed by the ancients; disarming them was a job for the magicians on the seeker's payroll, along with astrologers and geomancers who claimed the ability to pinpoint treasure locations.

In addition to rock-hewn tombs crammed with precious oddities, Egypt came furnished with peerless above-ground buildings seemingly made by giants, whose purpose and construction provoked both serious study and wild speculation. Consider the impression the monuments must have made on those who experienced them without the intermediary of photographs or illustrations, having heard stories but never seen anything like them. Under Arab rule, magic, religion, science and metaphysics were inextricably bound up with awe of the unknown and an insatiable appetite for knowing. Medieval Egypt was populated with connoisseurs of the marvellous, keen to unlock the past's secrets and experience the frisson of breaching the boundary between the material and metaphysical worlds. Treasure hunting promised this and more. Amateurs of every background tried their hand, from the poor fighting to survive cycles of plague and famine to the wealthy who hunted for entertainment and the scammers who preyed on both. How-to manuals were but a part of the literary corpus treasure hunting generated at a time when *The Thousand and One Nights* were less fantastical tales than heightened versions of current events. Chapter Three, 'The Seekers', tracks the coalescence of fact and fiction into the foundational myths of treasure hunting.

Egyptians have always mined their past to feed their present. The founder of Egypt's last ruling dynasty, Mohammed Ali (r. 1805–48), continued the tradition of recycling ancient wealth to fund national development, using antiquities as bargaining chips in exchange for Western technologies. Steamships facilitated travel, and thanks to photography the land of 'pharaoh the oppressor' leapt from the pages of the Bible into the popular imagination. Western museum agents and private collectors treated the country's treasure-strewn necropoli like shopping malls, gathering trophies to show off at home. Whereas tomb raiders once stole to enrich themselves and, later, to enrich the state, by the nineteenth century they were enriching the world, answering the demand for all things Egyptian. Chapter Four, 'Den of Thebes', documents a tomb-raiding clan headquartered in the Theban necropolis, and how they negotiated the forces gathering around them. These included their arch-rivals, the foreign officials placed in charge of antiquities, who were anxious to curtail or, failing that, to co-opt the raiders' discoveries, among them the most sensational find in the annals of treasure hunting, the Royal Cache.

Egypt's modernization relied on forced labour, crippling taxes and foreign financiers, exploitative tactics that ignited an army revolt in 1881 and ended with the British occupation. The popular uprising of 1919 failed to oust the country's overlords and it wasn't until the Free Officers Revolution of 1952 that Egypt finally rid itself of its monarchy and the British to boot. The new Egypt dealt with the old one expediently. In the 1960s it traded the annual Nile flood that informed its very being for electricity and other production-orientated benefits of the Aswan High Dam. Temples that might have finished beneath the dam's reservoir were salvaged in a Herculean international effort accompanied by a prolonged media extravaganza. President Gamal Abdel Nasser seized the opportunity to instate Egypt's monuments as icons of an influential, self-reliant nation while opening the floodgates to mass tourism. Related development transfigured the nation, with the needs of short-term, foreign guests taking precedence over those of average citizens.

Throughout time, when deprivation grew unbearable, Egyptians sought relief underground. In 2008, as the repercussions of the global financial crisis struck Cairo and its rigid autocracy began to crack, houses collapsed because people were tunnelling beneath them for treasure. Chapter Five, 'A House of Many Stories', is a first-person account of the sociopolitical tensions in the years surrounding Egypt's uprising of 2011 and the labours of latter-day raiders, highlighting the historic continuities present in the modern version of an age-old pursuit. Satellite imagery and social media were added to the kit, but the motivations and social dynamics behind tomb-raiding remain unchanged. It's hard to think of a country whose past has proved as enduringly lucrative as Egypt's. So great were its treasures and so compelling the narratives surrounding them that even if every last artefact had been conclusively unearthed, the search would carry on for generations.

There's a reason why treasure-related stories have thrived throughout the ages, from ancient tales of secret scrolls bestowing riches on the daring to novels, films and computer games along the same lines. The hunt for treasure is the quest for an ideal self, who we might be if we won the lottery, if only we could agree on what winning really meant. In these pages taken from Egypt's past, readers will recognize the foibles of today's politicians, demagogues, entrepreneurs and con artists, the consequences of yearning and gullibility, and the cycles of compliance and dissent in the face of injustice; in short, the set-pieces in humanity's recurring dream of civilization. Egypt's history is full of clues to that most subtle of treasures: a sense of who we were and have become, and of who we have always been. 'History is the record of the struggle between two polarities of mind,' wrote Barry Kemp, 'the rise and fall of civilization are present in each one of us.'[3]

Anubis, from the Tomb of Nebenmaat (TT219), 19th dynasty, Deir al-Medina, 2019 photograph. The yellow paint (appearing here in grey) is made from goethite, a locally available oxide ore composed of quartz grains with inclusions of iron and titanium, which was used as a substitute for gold dust.

ONE

NEVER SAY DIE

A pilot who sees into the distance,
will not let his ship capsize.[1]
– *INSTRUCTION OF AMENEMOPE* (c. 1300–1075 BC)

Tomb-raiding would not have begun had tombs contained nothing worth stealing. So why was so much treasure buried to begin with? The short answer is that religious tradition amounting to sacred law demanded it. Although the ancient Egyptians' emphasis on tombs and mummies suggests an obsession with death, the opposite was true: they loved life and intended it to go on forever. Heaven was conceived as a matter of picking up where you left off, albeit under improved conditions. To ensure an afterlife of ease and plenty, people figured they needed the same things they'd always enjoyed, starting with a body. They buried their entire household: furniture, linens and utensils, food and drink. They took board games, musical instruments, even mummified pets, everything they liked and could afford. The tomb was not a final resting place so much as a combination launch-pad and shipping container for that longest of journeys.

The weakness of such a system was obvious even to the ancients: while poor people's burials usually remained untouched, rich ones were systematically plundered. Yet for millennia they persisted in the belief that significant wealth and effort must be invested in the grave. Understanding the logic behind burial traditions and what tomb raiders risked in flouting them requires a brief excursion through a religious system whose influence lasted 3,000 years.[2] Christianity and Judaism will have to hang on for another millennium to catch up with it; Islam will have to tack six hundred years on to that. For ideological traditions to become lasting articles of faith they must be grounded in great truths. To the ancient Egyptians the greatest truth was all around them. They called it *maat*, or immanent order, the regulator of the stars in the heavens, the seasons on earth and ideally of a good and just society.

The Egyptians may appear to us a whimsical and esoteric people, with their high priests and funerary rites, their magic spells and animal-headed gods. But the ideology that arose in the Early Dynastic Period (beginning around 3000 BC) reflected a profound pragmatism rooted in the land and the river that ran through it. If social and religious systems revolved around a conviction that there was life after death, it was based on the observable phenomenon of renewal. The sun vanished each day only to appear the next. The stars moved predictably across the sky and the seasons maintained an orderly progression. What we call civilization connotes a distancing from nature, the building of cities and invention of technologies that bend nature to our needs. The Egyptians, whose civilization achieved outstanding longevity, chose instead to recognize nature's power and patterns. In this desert environment, the proper stewardship of land and water was so highly valued that the ancients' Book of the Dead, a guide for entering the afterlife, calls for the deceased to declare: 'I have not diminished the palm . . . [or] encroached on fields. I have not driven herds from their fodder . . . I have not stopped the flow of water at its seasons; I have not built a dam against flowing water.'[3]

The yearly calendar officially began with the Nile flood, which visited the parched earth in summer (*akhet*; June to September) when it was needed most, its waters reaching far enough inland to challenge the desert. The growing season (*peret*; October to February) started when the flood withdrew, having deposited a carpet of alluvial silt so rich and black it gave the nation its name: *Kemet*, 'the black land'. The harvest (*shemu*) corresponded with spring, bringing the promise of prosperity throughout another year, until the floods returned and the cycle repeated. Egypt was not as arid 5,000 years ago as it is today but it was still predominantly desert. The Nile was understood as a godsend, its presence an affirmation of divine will. The land flanking the river was carpeted with fields, and the annual floods more or less guaranteed at least one big crop of grain, in addition to pulse, roots, vegetables and fodder enough for a variety of domesticated animals.

Egypt's population was massive by ancient standards, reaching around 4 or 5 million in the New Kingdom (1549–1069 BC). The nation developed in relative isolation, able to meet its own needs, protected to the west and south by difficult-to-cross desert, and to the north and east by open sea. The ancients considered this circumscribed territory ideal, preferable to any other. The gods had made it that way, so, rather than try to improve things, they endeavoured to maintain the status quo. Conservative to a fault, once they settled on a ritual or a tradition, whether farming and irrigation methods or a style of burial, the Egyptians stuck to it literally for ages. Innovations might come along, but they rarely replaced original ideas and were merely added on as extensions of an already familiar concept; change was presented as continuity.

Egyptian beliefs were informed by a love of order and stability alongside an intimate rapport with their surroundings, a connection to the land that is hard for us to imagine. This is partly because Egypt was a nation of farmers. But the Egyptian religion, like other so-called primitive belief systems, was also an acknowledgement of the benefits they accrued from their environment. There are few places left on earth, perhaps the swamps of South Sudan's Sudd, or the wetlands of Lake Victoria, that provide a hint of what parts of Egypt were like in antiquity. Even today along the Nile in Upper Egypt, dawn brings a cacophony of birdsong so raucous and insistent that one can almost imagine being part of a world seething with life and placed there to bear witness to nature's endlessly inventive bounty. The river roiled with fish. The Nile Delta was a marshland, a maze of dense papyrus groves with tall, slender stalks and feathery fan-like tips, a favourite resting place for the migratory birds that came twice annually in their millions, and were hunted with nets strung up between the 5-metre-high (16 ft) papyri.

Yet then as now, at an hour's walk from the river, this verdant, animated realm came to an abrupt halt. The desert was everywhere at the corner of one's eye: vast, empty and silent, the negation of life, nature at its most fiercely indifferent. No wonder the ancient religion expressed itself in dualities; the contrasting realities of life and death are etched in Egypt's topography. The Nile floods, however reliable, could be capricious. Too little or too much water spelled disaster. Nature's order encompassed an element of disruptive chaos that needed to be held in check. That's where the wise rule of kings and close attention to ritual came in. Death, the ultimate disruption, could only be negotiated by unwavering belief in a divinely ordained way of life. In the sun's ferocity and the Nile's surging flood, the ancients saw the power nature wielded, and they wanted to keep it onside. Order meant control, as expressed in the strictly observed canons of their religious art, the design of their monuments and their rigorous devotion to bureaucracy.

According to an Egyptian creation myth, life began on an islet that rose from primordial waters. Both writing and religious architecture embodied this cosmology. The ceilings of Egyptian temples represented a star-studded heaven, the pillars mimicked papyrus stalks, the floor was the fertile mound from which life emerged. The pylons at the temple's entrance were shaped like the hieroglyph for horizon, and the whole edifice, like the horizon, was the nexus of heaven and earth, divine and mortal, order and chaos. The temple held these polarities together, captured in stone. So long as the rites honouring the gods were enacted, order held sway and harmony and balance were maintained. The ancients accepted that even the gods must one day die, returning the world to its chaotic origins, but the observance of sacred ritual could forestall that time indefinitely. Yet priests and kings were not alone in preserving *maat*; everyone contributed to it through right conduct, that is, adherence to law and tradition. *Maat* was conceived as reciprocal: you get as good as you give.

Lest the demands of order prove too restrictive, Egyptians marked the march of the seasons with rituals and celebrations lasting up to 24 days. If you count full-moon festivities and the two-to-three-day weekends that punctuated the ten-day work week, Egyptians could look forward to ample time off for good behaviour. People feasted and danced, drank beer and wine, wore their finery and flowers, and the afterlife was understood as more of the same sort of party in a perfect Egypt. Heaven was associated with the west, where the sun set; it was 'the fields of reeds' or 'field of offerings', a place where crops grew to gigantic proportions, and magical helpers (*ushabti* or 'answerers') did most of the work, where everyone would 'eat of that wheat and barley and his limbs be nourished by it, and his body be like the bodies of the gods'.[4] Pharaohs would dwell in an upscale heaven, cruising nightly across the sky with fellow gods in a solar boat, but for everyone else, paradise was a mirror image of ordinary life minus sickness and conflict, calamity and hardship.

'Make your dwelling place in the Necropolis. Perfect your place in the west. The dwelling place of death is for life,' said the Old Kingdom sage Hardjedef. If his advice sounds like a sales pitch for a holiday home, it's because the Egyptians envisioned heaven as an extended holiday. 'Little is in life on earth,' admonished another wise man, 'eternity is in the Necropolis.'[5] Death, like a long and fruitful retirement, required a lifetime of planning and was consequently not taboo as it was in Western culture. To dream

Music and dancing, relief from the Tomb of Nenkheftka, Saqqara, 5th dynasty, the Egyptian Museum, Cairo.

oneself dead, according to ancient interpretations, was a good omen, a sign that a long life awaited the dreamer. Dying was also not an abstract topic of philosophical debate but a singularly reliable event of which the elaborate process of preparing one's tomb might serve as a constant reminder.

From an ideological point of view the price of admission to paradise was affordable – a light heart: the deceased's had to balance with a feather symbolizing *maat* when weighed on a cosmic scale. Meeting the other conditions was more complicated. Most graves dating to the pre-dynastic period were little more than shallow pits containing the body lying on its side in a fetal position, with a few possessions in clay jars placed beside it. At that time Egypt was still a series of farming communities, with several larger settlements or chiefdoms in the north and south. But by the first dynasty, when the country was unified under one ruler, some people were wealthy enough to envision an afterlife with all the furnishings, adornments and comforts to which they'd grown accustomed, the goods irresistible to thieves.

Early tombs of the ruling class consisted of a boxy mud-brick building (*mastaba*) that served primarily as a warehouse for afterlife supplies. A first-dynasty tomb belonging to Queen Neithhotep from Nagada in Upper Egypt had twenty above-ground rooms, including the burial chamber in the middle. A slightly later tomb in Saqqara had 27 storerooms on the ground level, but now the burial chamber and four more storage rooms were sunken, like a basement, a practice that became standard. Two tombs in Saqqara had 45 storerooms, as full of household items as a department store, and despite their thick mud-brick walls and sturdy roofs, almost as accessible to thieves. Around the middle of the first dynasty (3050–2815 BC) all the storerooms were moved underground.[6] During the second dynasty (2813–2663 BC), the *mastaba* became a solid brick box or else was filled with rubble to thwart theft, but with substructures so spacious and well-equipped they amounted to a fully furnished bunker.[7] The ancients literally placed stock in eternity, blurring the line between the material and the metaphysical.

The item most essential to the deceased's continued existence was a body, a requirement underlined by the myth of Osiris, one of the four children of Earth god Geb and Nut, goddess of the sky. Osiris was married to his sister Isis, and his sister Nephthys was the wife of his brother Seth. Geb gave Osiris dominion over earth, and a jealous Seth plotted to take it for himself. He threw a party and in the midst of the revelry brought out a fancy coffin, promising to give it to whomever it most perfectly fitted. Everyone tried it on for size, but when the unwitting Osiris was inside, Seth, the original killjoy, trapped him there, chopped his body into pieces and scattered them around the country. Isis laboriously gathered her husband's parts (except his penis, which was eaten by a fish) and Anubis, jackal-headed deity of burials, reassembled and bound Osiris in cloth wrappings. Through Isis' intercession and with the help of the almighty sun god, Ra, Osiris was resurrected as ruler of the underworld. As the prototypical mummy, he represents the will to pull oneself together to not only survive death but to be favourably and forever transformed by it, the concept behind mummification.

Although it was integral to their burial customs, the Egyptians, who recorded everything, were reticent on the topic of mummification; embalming secrets were passed from father to son. Most of what we know about the process is derived from the account of Herodotus (who visited Egypt *c.* 460–455 BC) along with modern analyses of mummies and of the embalming materials found buried in necropoli. Herodotus outlined three mummification techniques, one for the very rich, another for the well-to-do and a third for the somewhat less fortunate. 'The most perfect' technique involved evisceration (a practice that began during the Old Kingdom) via an incision on the flank and the brain's removal via the left nostril with a hook (a practice dating to the Middle Kingdom). The resulting cavities were washed with palm wine, followed by an infusion of herbs, and filled with linen, myrrh and other aromatics. The corpse was sewn up and covered in natron for forty days, after which it was washed, wrapped in linen strips and presumably left to air, the total process lasting seventy days. Natron, a desiccant with defatting properties that the ancients called 'divine salt', was readily available in Lower Egypt. The embalming tables were spread with piles of it and the corpse placed on top and covered with more. As it absorbed the bodily fluids, the natron had to be changed repeatedly.[8] Toes and fingers, apt to fall off in the drying process, were secured with string. Royal phalluses were sometimes bound to the inner thigh for preservation and, in the case of Tutankhamun, wrapped upright on the mummy in a permanent erection.[9]

Rather than surgically removing the intestines, the more affordable second technique Herodotus mentions (introduced in the Middle Kingdom) made use of juniper oil injected into the anus, which, when drained, 'brings the viscera with it in a liquid state'.[10] The body was then treated with natron. According to Herodotus, those travelling economy kept their intestines, which were rinsed with water before their bodies were dried in natron. Not everyone could afford even the most rudimentary mummification; for preservation, commoners relied on a shroud or a few bandages and a long bake in the hot desert sand. Embalming ingredients were costly, including fir and cedar resins from the Levant, and locally produced lettuce and castor oils that served to deodorize the corpse and render it pliant for wrapping in linen bandages. These too constituted a significant expense, since the wrappings consisted of strips 1–3 centimetres (⅜–1¼ in.) wide tied together into lengths that could exceed 1 kilometre (½ mi.). The mummy of an early Middle Kingdom nobleman named Wah used 325 metres (1,060 ft) of linen. Some of it was stained with the tarry fingerprints of the embalming priest, and a mouse, a cricket and a lizard were accidentally swept up in the course of the wrapping.[11]

Concern for the appearance of the deceased was evident as early as the pre-dynastic Naqada II Period (3150–3000 BC), when mummies were given hair extensions and toupees. During the Old Kingdom, wrappings were sometimes sculpted to show facial and body contours, including genitalia. Some wrappings were coated with plaster that was itself modelled and painted to represent the deceased, transforming 'the body into an image of itself'.[12]

Never Say Die

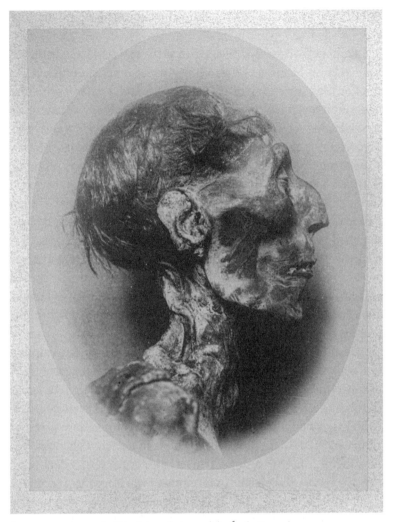

Ramses II unwrapped, 1889, Cairo, photograph by Émile Brugsch.

During the New Kingdom more expert and pronounced cosmetic attentions amounted to a total makeover of the deceased, using facial and body contouring (by means of sawdust or cloth stuffing), skin paint and cosmetics. More a matter of perfecting than preserving the body, mummification made it the medium for a statue-like idealization, sealed in resin, tightly wrapped, more resplendent and lasting than and therefore superior to the body itself, mirroring the divine state the deceased would acquire through death.[13]

Ramses II's nose was filled with seeds and reinforced with an animal bone. Ramses IV had onions inserted beneath his eyelids to offer the impression of closed eyes, though stones were more commonly used for that purpose. Body contouring was accomplished using combinations of resin, linen, mud, sawdust and sand. Sometimes faces were filled too enthusiastically and later burst. The mummified wife of a 21st-dynasty high priest was plumped with sawdust bound in the linen wrappings. Her face was packed through the mouth, and she was given eyebrows made of human hair to replace those lost in the natron treatment. An elderly woman who had been bedridden prior to her death had bedsores on her back carefully patched with gazelle hide.[14] A passage from a funerary text included in burials expressed the timeless wish for renewal embodied in the mummification process: 'You live again, you revive always; you have become young again. You are young again and forever.'

Despite many a no doubt gooey initial failure, the embalming arts achieved a high standard, with methods and materials differing over time according to current trends and availability. Whereas the organs were previously dried in natron and buried in separate containers, embalmers of the 21st dynasty simply wrapped and returned them to the torso, like giblets in a frozen chicken. The most significant shift occurred in the Late Period when a dark resin (often erroneously referred to as bitumen) was introduced to encase the body, a technique that did not preserve the flesh but greatly expedited mummification.[15] Maggots found embedded in the resins used to fill the torso cavity of some mummies suggest that the corpses had decomposed while awaiting treatment. Mummies containing the bones of more than one individual likewise suggest hasty production-line embalming resulting from higher demand. Greco-Roman period burials consisted of communal crypts with mummies packed floor to ceiling. Embalmers were apparently numerous and influential enough to form their own guilds, but their profession had lost its mystic sheen. Known as 'slitters and curers', their title was the same as that of the people who made a living salting fish.[16] Embalmment standards may have shifted but the mummy's appearance remained paramount. Attention was increasingly devoted to wrappings; Greco-Roman mummies had the most intricate ones, diamond-shaped patterns with gilded studs. Never in human history has the body's presentation held such a prominent, pervasive place in a spiritual corpus.

The preoccupation with looking one's best for the afterlife reflected the ancients' love of beauty and grooming while alive. Warm weather heightens awareness of the body; the Egyptians shaved their heads to stay cool and were meticulous in their toilet, using deodorizing ointments and a toothpaste applied with a frayed twig. Men went about bare-chested in wraparound skirts, while women wore tube dresses likewise made of a fine, semi-transparent linen, sometimes with a central strap leaving the breasts uncovered, sometimes with shoulder straps that lightly concealed them. The cosmetic arts were highly developed and, then as now, the wealthy had recourse to special products. Anyone who has lived in a dry climate can appreciate the value they placed on unguents for the face, hair and body, which were sometimes stored in gold and silver or alabaster jars.

They loved perfumes, which, beyond a pleasurable fragrance, were concocted to affect the senses in subtler ways. A word for perfume, *senetjer*, means 'to render divine'. Plutarch wrote that a scent called *kyphi* 'purifies and polishes like a mirror the faculty which is imaginative and receptive to dreams'. Perfume was often mixed with wax and shaped into a cone that was placed atop the bewigged head, where it melted gradually, drenching the body in scent. Wigs were considered erotic: 'Don your wig and let us spend a happy hour' was an expression used to invite a woman to bed.[17] The wealthy wore elaborately styled ones of (mostly black) human hair, sometimes woven with gold strands and jewels, while the poor coiffed themselves with tufts of wool. Both sexes used eyeliners concocted from pigments like powdered green malachite and black galena, which helped deflect the sun's glare. People were so fond of perfumes, wigs and cosmetics that they literally wouldn't be caught dead without them and plenty of these costly accessories were taken to their tombs.

Next to the mummy, food and drink were the most essential features of the burial. The mummy was the meeting point for the individual's *ka* (his or her animating force or vitality) and *ba* (the spirit, or essence), which, like living bodies, needed nourishment for survival. In case the mummy was destroyed, the tomb contained a sealed room (*serdab*) with a *ka* statue resembling the deceased that could act as the body's double and receive the necessary offerings. These came at first in the form of actual meals laid out like picnics before the tomb was sealed. The menu from an Old Kingdom tomb found in Saqqara included bread, wine, porridge from ground barley, a cooked fish, pigeon stew, a cooked quail, two cooked kidneys, ribs and legs of beef, and for dessert, stewed fruit, fresh *nabaq* (a local crab-apple) and small cakes with honey and cheese.[18] So long as this feast remained untouched in the tomb it could be enjoyed forever. Tombs were also stocked with quantities of amphorae filled with liquid refreshment, both wine and the soupy, mildly alcoholic beer that was a staple of the ancient diet.[19] Much of our understanding of early dynastic administration comes from the clay plugs of these vessels, which were inscribed with data related to the reign, date and place of their origin.

The Egyptians were the prototypal bureaucrats, committed to documenting the minutest transaction. Without the diligent handling of people, goods and resources at which they proved so adept there would be no pyramids or temples, or rock-cut tombs. Food was a key component of the burial because it held particular significance in life; aside from building, the production and distribution of foodstuffs was the principal occupation of the people and the state. The ability to feed a growing population while storing surplus food determined Egypt's strength as a nation. Yet drought and famine were not so rare as to ever be forgotten, and neither was their destabilizing effect on society underestimated by those who held and wished to maintain power. Bulk provisions, like those stored in many Old Kingdom tombs, provided additional insurance that the dead and their households would not go hungry. Victual

Never Say Die

mummies offered another form of lasting nourishment: joints of beef or mutton and whole geese, duck and pigeons preserved in salt and resin-coated bandages. New Kingdom pharaoh Tutankhamun was buried with forty cases of victual mummies. The fowl were prepared for cooking before wrapping, with the heads, wing tips and feet removed; in some cases the bird was soaked in oil, ready to roast.[20] But even these forms of food might not last an eternity.

An above-ground portion of the tomb served as an offering chapel where priests and family members could bring ceremonial meals. Royals and the wealthy bequeathed a piece of land whose proceeds would cover the costs of the ongoing rituals and food delivery service. Feeding the dead was an obligation of the living, who ate and drank the offerings once they were dedicated, but it was understood that proper services would not go on forever. Just as a *ka* statue bearing the deceased's name could double for a missing mummy, so the walls of the tomb were carved with reliefs or

Bewigged daughter of Ramose, relief in funerary chapel of Ramose, Theban Necropolis, 1350 BC.

25

Offerers, relief from the temple at Dendera, Upper Egypt. The temple complex dates from the period between Dynasty XXX (380–343 BC) and the Roman Period (30 BC–AD 395).

covered in paintings showing food and drink in various stages of preparation that could serve as a replacement for the real thing. Offering tables were carved with images of nutriment, another means of ensuring provision. More than decorations, these were incantations that could magically act as the depicted things in case real ones weren't supplied.

Likewise, tomb walls showed scenes from daily life so that familiar and beneficial pursuits might continue after death, and the detailed, miniature wooden models placed in tombs beginning in the Middle Kingdom represented activities or services the living valued. Among the most popular were model boats complete with crews, and models of bare-breasted servants carrying baskets of foodstuffs on their heads. Breweries were another common subject of the models, as were bakeries and farming activities like ploughing and husbandry. To bolster these means of magical provisioning, the tomb was inscribed with the owner's name and many chapels had this entreaty carved on the outer walls:

> O ye living who are upon earth, who shall pass by this tomb,
> so surely as you wish your gods to favour you, may you say:
> a thousand of bread and beer, a thousand of flesh and fowl,
> a thousand of alabaster and clothing for the *ka* of [name of
> the deceased].[21]

Re-membrance, the message embodied in the mummiform image of Osiris, was the key to eternal life, to have one's name spoken by the living. If the name was destroyed, all was lost.[22]

From the pre-dynastic period onwards, graves contained jewellery, from modest adornments of ceramic beads and seashells to pieces fashioned with faience (a blue- or green-glazed earthenware), precious metals and semi-precious stones. While some of the jewellery belonged to the deceased in life, other pieces made specifically for the burial were flimsier and symbolic, representing the myriad necklaces, ankle bands and bracelets the deceased would wear in the afterlife. Portions of mummy casings were sometimes gilded, and outfitted with golden finger and toe stalls, pointy encasements that looked impressive while keeping these desiccated extremities from falling off. Some royal coffins were made entirely of silver or gold. The tomb of Tutankhamun, a young, unaccomplished and short-lived pharaoh, offers an indication of the quantities of precious metals that accompanied the royals to their graves. In addition to his famous mummy mask and an assemblage of finely wrought jewellery, the innermost of Tut's three coffins was made of 1,110 kilograms (2,440 lb) of 22-carat gold.[23]

The ancient Egyptians equated incorruptible gold with the flesh of gods; it was the ultimate status symbol, especially if it was a gift from pharaoh. Loyal nobles and generals were publicly decorated with ornaments of different kinds, especially during the

New Kingdom. Considered the apex of Egyptian civilization, the New Kingdom was a period of unsurpassed wealth due to military conquests of neighbouring countries. Amenemheb, a general under New Kingdom pharaoh Thutmose III, was 'arrayed' six times, in one case receiving 'a golden lion, three necklaces, two golden bees and four bracelets'. Amenhotep I gave his general Ahmose four bracelets, one ointment jar, six bees, a lion and two hatchets, all in gold. These awards were worth more than their weight in the precious metal, as they were granted in the presence of pharaoh and his confidants. At least a portion of such treasured items would have accompanied the receivers to their graves.[24]

Extravagant gift-giving went both ways, and it was customary at the start of the new year that 'the house should give gifts to its lord.'[25] A high official's tomb dating to the New Kingdom reign of Amenhotep II contains a long list of the tributes (or kickbacks, depending how you look at it) that he offered to his boss: 'carriages of silver and gold, statues of ebony and ivory, [necklaces] of all kinds, jewels, weapons and works of art'. The list goes on with quantities of axes, daggers and armour, hundreds of leather quivers, thirty clubs of ebony inlaid with silver and gold, 360 sickle-shaped bronze swords, 220 ivory whip handles and 680 shields

Finger ring depicting King Akhenaton and Queen Nefertiti as Shu and Tefnut, c. 1353–1336 BC, New Kingdom reign of Akhenaton, Flinders Petrie excavations (1891–2), gold.

'made of the skin of some rare animal'. There were two large carved pieces of ivory representing gazelles with flowers in their mouths, and finally the *chef-d'oeuvre*, a decorative item in the form of 'a building overgrown with fantastic plants bearing gigantic flowers, amongst which tiny monkeys chase each other', all in precious metals. Items such as these would likely have been buried with the king in his tomb.[26]

There was plenty of booty to go around and palace courtiers, high-ranking priests and military officials were living like kings themselves, in villas with gardens, servants and slaves in great numbers. Rather than dispense with lavish burial goods that tempted thieves, the ancients went to increasing lengths to protect them in safelike tombs. The vision of a luxurious afterlife was seductive, and the wealthy could afford it. To replicate the pleasures of their household in the afterlife, some of the ruling class mummified their pets. Prince Djhutmose, eldest son of Amenhotep III, had a limestone sarcophagus carved for his cat Tamyt. The wife of a 21st-dynasty high priest was buried with her gazelle. A Late Period nobleman was buried with his mummified dog curled up at his feet, like the knights in medieval tomb carvings.[27] The accoutrements constituting a fine burial reflect an attachment to leisure and the display of wealth, an elitism believed to extend to the hereafter where class distinctions would be preserved. Kings would still rule, nobles would continue to enjoy privileges and farmers would still farm, albeit with the help of servants, represented by *ushabti*, miniature mummiform figures commonly made of clay or faience. Magical servants accompanied both rich and poor to their graves to act on their behalf when called upon. Some New Kingdom tombs contained entire sets of *ushabti* buried in boxes, one for each day of the year, in addition to overseers, carrying whips.

Indeed, the lifestyles of antiquity's rich and famous came at the expense of much hardship on behalf of the common folk who comprised nearly all of Egypt's population. Major tomb- and temple-building projects were accomplished with the use of conscripted labour. Men and women worked in lieu of taxes or for food rations during the flood season when their fields were underwater, and there were prison penalties for those who did not comply. Mobilizing labour was an Egyptian speciality; for a Middle Kingdom expedition to Eastern Desert quarries, more than 18,600 citizens were rounded up.[28] Convicted criminals and prisoners of war provided additional manpower, usually in quarries or gold mines in the sweltering southern provinces. The Greek historian Diodorus visited Egypt's gold mines in around 100 BC, describing working conditions that were probably much the same in previous millennia.

> The vast numbers employed in these mines are bound in fetters, and compelled to work day and night without intermission, and without the least hope of escape; for they set over them barbarian soldiers, who speak a foreign language, so that there is no possibility of conciliating them by persuasion, or the kind feelings which result from familiar converse... No attention is paid to their persons; they have not even a piece of rag to cover themselves; and so wretched is their condition that everyone who witnesses it deplores the excessive misery they endure.[29]

According to Diodorus, the miners (men, women and children) illuminated their paths in the pits and 'dark windings' by fastening oil-burning lamps to their foreheads. It must have been an added torture to know that much of the gold extracted by 'such great toils' was destined to be buried again. 'Nature', Diodorus concluded, 'teaches that as gold is obtained with immense labor, so it is kept with difficulty, creating great anxiety, and attended in its use both with pleasure and grief.'[30]

Such anxiety is evident in a host of burial traditions. The ancients understood that just as nature contained a degree of chaos that needed to be held in check, so human weakness could upset the most carefully laid plans for eternity. Consequently, burials were furnished with magical fail-safe mechanisms to protect their contents in case of theft or some other disaster. Mummies were peppered with amulets placed in strategic positions on and within the body and its wrappings. These variously shaped objects provided protection to help ensure a safe transition from temporal to eternal life.

The popular 'eye of Horus' (𓂀), evoking the falcon-headed son of Isis and Osiris and still used in Egypt to ward off misfortune, was placed over the evisceration incision on the body's left flank. The 'djed pillar' signifying stability and associated with Osiris, was usually placed on the throat. Depending on one's budget, amulets could be made of faience or clay or of materials deemed magically potent, like carnelian, feldspar or gold. The golden heart scarab, an amulet introduced in the Middle Kingdom, protected the organ held as the seat of intelligence, where the sum of a person's experience resided. During the affluent New Kingdom, more amulets were used than ever. Tutankhamun had 140 embedded in his mummy wrappings, making his body a veritable treasure chest.[31]

The use of magical devices like substitute statues, amulets and representations of afterlife necessities betrays both vulnerability and self-knowledge. However important funerary rituals might have been, it was understood that in time they would be neglected. Worse, the tomb with its costly burial equipment might attract the very destruction it sought to prevent. Magic was insurance against the propensities for greed and forgetfulness in others, but one's own weaknesses could also reduce the chances of reaching paradise. Among the most important pieces of burial equipment were papyri and coffins inscribed with texts that served as maps to the afterlife with instructions on how to behave en route. The so-called Pyramid Texts were inscribed on the burial chamber walls of pyramid tombs, beginning with that of King Unas (c. 2350 BC) in the Old Kingdom. The texts comprised a series of spells to protect the body from scorpions, snakes, crocodiles and other dangers, and to reanimate it when it reached its destination.

They went by many names over time, but the ancients referred to what we call the Book of the Dead as the Book of Coming Forth by Day, a title that conveyed its purpose of explaining how to overcome death's obstacles. The underworld, like a foreign country, was full of traps and pitfalls. To successfully navigate the terrain you needed the right directions, to know what to say and do at every turn of the path. The journey began with an official judgement, when the heart was placed on the left pan of a scale and the feather symbolizing truth, justice and order (*maat*) on the other. Anubis supervised the weigh-in, with Thoth, the Ibis-headed god of writing and wisdom, recording the results. Given the ancients' bureaucratic propensities, it is unsurprising that no fewer than 42 'assessor gods' helped decide the deceased's fate, but so long as each was addressed by name, their approval was guaranteed. The Books of the Dead contained all the passwords required throughout the process, including the names of gates and halls that demanded recognition, down to the bolts on the doors.

While some religions demand that the deceased beg pardon for their shortcomings before entering heaven, the Egyptians sought no such forgiveness. The Books of the Dead included negative confessions: lists of all the wrongs they'd have to claim they'd never done. In case you forgot to be good in life it was enough to recall, when interrogated by the assessors, what good consisted of and to deny having departed from it. The answers to all death's queries were included in the funerary texts, which acted as a kind of cheat sheet for the most final of all exams. Those who failed faced Ammit, a fearsome creature with a crocodile's head, a lion's foreparts and a hippo's rear end, also known as 'the eater of the dead'. Yet it seems Ammit usually went hungry. The funerary texts assured that everyone who followed their instructions could pass, no matter how they'd behaved in life. So long as you included them in your burial, heaven meant never having to say you were sorry.

At first this privileged information was reserved for pharaohs only, but the use of funerary texts, like most burial trends, began with the royals, was eventually adopted by nobility and finally trickled down to the greater public. Expensive sarcophagi, for instance, were originally tailor-made for a royal or high official, but prêt-à-porter coffins inscribed with the funerary texts were later mass-produced. Likewise, papyrus versions of the Books of the Dead, once commissioned specifically by and for well-to-do individuals, became available in off-the-shelf copies with blank spaces where buyers could fill in their names. The burial

Weighing of the heart (Ammit is on the far right), detail from the Book of the Dead.

commodities so useful for achieving the afterlife were democratized by market demand over the course of centuries, especially during the First Intermediate Period, a time when central power had collapsed, along with the elite's monopoly on forever.

The ancient Egyptians did not use money; wages took the form of food rations, and goods and services were bartered. Taxes might consist of a portion of a farmer's grain crops, livestock, pigeons or honey, things like hempen rope, reed mats or, in the case of the wealthy, linen and precious metals. Although volatile at times due to circumstances like unrest or drought, commodity values were generally stable. A pair of sandals might trade at the same price for 150 years. Barter was not arbitrary but based on precise values calculated in *debens* (a unit of measure equalling approximately 91 grams/3 oz of copper) and achieved by agreed-upon combinations.[32] An ox worth 50 *debens* of copper, for example, was purchased with a combination of scraps of copper and bronze weighing (and therefore worth) 5 *debens*, two tunics valued at 10 *debens*, a quantity of vegetable oil worth 5 *debens*, and a large clay jar of fat, worth a whopping 30 *debens*. It took a whole spit-roasted young bull to produce a jar of fat; for the same price you could get a small sheep. The cost of an anthropoid wooden coffin inscribed with funerary texts was apparently half an ox, or 25½ *debens*, paid in one case with copper scraps, two goats, a pig and two sycamore logs, perhaps used in the coffin's construction.[33]

Building and filling a tomb with the most propitious equipment was an ambitious enterprise that involved significant investment, but everyone who hoped for immortality did their best to provide an attractive burial according to their means. It was a time- and effort-consuming activity, doubtless the topic of dinner-time conversation and consultations between family members. The ancients were house-proud, especially the well-to-do, and they could not help also being tomb-proud. Just as keeping up with the Hoteps meant having a quantity of servants and luxury items such as imported wines and Nile-going boats, competition among peers surely upped the ante of what constituted a good burial. Vast amounts of goods were meanwhile placed out of circulation, only to become a powerful incentive for theft.

Every religion pins its hopes on the soul's survival, but the Egyptians' lives, and significant aspects of what may be understood as their economy, revolved around it. The practicalities of death helped organize life, not least since they generated employment for masons, carpenters, goldsmiths, weavers, hunters, farmers, wine and beer brewers, bakers, embalmers, priests, scribes and many others. People adhered to burial traditions not only for whatever spiritual comfort they may have provided but because they belonged to an established order that coincidentally ensured their livelihoods. Just as many of us cannot imagine functioning without a car, however destructive the forces this collective dependency has unleashed, so the ancients were stubbornly attached to what they perceived as their vehicles of existence for this life and the next.

According to an ancient custom similar to a mealtime prayer, a wooden likeness of Osiris was shown to those seated and waiting for their food to be served. Everyone had a chance to admire the memento mori or ignore it as they wished. There is nothing like mortality to stimulate the appetite; to the Egyptians it was the very spice of life. Reminders of death were everywhere, not only in religious traditions but in popular pursuits. A board game called *senet* ('to pass') involved property, like Monopoly, but the goal was a piece of paradise and the opponent death itself. Instead of dice, players rolled the ankle bones of sheep, the sides of which were assigned numeric values. Moving across the board, you might land on a propitious square, allowing you to 'tread the staircase of the souls in Heliopolis' or 'ferry across the lake without wading'.[34] Then again, you might lose your *ba* or *ka* and end up as dinner for Ammit.

The ancient Egyptians were intimate with death's promise practically from birth. The average lifespan was 35 to 40 years. Their solution to mortality's dilemma was to live life to the fullest, while bolstering trust in the afterlife with comforting quotidian traditions. The hope for immortality clearly influenced the ancient Egyptians' approach to living and dying in a variety of ways. But in the words of Egyptologist Pascal Vernus:

> The word 'hope' entails a shade of uncertainty which well suits the situation in Pharaonic Egypt. The exceptional importance of funerary beliefs did not prevent the development of a skeptical attitude towards them. Though this skepticism was overtly expressed by intellectuals, we have every reason to believe that this attitude was not limited to them. Skepticism did not lead to a rejection of these beliefs, but rather to a sort of compromise ... postmortem survival was not assured ... but that was all the more reason to increase the odds in its favor by attempting to fill all the conditions required by tradition.[35]

Some were convinced they could achieve eternal life or were at least willing to give it their best shot by providing the necessary equipment no matter the cost. As for the sceptics, society is a powerful arbiter of behaviour; even if one does not share the beliefs of one's fellows, one may still act as if one does. Whether through belief or conformism, fulfilling the conditions for a good burial was, for millennia, a respected norm.

The existence of 'the field of reeds' and the value of burial traditions for attaining it may have been questioned, but the punishment for spoiling someone's chances of getting there was very real. People knew what to expect if they were caught breaking the law. According to ancient documents, 'his crime seizes him, it overtakes and undoes him.'[36] Diodorus recorded being told that the god Thoth authored Egyptian law, which has an Old Testament 'eye for an eye' feel. Those found guilty of treachery had their tongues removed; forgers lost a hand. Delinquents were condemned to hard labour in the quarries or the mines. Alongside murder and perjury, tomb-raiding ranked as the most reprehensible of crimes. Such transgressors would face 'the five cuts', mutilation of the nose, ears and lips, as a prelude to 'the great punishment of death, of which the gods say "do it to him"'.[37] In the case of tomb raiders this meant public impalement on a sharp wooden stake. For good measure, the names of the convicted were erased and their existence, in this life and the next, annulled.

Amenhotep II composed a curse for the funerary chapel of a favourite courtier, warning that if anyone disturbed his remains or neglected to bring his regular offering meals:

> The royal snake, the fire-spitter sitting of the head of the king, will devour them ... they will burn in holy flames and their bodies be engulfed by the sea and hidden from decent burial. Never again will they hear the voice of their king, the nobles will not visit their houses, the sons will not succeed their posts at court, their wives will be raped before their eyes.[38]

This admonition reached to the heart of society's greatest fears: of loneliness, illegitimacy and the extinction of family lines, not to mention the death of the spirit. But tomb raiders weren't buying it. They tore mummies apart to reach the treasures bound in the

Plundered tomb of Prince Khaemwaset, son of Ramses III, Valley of the Queens, 1903, photograph by Ernesto Schiaparelli.

wrappings, wrenching arms and fingers from their sockets to get at bracelets and rings. They even set mummies on fire to better examine their loot by the light of the flames.

Despite customs and beliefs, the threat of death and annihilation, the presence of priests and guards in the necropolis and laboriously secured underground burials, tombs were robbed throughout antiquity. Egyptologists have found some sealed from the outside yet stripped of their inner treasures, meaning they were robbed before they were officially closed. Some Middle Kingdom coffins were equipped with locks, not to thwart raiders who would simply have broken them open, but from an apparent fear that someone might pinch a few trinkets on the way to the tomb. Modern examinations of mummies with intact wrappings have revealed that embalmers stole the amulets they were meant to bind to the body, replacing them with similarly shaped clods of mud. Less egregiously, embalmers sometimes cut corners on expensive materials, and not everyone got their mummy's worth in terms of quality of preservation. But for a society that upheld the sanctity of the tomb and its promise of immortality, little enough was sacred. The fact that so many tombs were pillaged in antiquity suggests that there were plenty of individuals less interested in eternity than in seizing the day. Popular wisdom rang from a tune that was sung for centuries: 'Follow your desire, allow the heart to forget . . . Celebrate [and] remember: no man takes his goods with him, and none have returned after going.'[39]

Archaeologists often note the irony that so much of our knowledge of ancient Egyptian lives has been derived from tombs. Their decorated walls are biographies of the people who built them, relating their beliefs, activities and accomplishments. The paintings or carved reliefs portray able-bodied servants farming the fields and preparing food or drink for a tomb owner sitting contentedly at table, surveying his vineyards, crops or cattle. There are picturesque scenes of bird hunts, sailing trips, familial gatherings and pious offerings to the gods. But the tombs that have helped paint our picture of the past belonged largely to the rich or relatively well off. The masses disappeared leaving barely a trace.

Temples are likewise books in stone describing valiant conquests and the fatherly rule of muscular kings working shoulder to shoulder with ancestral gods in the interests of humanity. Much has been learned from the inscriptions in tombs and temples, in addition to numerous papyrus documents containing the bureaucratic minutiae the Egyptians compiled in their ceaseless quest for order. No other ancient people have so generously supplied us with the remains of their great day. But wealth and skills like writing were concentrated in the hands of the few. Most of the voices we hear are of powerful figures, those who could command what would be written. The glamorous processions of scantily clad, lotus-sniffing royals that comprise so much of ancient Egyptian religious art existed worlds away from ordinary folk. Much of what we know about ancient Egypt is a kind of propaganda written exclusively by men representing themselves in the most flattering of all possible lights.

The majority of individuals who wished for an afterlife had to struggle to get by in this one. Motivated by need and greed but also disillusionment, tomb-raiding redressed the imbalance between rich and poor, while signalling contempt for social hierarchies so deeply engrained they were believed to be eternal. In violating tombs and destroying mummies, raiders theoretically spoiled the tomb owner's chances for immortality, while effectively undermining a system geared towards the accumulation of literally dead capital. More than thieves, they were transgressors, the original outlaws in the most precise and thorough sense of the term. In a world devoted to order, raiders were on the side of chaos, in conflict not only with society's treasured traditions but with its fondest hopes for itself. They were havoc personified like the god Seth, 'dismember-ers' who didn't give a damn if their names were forgotten. Their actions speak volumes about the unrecorded realities of life in ancient Egypt, the tensions between tradition and change, spirituality and cynicism, faith and demagoguery.

Ancient Egypt may appear in some ways ideal: people living close to the land, working in concert to create wondrous expressions of their cultural values over the course of millennia. But the truth of a society lies in its contradictions, not its idealized self-image. Raiders were a symptom of dysfunction, a ticking bomb, the antagonists with whom society had to contend in one way or another. Their actions illumine the fault lines of a culture whose evolution they profoundly influenced, forcing changes in how tombs were built, and calling the values driving long-held beliefs into question.

Scratch the surface of many an archaeologist and you'll find an Indiana Jones, determined to reveal what time has hidden, savouring the anticipation of fresh insight or discovery as reward for dogged and sometimes perilous work. And what emotion could surpass that of bearing witness to places where time has literally stood still? Excavating for the Louvre, Auguste Mariette unearthed the rock-hewn burial galleries of the sacred Apis bulls in Saqqara (necropolis of Memphis) in 1852, and described entering one of the rooms:

> Although 3,700 years had elapsed since it was closed ... the finger-marks of the Egyptian who had tested the last stone in the wall built to conceal the entry were still recognizable on the lime. There were also the marks of naked feet imprinted on the sand which lay in one corner of the tomb-chamber.[40]

Wonderment is also present in an account of excavations written by Egyptologist Arthur Weigall, British inspector of the Antiquities Services in the Theban necropolis on Luxor's west bank in 1905, during the discovery of the tomb of Yuya and Tjuyu (Amenophis III's in-laws). That the tomb was lightly ransacked in antiquity only heightened the drama:

> We slipped and slid down the long steep passage ... and with some difficulty crawled into the inner chamber ... as our eyes got used to the candlelight we saw a sight which I can safely

say no living man has ever seen ... in the middle of the room were two enormous sarcophagi of wood inlaid with gold. The lids had been wrenched off [and] the two mummies were exposed. The plunderers had evidently very hurriedly searched the bodies for the jewels but had not touched anything else. All round the sarcophagi – piled almost to the roof – were chairs, tables, beds, vases and so on – all in perfect condition ... The room looked just [like] a London house shut up while people were away for the summer. [We] stood there gaping and almost trembling ... and I think we were face to face with something that seemed to upset all human ideas of time and distance.[41]

Weigall was fortunate to have found a tomb that thieves had barely touched. More often than not, archaeologists are obliged to measure, catalogue and publish the debris that raiders left behind.

Egyptologists grew accustomed to the scenes of devastation that greeted them in ransacked tombs. When Flinders Petrie excavated Senwosret II's Middle Kingdom mud-brick pyramid at Fayoum (1889) he found an empty sarcophagus, but lying on the ground in an adjacent room was a gold- and jewel-encrusted royal cobra that someone in a hurry had dropped on the way out. Jacques de Morgan, who excavated at Senwosret III's pyramid at Saqqara (1894–5), dug exploratory tunnels to locate the entry shaft, but the first passage he hit was dug by raiders. When he finally reached the burial chamber, he found a sarcophagus of red granite with nothing in it, 'not even dust'.[42] However frustrating the experience of being beaten consistently to the punch, archaeologists have learned a lot from tomb raiders, enough to admire their tenacity and ingenuity, to recognize their influence on tomb design and to understand that some must have had inside information.

Just as national security is among today's chief preoccupations, so tomb security absorbed the ancients. Society's laws were never enough to protect the dead, and neither were the curses and invocations inscribed on tomb interiors a deterrent to their destruction. Tomb architecture evolved as a more practical means of evading raiders, and the finest craftsmen in the land were charged with securing the 'horizon of eternity', as the pharaohs' resting place was called. The tomb builders worked under sweltering, claustrophobic conditions, splitting rock with cedar hammers and metal spikes that sent stinging chips ricocheting through the air. Using heavy wood-handled copper adzes, they tunnelled like gophers, displacing countless tons of rock and sand to carve shafts and corridors and colonnaded rooms.

To be pharaoh entailed a degree of vanity that, like burying masses of gold and expensive goods, was a fatal weakness embedded in the funerary cult. The 'principal public statement on the nature of kingship', the tomb was the place where the pharaoh, the intermediary between gods and men in life, became himself a god.[43] The lieu of divine transformation demanded a particular kind of architecture, austere yet exalted and in every way possible locked down. Funerary monuments like pyramids, a building trend initiated by the architect Imhotep around 2600 BC, may have been suitably impressive but they also screamed 'x marks the spot'.[44] However cunning or physically daunting the deterrents and booby traps installed for protection, raiders eventually exposed the flaws in each tomb's design.

The most basic security technique was to fill the tomb's access shafts with rubble after the burial, a method that only delayed the inevitable. Architects tried portcullises, precision-cut limestone slabs lowered by ropes along grooves in the walls of the underground passage, but the limestone was soft and raiders chipped their way through. When giant plugs were inserted at intervals along the entry passage, the thieves simply tunnelled around them. The shaft to the burial chamber of the Old Kingdom tomb of Ny-ankh-Pepy at Saqqara was blocked with a red granite boulder, so the raiders just tunnelled deeper, closer to the shaft's base where it met the burial chamber. Architects got trickier, using dummy doors, secret rooms, decoy passages and 36-tonne (40 T.) stone trapdoors, but raiders were motivated and relentless. If they hit the wrong chamber or a dead-end passage they backed up and started again.

Never Say Die

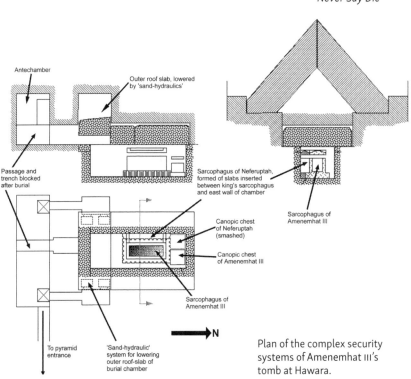

Plan of the complex security systems of Amenemhat III's tomb at Hawara.

The Middle Kingdom architect of the mud-brick Hawara pyramid in the oasis of Fayoum (built for twelfth-dynasty pharaoh Amenemhat III) went to obsessive lengths to stymie the raiders. The stairway descending from the tomb entrance on the north side led to an apparently dead-end chamber, but a stone in its roof slid sideways, opening to a room above. From here, a dummy shaft, carefully blocked with rubble to resemble a real shaft, led away from the burial chamber, not towards it. Raiders would have spent days clearing the trick shaft, increasing their risk of exposure, before finding the correct shaft, which had yet another trapdoor embedded in the ceiling, opening to a passage with a third, final trapdoor leading to a burial. The *pièce de résistance* was the burial chamber itself, cut entirely from a monolithic block of quartzite that had been lowered into place by sand hydraulics before the pyramid was built on top.[45] Egyptologists found two sarcophagi inside, both empty.

In wealthy burials, a stone sarcophagus was the mummy's last material line of defence and raiders must have smiled when they saw it, considering all they'd done to get that far. Limestone is soft and easily penetrated by chisel; granite or quartzite are a lot more challenging. For the latter the looters used wooden levers to raise the heavy lids that they propped open with rocks, or else they rolled the lid back on inserted wooden mallets, as if on ball bearings. The simplest and perhaps most popular method was to lever the whole sarcophagus up and tip it over, sending the lid crashing to the ground. It's worth pausing to consider, on the one hand, the arduous effort to create these subterranean tombs with their rooms and passages, alongside the backbreaking delivery and damage-free installation of costly items by the ton, and, on the other, the apparent zest with which raiders smashed it all to smithereens.

Horemheb's sarcophagus (KV57), 18th dynasty, West Bank, Luxor, photograph by Francis Dzikowski, 1996.

Tomb raiders suffered injuries in the line of duty, and sometimes paid the ultimate price. When Reginald Engelbach excavated a Middle Kingdom shaft tomb at Riqqa (south of Cairo, 1912–13), he discovered that the roof of the burial chamber had given way at an inopportune moment. A thief had apparently just removed the mummy from its coffin and was about to rifle its wrappings. He must have been standing over his prize, admiring it, when several tons of rock and rubble came crashing down on his head. His pulverized bones were found mixed with those of the mummy he was about to desecrate.[46] Only a fluke of fate or *force majeure* could protect a tomb indefinitely, for instance when buried beneath the rocky sludge delivered by a flash flood, as was the case in the tomb of Tutankhamun, unearthed in 1922.[47] Tomb security was a cat-and-mouse game that architects couldn't win; they had only one go at it while their opponents had forever, yet they kept trying to outwit the raiders. Given the labour and expense involved, the insistence on tomb security was sheer arrogance, as if deploying superior technology could somehow cow the thieves.

A twelfth-dynasty (1994–1781 BC) *mastaba* tomb at Lisht (80 kilometres/50 mi. south of Cairo) belonged to Senwosretankh, a 'Royal Sculptor and Builder' who had apparently mulled its innovative features throughout his career.[48] The substructure began with a sloping descent to a horizontal passage. Before arriving at the burial chamber, this passage ran beneath a vertical shaft packed with gravel and sand. The more the raiders tried to clear the passage, the more rubble fell from the shaft to replace it. After that, there were four portcullises that cleverly locked into place when lowered. One imagines the raiders shaking their heads as they burrowed straight down into the bedrock then directly into one of the burial chamber's side walls. They were expert tunnellers, intimate with the properties of sand. Heavy, unwieldy, it doesn't stay where you put it, is susceptible to wind and follows the path of least resistance like water. Just as Senwosretankh harnessed gravity to protect his tomb, so tomb builders got sand to work for them. Massive stone slabs in the Hawara pyramid were lowered into place by releasing sand via shafts from the space beneath them, the same system used to seal the burial chamber of the mud-brick pyramid of King Khendjer (thirteenth dynasty, Saqqara).

Sand hydraulics was eventually adapted as the ultimate security device, as evidenced in a 26th-dynasty (54 BC–AD 1) tomb belonging to a wealthy individual.[49] The burial chamber with its stone sarcophagus was placed at the bottom of a giant pit, around 10 metres (33 ft) wide and 30 metres (100 ft) deep. Next to the pit was a shaft leading from ground level to the burial chamber, just wide enough for a man to crawl through. The roof of the burial chamber was fitted with a series of clay pots and the pit above it filled with sand. The workers exited with the help of ropes up the narrow adjacent shaft, which was likewise filled with sand. The last workman out broke the pots that allowed the sand to flow from the pit above to engulf the burial chamber below. Anyone who tried tunnelling into this burial chamber would be overwhelmed by a deluge of sand. The only way to gain access would be to clear the entire pit, 'a lengthy process as archaeologists know to their cost', one that would have risked too much exposure for the thieves.[50] This burial was in fact found intact, but without a single object in the chamber or on the person of its occupant. A proud and pious man, he went to the grave alone and unadorned, wishing to cheat not only death but whomever dared to interfere with his journey to the afterlife.

Theft had long since forced architects to move further underground, but now they sought more discreet burial locations. In the early New Kingdom, Ineni, superintendent of Thutmose I's building projects, chose a portion of the desert badlands on the west bank of Thebes (Luxor), north of a burial ground used in centuries past by kings of the eleventh and seventeenth dynasties. The formal name of the new necropolis was 'the great and noble necropolis of millions of years of pharaoh on the west of Thebes', aka 'the great place', and the 'the place of truth'. The area dedicated to royal women and children was 'the place of beauty'.[51] The mountain guarding the necropolis was called 'a gate of heaven', home of the Theban cobra-goddess Meretseger, 'mistress of silence'. Set amid stark, labyrinthine hills and gulches, what we call the Valleys of the Kings and Queens must have seemed a safe haven for royal burials, but their remoteness served less to deter theft than to invite it.

Ineni devised an additional security measure by doing away with the funerary chapels typically built above tombs. Daily food offerings and ritual maintenance now took place in temples on the edge of the floodplain, a liminal space appropriate to the congress of the living with the dead and a shorter walk for priests and family members. Aside from the funeral procession that accompanied the deceased to his/her resting place, regular visits to the tombs literally beat a path to their doors, so the fewer of those the better. But the necropolis police, the Medjay, meant to guard against intruders, were either on the take or slept a great deal on the job, because they did not protect the tombs of royals and nobles from pillage.

The Valley of the Kings tomb of Seti I, father of Ramses II, New Kingdom pharaohs who presided over Egypt at the New Kingdom zenith of its wealth and power, boasts a stunning array of magical decorations and security devices, including the longest underground passageway (147 metres/480 ft) of any known tomb.[52] A stairway leads from the entrance to a corridor, followed by another stairwell and a second corridor leading to a shaft opening down to an 8-metre-wide (26 ft) room with four pillars. On one side, a truncated stairway where wall decorations continued uninterrupted suggests the tomb ends there. But behind the blockage lay a third corridor and another stairway opening to an antechamber, then a six-pillared burial chamber with a ceiling portraying the constellations of the night sky. The anthropoid sarcophagus, a masterpiece in alabaster intricately carved with funerary texts (now in London's Sir John Soane Museum), was found empty, the mummy removed pre-emptively by priests to protect it from theft.

The author of the *Admonitions of an Egyptian Sage*, Ipuwer, whose late Middle Kingdom text was reproduced for centuries, lamented a situation that matched the one confronting New Kingdom rulers:

> Behold, those who once owned tombs
> Are thrown out into the desert

> While he who could not make a tomb for himself
> Is (now) the owner of a treasury.[53]

Implying ill-gotten gains, Ipuwer complained how 'paupers have become men of affluence, and he who could not provide sandals for himself is (now) the possessor of wealth.' No one could be trusted and thieves acted with impunity. Ipuwer saw tomb and temple theft as anarchy that sabotaged society and its traditions. 'A man of integrity goes mourning for what has happened in the land, but [a man of depravity] goes about [in glee],' he wrote, appealing to pharaoh to restore law and order before it was too late.[54] Ipuwer's diagnosis of a sickly state was well known to New Kingdom leaders, who nonetheless ignored the symptoms. The ancient Egyptians didn't learn from history any more than we do. By the end of the New Kingdom, systemic corruption in palace and temple institutions made raiding a going concern that fuelled a veritable underground economy. With some taking far more than they gave, the reciprocity of *maat* was an empty concept and theft became the order of the day.

TWO

GRAVE MATTERS

Do not set your heart upon seeking riches . . . if riches come to you by thievery, they will not last you through the night.[1]
– *THE INSTRUCTION OF AMENEMOPE*, NEW KINGDOM

The New Kingdom lasted five hundred years (1549–1060 BC), a time of imperialist expansion under clever, ruthless leadership with Thebes (ancient Luxor) as its religious capital. Think of Thebes as a bit like New York; when people referred to 'the city' (*niwet*), they meant Thebes.[2] It wasn't Egypt's administrative centre and the pharaoh maintained residences in the city but didn't always live there; except for during the religious festivals requiring his presence, he and his court resided in Memphis or elsewhere in the north.[3] But Thebes' magisterial architecture, and the wealth and spectacle in which its temples were enveloped, made it a storied city in its day. One can almost hear Frank Sinatra belting out these lines, composed by a 'metropolitan scribe':

> What do they say every day in their hearts,
> Those who are far from Thebes?
> They spend their day blinking at its name,
> If only we had it, they say –
> The bread there is tastier than cakes made with goose fat,
> Its water is sweeter than honey,
> One drinks of it till one gets drunk.
> Oh! That is how one lives at Thebes.[4]

Referred to in the Bible as No-Amon, 'situated among rivers, the waters round about it', the city straddled the Nile, the conduit

Ramses III funerary complex, Medinat Habu, West Bank, Luxor, 2019.

for commerce and communication that made Egypt an empire and Thebes its throbbing heart.[5] It was barely a village during the Old Kingdom, when Memphis was the focus for monumental building and the codifications of writing systems and artistic representations that characterized that half-millennium. During the Middle Kingdom, its east bank was the cult centre of Amun, the creator deity who grew in prominence to become the king of gods and eventually the sun-god, Amun-Ra. His earthly address was Karnak, a temple and religious complex whose size, wealth and influence expanded during the New Kingdom, making it one of the largest in the world.[6]

New Kingdom pharaohs reconfigured Thebes as the stage for history's most extravagant religious theatre, adding much of the monumental architecture that remains a source of wonder on its east and west banks. At the height of the New Kingdom, Egypt extended its control 1,300 kilometres (800 mi.) northeast to the Sinai Peninsula, Palestine and Syria. In the mainland south, the empire stretched another 1,300 kilometres (800 mi.) up the Nile to what is now Sudan, encompassing the Red Sea coast and the

Western Desert oases, way stations for caravans of slaves and goods from the south. Their palace coffers fat with trade, plunder and tributes from conquered lands, pharaohs launched building sprees to thank the gods for their triumphs and ensure their own lasting adulation, raising larger, more magnificent monuments and equipping them more sumptuously than ever before. Works of ideological and ego-driven genius, these buildings represent a degree of architectural exactitude, artisanal rigour and crushing physical labour on a scale nearly unthinkable today that back then was just a matter of following orders.

Thebes rivalled Memphis as Egypt's largest city during the New Kingdom, with the bulk of its population comprising farmers and labourers. Swaths of their humble dwellings on the east bank were levelled to clear the way for Luxor Temple, begun during the reign of Amenhotep III (1388–1348), a prodigious builder. Pharaoh's coronation was re-enacted there annually, and propitiously linked to the rebirth of Amun-Ra. Karnak's Temple of Amun-Ra, the most ambitious building of its time, was begun in the early Middle Kingdom but supersized by successive pharaohs, including Seti I

Alley of Sphinxes, Karnak forecourt, East Bank, Luxor, 2020.

(1296–1279 BC), who gave the temple its 5,000-square-metre (53,820 sq. ft) hypostyle hall, with 134 thick columns, some of them 21 metres (63 ft) high, supporting architraves each weighing 63 tonnes (70 T.), all intricately carved with hieroglyphs and depictions of impassive pharaohs and deities absorbed in ritual.[7]

Thebes' west bank was likewise transformed with the construction of Amenhotep III's palace city, including a Nile-fed harbour, 2 kilometres (1⅓ mi.) long and half as wide, used for the religious festival set-piece of the pharaoh parading on his gilded barge. The Colossi of Memnon, each carved from an 18-metre-tall (60 ft) block of quartzite, stand guard at the entry to the recently excavated remains of Amenhotep III's funerary temple, where a tall stone slab was raised and inscribed with a proud dedication:

> Come Amun Ra, Lord of the Thrones of the Two Lands, Foremost One of the Temple of Karnak, that you can see the temple I have made for you . . . when you shine in the morning, your beauty is inside it, unceasingly . . . My majesty filled it with monuments from what I had brought from the mountain of marvels . . . Greatness is what I made with gold and every noble and precious stone without limit . . . no goodness is lacking . . . Did I not make it as an excellent work?[8]

Of the many royal funerary monuments erected on the west bank, those of Hatshepsut, Ramses II (the Ramesseum) and Ramses III (Medinet Habu temple) still testify to the wealth, industry and narcissism-inflected religious convictions that brought them into being. At the end of Ramses II's reign, Thebes was called 'the pattern for all cities':

> Both water and earth were within her from the beginning of time. There came the sands to furnish land, to create her ground as a mound when the earth came into being. And so mankind came into being within her, with the purpose of founding every city in her name for all are called 'city' after the example of Thebes.[9]

Tying Thebes to the Egyptian creation myth historicized the city's importance, and by extension the legitimacy of pharaoh's rule.

Whether built in the name of a living god or to memorialize a deified pharaoh, temples were the engines of the land-based economy, acting as a federal reserve where grain was stored. Incomes came largely from crops produced on land endowments spread throughout Egypt and sometimes in occupied territories. Temple land was leased to farmers, large and small, in exchange for 30 per cent of crops, transported at harvest time by barge to temple storage areas. The Ramesseum alone had more than 8,000 square metres (86,111 sq. ft) of mud-brick granaries, enough to support about 3,400 families. Temple holdings included herds of cattle, fishing and fowling rights, flax fields, orchards, vineyards and beehives. Temples employed traders to exchange surplus grain or linen for needed goods, including high-demand items such as papyrus rolls. Pharaohs who wished to express their piety augmented temple wealth with gifts such as precious metals or portions of booty from foreign lands, including slaves. The temples of Seti I at Abydos and Karnak in Thebes were endowed with the rights to gold mines in the Eastern Desert.[10]

Although life revolved around the temples, Egypt 'was no spiritual state. Religion was the language of power.'[11] An interwoven hierarchy of high priests, scribes and governors managed temple affairs, with priests sometimes doubling as governors. Schools and libraries known as 'the house of life' were attached to temples but while priests studied and may have copied or written religious texts, they married and had families and most had administrative duties. Women (including some of the priests' wives) could serve as priestesses or chantresses involved in temple ritual but men ran the show. They were talented logisticians; the daily offerings for Ramses III's funerary temple involved the marshalling of 5,500 loaves and 204 jars of beer in addition to a long list of gourmet delicacies, and there were many other tombs and temples that needed servicing.[12] In the course of a year tens of thousands of head of cattle, geese and other fowl were slaughtered for offerings. Once dedicated, these foods were allotted to temple and necropolis staff, requiring another level of bureaucracy, more apportionment and delivery. The labour-intensive activities surrounding the temples generated countless livelihoods while ensuring people's dependence on and presumed compliance with the institution they served.

High-ranking temple and palace officials lived in relative luxury, with plenty of servants, *divertissements* and the prospect of a fine tomb. The bulk of Thebes' population living in mud-brick hovels may have narrowed their eyes at their conspicuous consumption, but it is unlikely that the grandeur of the temples and palaces surrounding average subjects was a source of particular awe. Having contributed to and/or witnessed their construction which lasted many years, the people's pride of place or achievement was surely leavened with a pragmatic assessment of their own insignificance, aside from labour and taxes, to the state. Temple facades were covered in larger-than-life, vividly coloured portrayals of pharaohs and gods, but ordinary folk could only catch glimpses of them beyond the surrounding walls. Temple interiors were off-limits to subjects, reserved exclusively for 'ritually pure' priests, priestesses and kings. Temple gateways, as big as aeroplane hangars, were plated with shining metals and flew pennants on pinewood masts tipped with glittering electrum.

The title of pharaoh derives from the word for palace (*per'o*) or 'the great house', and his job was to administer the house of the state. Revered in the Old Kingdom, he wore a knee-length kilt with a bull's tail protruding from the backside, signalling fecundity and ferocity; courtiers were accustomed to kissing the floor at his feet. Elaborate hierarchies were born in the Old Kingdom and scores of bureaucratic positions invented. The head of the pharaoh's advisory committee was 'the chief of secrets' and the head of the treasury was the 'governor of all that exists or does not exist'. The ranks of the less poetically titled grew rapidly, so that there were not only scribes, for example, but the superintendent of scribes who had sub- and deputy superintendents. So great was the number of titled individuals that some added the word 'real' to their names, for example 'the real judge of the district', to give themselves a competitive edge.[13] As Egyptologist Barry Kemp noted, 'a developed bureaucratic system reveals and actively promotes a specific human trait: a deep satisfaction in devising routines for measuring, inspecting, checking and thus as far as possible controlling other people's activities.'[14] The ancients discovered that one of the best means of state control, popular in Egypt until now, was to employ as many people as possible.

Old Kingdom pharaohs are perhaps easily imagined as embodiments of the belief that immortality was within mortal reach, with wilful accomplishments like the Giza pyramids as compelling proofs. The king's role in temple matters was paramount among his duties; he was the highest of high priests and held the power to ensure an orderly life in this world and the next through the repetition of sacred ritual. But as every Catholic knows, there are only so many times you can see the priest raise a communion wafer and think it's the body of Christ. In the New Kingdom, the state matured and the pharaoh's persona altered as Egypt embraced its new identity as a military state profiting briskly from wars in the north and south. Attention to temporal, pecuniary affairs eclipsed that devoted to the sacred and eternal, a shift that may have affected people's faith in their religious leaders. Commander of a standing army, the pharaoh was now immersed in foreign affairs; in correspondence with fellow leaders in Babylonia, Assyria, Asia Minor and elsewhere, they addressed one another as 'brother'.[15] In addition to his role as living god, the pharaoh was a world-class player.

Generals could acquire lofty court positions even without noble lineage providing they were victorious, and humbly born men could rise to prominence within New Kingdom institutions if sufficiently competent and obeisant. 'Bend your back before your chief,' runs an ancient Egyptian proverb, and boy, did they ever. In letters to their inferiors, higher-ups issued brusque orders, 'do this' or 'do that', but the responses were couched in unabashedly sycophantic terms. 'I am as a horse pawing the ground,' wrote a subordinate to his boss, 'my heart awakes by day and my eyes by night, for I desire to serve my master.'[16] Likewise the titles accrued to the pharaoh dripped with unctuous praise. Honorifics appended to the king's name on a stela erected under Ramses II ('the great') offer an example:

> In the third year of His Majesty Horus: the strong bull, beloved by the goddess of truth . . . who protects Egypt, and subdues the barbarians, the golden Horus: full of years, great in victories . . . strong in truth . . . giver of everlasting life . . . shining daily on his throne amongst men . . . the beautiful silver hawk, who protects Egypt with his wings, providing shade for mankind, the castle of strength and of victory, who came out terribly from his mother's womb . . . Heaven rejoiced at his birth . . . his name is famous in all countries because of the victories his arms have won . . . at the mention of his name, gold comes out of the mountains.[17]

Aside from his expansionary military campaigns, Ramses II was a great builder, with the temples of Abu Simbel to his credit, among many others. But glorifications such as those engraved on his stela were used for subsequent, far less accomplished pharaohs, suggesting that genuine deference may have been reduced over time to tedious formalities.

Like modern CEOs, pharaohs were exceptionally mobile, travelling abroad to wage battles and plying the Nile in luxurious sailboats to fulfil their domestic duties, stopping at royal rest houses along the way. They had large families to think about. The royal harem housed hundreds of women, high-born Egyptians and foreigners given as tribute. The women did not want for their lord's attentions, as suggested by the titles awarded to some royal consorts, 'she of numerous nights in the city of the brilliant Aten', 'she who appears in glory' and 'she who strikes with fury for the brilliant Aten'.[18] 'Aten' is the sun disc, an aspect of the god Ra, and in this case, a possible reference to the pharaoh's brilliant manhood. Ramses II reportedly had two hundred children, among them 111 sons.[19]

When the royal family resided at Memphis, young princes could hunt lions (introduced to the area for sport), or ride horses and practise chariot warfare on the nearby Giza Plateau, in the company of the pyramids and Sphinx. At curtain time, the royals packed their wigs and sailed to Thebes to star in lavish displays of pomp, wealth and celebrity. The vizier, pharaoh's number-one man, was responsible for organizing these city-wide religious festivals, including food and drink for the masses who celebrated with such revelry as befits hardworking, bare-chested folks on vacation. Opet, the first and longest festival of the year, was held in summertime, in the second month of the flood. On this occasion, the statue of Amun-Ra, kept in the innermost, stone shrine of his temple, left Karnak for a ceremonial journey to Luxor Temple, accompanied by his divine wife Mut and son Khonsu. Karnak's doors were flung wide to make way for white-robed priests carrying litters with the gods' statues in ponderous gold-coated cedar boxes that were placed aboard 4-metre-long (13 ft) portable replicas of the solar boat. Shaven heads held high, the priests marched along the ceremonial sphinx-lined boulevard to Luxor Temple, hemmed in by an admiring crowd, then proceeded to the Nile, where they installed their cumbersome loads on the royal barges. Accompanied by a crowned and bejewelled pharaoh, resplendent in his headdress and dramatic eyeliner, the god and his family were towed the short distance back up the Nile, their conveyances trailing clouds of aromatic smoke. Subjects thronged the riverbanks to cheer for this prototype of all parade floats, enjoying entertainments en route: drummers, harpists and lady lute players, dancers, wrestlers and acrobats.

The celebrations extended to the west bank village of the royal tomb builders, valued craftsmen who were feted with a banquet to reward their monumental labours. Since their homes were small, the Opet feast was served outdoors after sunset. Copious amounts of foods were prepared throughout the day: honey-basted roasted ox and gazelle, chickpeas and lotus seeds spiced with marjoram, heads of roasted garlic and loaves of bread to dip in delicacies like sesame paste (*tahina*) and balls of animal fat dressed in cumin-flavoured radish oil. Salad came fresh from the fields: parsley, onions and lettuce (an aphrodisiac). For dessert there were honey cakes and sycamore figs. Nearby vineyards supplied wine, a special treat, and a pomegranate-flavoured beer was prepared especially for Opet. There was music and dancing beneath a nighttime sky ablaze with stars, everyone slick with perfumed oils and wearing woolly brown wigs, the women's as wide as their shoulders.[20]

Although Opet and other festivals were religious in nature and marked traditions that by the time of the New Kingdom were already ancient, they also functioned as bread and circuses, offering people time off from work, and distraction from ordinary cares and the signs of dysfunction of the institutions that governed them. The Egyptians understood the power of spectacle, and the ruling elite relied on it with increasing frequency. At the start of the New Kingdom, Opet lasted eleven days; by its end, it occupied the better part of a month.

The tomb builders' village (Deir al-Medina in Arabic) is tucked away between the sun-baked hills on Thebes' west bank, a sturdy trek of several kilometres from the royal necropolis where they worked. The community was probably founded under the reign of Amenhotep I, who was honoured there, though his successor Thutmose I is credited with formalizing the town by surrounding it with a protective wall. A footprint of the village remains: a maze of houses tightly bundled in a walled rectangle (132 × 50 metres/433 × 164 ft) bisected by a narrow main street. There were around seventy mud-brick and stone dwellings within the wall and another forty or fifty outside it, all whitewashed with wooden doors painted red. Every household had a shrine in the vestibule (for votive objects and daily offerings) and four small rooms, 3–5 metres (10–16 ft) high, that must have been suffocating in summer. Families were large, with as many as fifteen children, and they slept on their roofs in hot weather, as some residents of the remaining pastoral portions of Luxor's west bank still do today.[21]

The village thrived throughout the New Kingdom alongside demand for the residents' special craft, but by the end of the Third Intermediate Period (c. 525 BC) it was a ghost town that was slowly subsumed by the desert. Its existence remained unknown until latter-day raiders began unearthing antiquities at the site, including a trove of papyri found in the mid-1800s. The sheer quantity and sensational nature of the artefacts found at that time left these documents unstudied for decades. Impassioned scholarship has since revealed their contents, shedding light on every piquant detail of the tomb builders' lives: their work methods, the unfolding of their careers and professional rivalries, the minutiae of their households, their preoccupations, illnesses, sex lives and dreams, their quarrels with their neighbours, their acts of piety, the oaths they took and sometimes broke.

Foremost among those who resurrected this remarkable community is Czech Egyptologist Jaroslav Černý (1898–1970); the first to identify Deir al-Medina as the royal tomb builders' home, he devoted his life to understanding theirs. Černý deciphered and correlated thousands of texts from papyri and from inscriptions in the builders' tombs and on stelae, in addition to the drawings and texts scribbled on ostraca, the limestone chips produced by

Deir al-Medina, royal tomb builders' village, West Bank, Luxor, 2009.

quarrying that villagers used as notepaper. During thirty years of archaeological missions with Bernard Brueyère, who conducted systematic excavations of the site (1922–51), Černý became intimate with the tomb builders and their families, 'sifting through the very dust of their lives', piecing together their genealogies and interactions. After retiring from his position at Oxford University as the Edwards Professor of Egyptology, he returned to the village to track the thousands of graffiti villagers left scattered throughout the Theban hills. Černý's last years were spent combing the necropolis for inscriptions, as if hungry for news of old friends.[22]

More than labourers, the tomb builders were master masons, carpenters, draughtsmen, painters and sculptors employed by a royal enterprise known as the Institution of the Tomb ('the Tomb' for short). Their title was 'Servant in the Great Place', the royal necropolis, but to each other they were 'the men of the gang', an ancient term for ship crews. Like ship crews they were divided into two groups (right and left) of thirty to sixty men, each led by a foreman who answered to the vizier, a step away from pharaoh. Their positions were hereditary, and a foreman might remain in charge for longer than the reigns of some pharaohs. Over the course of 420 years, successive generations of village workmen produced tombs for pharaohs, in addition to tombs for royal mothers, favourite wives and other family members, many of which were of monumental proportions.[23]

Their job began when a king was crowned. The first step was the choice of location, followed by the tomb's design, usually by a royal architect. In some cases, the tomb builders assisted in the planning, based on the quantity of goods the tomb would have to hold. Secrecy was paramount; in an official progress report to Thutmose I, the architect Ineni proudly declared:

> I supervised the excavation of the cliff-tomb of His Majesty alone, no one seeing, no one hearing ... I was vigilant in seeking that which was excellent ... It is a work such as the ancestors had not which I was obliged to do there.[24]

The scribe of the Tomb was on hand to document the construction from the moment of 'the piercing', when quarriers began carving out the space with their bronze chisels and cedar mallets, tearing out soft limestone that hardened in the sun. Close at their heels came the plasterers, who smoothed the rough chipped walls with a layer of gypsum and whitewash, preparing them for decoration. The draughtsmen were next, sketching the appropriate scenes in red ink that the master draughtsman corrected in black. Sculptors meticulously carved the drawings into detailed reliefs, which were turned over to painters, who coloured them in vivid, mineral-based pigments. All aspects of construction proceeded simultaneously in different tomb rooms, the two crews spelling each other for maximum efficiency; since no one knew how long a pharaoh might live they had a literal deadline to meet.

The tomb of Ramses II was ready long before his death, probably when he was in his late eighties. To live so long was unusual; the elderly suffered from familiar ailments like arteriosclerosis and arthritis, but dental problems affected everyone. Teeth were worn down from the sand that crept into everything, especially bread, since millers added it to grain to grind flour more finely. Ramses II, that great pharaoh, is thought to have died of a bad tooth. By then, twelve crown princes had died and his thirteenth son and successor, Merenptah (r. 1212–1201), was in his mid-fifties. The men of the gangs leapt to work, digging a trench in front of the tomb site to deflect flash-flood waters, a rare but significant hazard in the hilly desert. By the second year, the entrance corridors were complete and work had begun on the burial chamber, with its laborious security system of nested coffins embedded in the living rock. In the seventh year, wooden funerary statues coated in buttery gold were delivered, prompting a brief celebration. When Merenptah died, having reigned just over ten years, his tomb was not quite ready, leaving the seventy-day mummification period the builder's last chance to finish as best they could.[25]

Despite rudimentary tools and the gloom of tomb interiors, the builders typically worked with great precision. The right angles in Ramses II's tomb, for instance, were accurate to within less than

Hypostyle hall in the Tomb of Vizier Ramose (TT55), built during the New Kingdom (18th dynasty) reign of Amenhotep III.

1 centimetre (⅜ in.). Light came from clay pots containing wicks of twisted linen dipped in castor oil or fat with salt to reduce soot that would mar the walls. The deeper they dug, the more light was needed and the number of wicks they used increased. These were carefully tallied by the tomb scribe, as were the tools that were weighed at the end of each day to ensure that no copper had been deliberately shaved off and tucked away. The irony of burying masses of gold while having to answer for every last linen twist and metal scraping is unlikely to have escaped the builders, who worked eight days a week, camping out by the site and returning to the village for two-day weekends. In the hot conditions, they worked naked or in a coarse linen mini-kilt and sturdy leather sandals. Their day was divided into two four-hour shifts with a noon break for lunch sent up from the village, though they sometimes took the afternoon off.

The tomb scribe assiduously recorded absenteeism and its reason. Scorpion bites and 'eye disease' (possibly dust-related conjunctivitis) were common causes, along with days off for the birth of children or a relative's death. A domestic argument could suffice as an excuse, as could brewing beer; someone took a day off expressly for drinking with a companion, another for a hangover, another to work on his house.[26] During long reigns when the king's tomb and those of his royal dependants were completed, the men worked for private clients to augment their income, while spending as much time as possible building and equipping their own tombs on the village outskirts. They also built and maintained a modest mud-brick temple on the village's north end, filling it with votive stelae and statues in wood and stone.

While they did not live as richly as palace or temple officials, tomb builders enjoyed a degree of prestige well above average. Some were literate and owned copies of popular stories and wisdom texts; some kept pets, a monkey or baby gazelle. They wore voluminous woollen cloaks in winter, and in summer they had sandals woven from reeds that turned up at the toes like a ship's prow. The food rations constituting their pay were hearty and varied, including fresh fish, dates, vegetables, milk and enough grain to set some aside for barter. Daily necessities were delivered to the village, including beer, oil, water and wood for cooking, sparing the women considerable work (though they still baked the family's bread in

Tomb of Sennedjem, 'servant in the place of truth', 19th dynasty, Deir al-Medina, 2010.

mud-brick ovens, as rural women do today). Extras like meat, sesame oil and salt were provided on special occasions. The villagers were fond of honey and kept their own bees, which they called 'the tears of Ra'. Except at times of famine when nearly everyone suffered, the tomb builders lived reasonably well and deserved it, given the demands of their work, which included being duly sworn to never 'overturn a stone in the Great Place of pharaoh', that is, to never steal.[27] Not everyone, however, was happy with his job. Aside from the danger of accident, the occasional broken or rock-crushed limb, or dreaded snake and scorpion bites whose pain was likened to fire, the most insidious occupational hazard was witnessing the burial of outlandish quantities of gold and useful goods.

Tomb foremen and the chief scribe had a higher pay grade, receiving a third more grain than workers. Some of their furniture was made of wood instead of cane or palm, their clothing was fancier and their tombs the finest in town. Some were more ambitious than others and exercised their power with greater freedom, including Qenhirkhopeshef (henceforth referred to as Qen), senior scribe of the tomb for over forty years. The scribal profession was greatly admired in antiquity. 'Behold, there is nothing that surpasses writings! They are like [a boat] upon the water,' according to a Middle Kingdom text, vaunting a career traditionally considered a cut above the rest.[28] 'Be a scribe so that your limbs may become sleek and your hands soft,' a New Kingdom author advised.[29] Even now, the scribe's modern equivalent, the civil servant, is envied for the respectability, absence of physical labour, short hours and guaranteed lifelong employment associated with the job.

Both Qen (c. 1262–1177 BC) and his father, the senior scribe Ramose, were adopted.[30] Infertility was a common complaint, and while childless couples petitioned the gods, adoption was deemed its best remedy. Although accepted as legitimate heirs, adopted sons may have felt compelled to prove their merit, as was the case with Ramose, whose dedication to his trade was reflected in his firm and even handwriting. Qen worked under his father's authority until he was around fifty, when he inherited Ramose's position, just as the building of Merenptah's tomb got underway. As senior

Tomb scribe, he was responsible for documenting and reporting the work's progress. Along with the foremen, Qen supervised removal of construction goods and tools from storehouses in addition to managing the builders' wage rations and monitoring deliveries. The tomb scribe and foremen sat on the local tribunal, adjudicating villagers' complaints and misdemeanours, a role that enhanced their prestige.

Qen was a history buff with a particular interest in the lineage of ancient kings. He kept a library of papyri in his home in Deir al-Medina, including some texts he had copied or written himself. Proud of his rank, he carved the words 'sitting place of the scribe Qenhirkhopeshef' in the shade of a rock cleft near the work site where he liked to rest. But compared to his father's handwriting, Qen's was fast and loose, in later life barely legible. He was not the most admired of authorities either, commandeering tomb builders to work for him privately while on the palace clock with apparently insufficient reward. 'What does this bad way mean in which you behave to me?' complained a draughtsman in a letter written on an ostracon and addressed to Qen. 'I am to you like the donkey ... if there is some beer, you do not look for me, but, if there is work, you do.'[31]

That scribes abused their power is evident in the stern warning against it in a popular New Kingdom text:

> Do not lead a man astray with reed pen on papyrus,
> It is the abomination of god.
> Do not witness a false statement,
> Nor remove a man (from the list) by your order:
> [Do not] make your pen false ...
> The beak of the Ibis [Thoth, god of writing] is the finger
>   of the scribe,
> Take care not to disturb it.[32]

Some 99 per cent of the population were illiterate, making scribal deceptions more feasible, but other forms of corruption were similarly denounced in wisdom texts, an indication of their prevalence.

Limestone statue of scribe, Tanis (Lower Egypt), 4th or 5th dynasty, photograph by J. Pascal Sébah, c. 1893.

There were several euphemisms for 'bribe' in the New Kingdom, ranging from 'a little something', to 'bonus', 'compensation' and 'fodder', another telltale sign that bureaucratic underhandedness was not infrequent.[33] Wielding rank for the purpose of extortion was common enough for Seti II (1201–1195 BC) to issue a royal decree that any priest found guilty of demanding 'something' from his underlings would be stripped of his title and sent to work in the fields.³⁴ Qen was accused of accepting bonuses to cover up for workmen's infractions on at least two occasions, and given the nature of his duties, there were likely other instances of false pen.

Like his fellow villagers, Qen wore an amulet around his neck as protection from Sehaqeq, a demon believed to cause headaches and illnesses. Able to breach the boundary separating the living and the dead, demons were hostile beings who had somehow offended the gods in life, the 'unjustified' who failed to pass the afterlife exam or spirits for whom the proper funerary rituals had not been carried out. Not all demons had names, but Sehaqeq was known as:

> He who has come forth from the sky and the earth, whose eyes are in his head, whose tongue is in his anus, who eats buttock-loaves ... who lives on dung, whom the gods of the necropolis fear.³⁵

Referred to as 'adversaries' or 'enemies' in spells composed to disarm them, demons could invade a place, a person or a portion of the body, causing pain or swelling. Associated with bleeding and miscarriage, they were also blamed for hangovers and vomiting. That they were widely feared is suggested by the availability of their repellents: garlic, beer, spit and amulets like Qen's, a spell inscribed on a bit of papyrus, folded repeatedly and bound with a flax string in a small leather pouch.

Qen thrived as chief tomb scribe to a ripe old age, supervising at least two royal tombs after Merenptah's. When he was around seventy he married a twelve-year-old girl, probably his first wife. While most girls married at twelve to fourteen years, their husbands were typically just a year or two older. If Qen felt himself at a disadvantage, he had recourse to popular remedies like a preparation for greying hair whose ingredients included 'the blood of young black oxen, the fat of black snakes, cats' wombs and raven eggs'.³⁶ Animal fats and ground tortoiseshell were believed to prevent baldness, while impotence was treated with various unguents and much prayer. As Qen approached the end of his life, the New Kingdom was likewise past its prime. Imperial expansion brought new (foreign) people, technologies and beliefs into play, in addition to more wealth and luxury goods for the elite. While initially invigorating, prosperity created appetites, and Ramses II's overlong rule whetted ambitions. Merenptah's brief reign was the coda to an era of relative stability and abundance; in the next twenty years the crown changed heads five times.

Secession disputes between those loyal to Merenptah's heirs, and supporters of Ramses II's other sons, resulted in deadly skirmishes near the necropolis, making work there unsafe. The tomb builders' village wasn't free of conflict either, with accusations of theft and misconduct causing family feuds that were not always easily resolved. Alert to widespread corruption, people regarded the courts with deep distrust. 'The judges are an insatiable belly. The speaking of falsehoods is like [fine] herbs for them, for such poison is pleasant to their hearts,' opined a Middle Kingdom author.[37] In a New Kingdom text, the condemnation was more pointed. 'Powerful though he may be,' the author warns, 'the matter lies with Sekhmet the Great.'[38] Enjoining the lion goddess of war to the cause of justice suggests that its enemies were so voracious that it would take an expert to vanquish them.

One of Qen's oldest and closest colleagues, the foreman Neferhotep, adopted an orphaned boy named Paneb, who was trained as a stonemason and eventually inherited his father's position as foreman of the right-hand gang. An individual of exceptional vitality who would supervise the building of five royal tombs, Paneb had a dark side. A brawler, philanderer, extortionist and a violator of his oath to never raid tombs, he was denounced by his father, uncle and son in formal complaints to the vizier. Qen shielded Paneb from the consequences of his actions on at least two occasions (in exchange for a bonus) but when he died, others colluded with Paneb to evade the law. Like the Greeks, the Egyptians conceived their gods as subject to the same wickedness as humans; among them were cheats and liars prone to greed and lust. In this regard, Paneb (c. 1225–1175) was a god among men. Infamous in his day for his exploits, Paneb was but a symptom of the malaise that would prove fatal within the next century.

The earliest study of human temperament on record is a portrait of an angry man. Qen kept a copy of the already ancient, Middle Kingdom text, in his library in Deir al-Medina and it surely reminded him of Paneb.[39] The ideal Egyptian in social terms was 'the silent man' (*ger ma-a*), a law-abiding 'follower of Horus', the falcon-headed god of the sky, and of the kings who maintain order.[40] The papyrus in Qen's library described instead the 'followers of Seth', the silent man's nemesis. In the course of an epic battle with his young nephew Horus, Seth buggered him and stole one of his eyes. He was a thief; in sexual and other matters 'the enemy of boundaries', the god of foreigners and foreign lands.[41] And he was a sore loser. When sun god Ra named Horus the battle's winner and king of kings, Seth was banished to the desert where he did his best to raise hell. Lord of the tempest, his sand-laden winds bruised Horus' skies, blackening the eye of Ra, and delivering the rainsqualls that sent juggernauts of muck and rubble thundering down from the hills.

Civilization may be described as the act of reconciling contradictions. Egyptian culture at its best was characterized by a dedication to equilibrium and the continuity this implied. The dualities that informed the ancient ideology (divine and mortal, fertile and barren, order and chaos) were recognized as aspects of a greater whole. Seth's role as the sower of discord was consequently integral to the Egyptian concept of order, lending balance to portrayals of both nature and the gods, neither of whom were always beneficent. In parts of Egypt a pair of falcons was worshipped as a dual god, Horus-Seth, order and chaos united.[42] But the conciliatory aspect of Seth's character was less pronounced than the divisive one, which was required to counter the stringent ethics of Horus, his arch-rival. Although sometimes depicted as a wild boar, in hieroglyphic writing the Seth-animal (resembling a canine with large, erect ears, an elongated snout and forked tail) signified confusion, the opposite of order, and it appears in words such as rage, tumult, to boast, to be harsh, to roar and to deceive.[43]

Mirroring the god's bellicosity, Seth's followers were described as hot-blooded and unpredictable, given to drunken rage and violence, and often red-headed. 'As to any man who opposes him, forthwith he pushes ... massacre arises in him,' according to the ancient text.[44] While we do not know the colour of Paneb's hair, he was as cold-blooded as the lizards said to be ruled by Seth, as toxic as the scorpions under the god's command and as havoc-wreaking as the crocodiles and hippopotami believed to be Seth's helpers. In a long complaint detailing Paneb's disorderly conduct to the vizier, his uncle, the tomb builder Amenakht, declared him 'unworthy of his office', remarking, 'he is keeping well, though he is like a mad man.'[45]

However he may have registered the loss of his parents, Paneb's adoption by Neferhotep granted entry to a more comfortable, promising world. But he wasn't satisfied and, for some unmentioned provocation, he attacked Neferhotep, according to Amenakht,

> though it was he who had reared him, and [Neferhotep] closed his doors before [Paneb, who] took a stone and smashed his doors. And they caused men to watch [over] Neferhotep, because Paneb said 'I will kill him in the night.'[46]

Paneb fought with a group of nine men that same night, and apparently had the best of them. Shaken by his behaviour, Neferhotep complained to the vizier and Paneb was reprimanded. But he retaliated, accusing the vizier of mistreatment, and the vizier himself was dismissed. This may have resulted from the attrition rate in high officialdom at the time more than the accusations of Paneb, who was not yet foreman. But that he should dare rebuke the pharaoh's main man offers an indication of both Paneb's self-assurance and how previously strict hierarchical authority had grown lax.[47]

Neferhotep died under uncertain circumstances around 1200 BC and although Amenakht insinuated Paneb was behind it, he was probably an innocent victim of the melees on the village outskirts after Merenptah's death. Paneb became foreman during the reign of Seti II (whose name means 'of Seth') and his career unfolded at a time when the tomb builders could barely keep up with the coming and goings of short-lived rulers. Seti II's six-year reign was followed by four years under Amenmesse, probably a son of Ramses II. Next came Siptah, the young, lame son of Seti II, who lasted six years with the help of his stepmother and a Syrian chancellor, and who ordered royal tombs be built for all three at once.[48] The pace of work in the necropolis was frantic; tool inventories showed 37 chisel heads worn to a nub in a single year.[49] The crews of Paneb and his left-hand gang counterpart, Hay, removed 1,060 tonnes (1,170 T.) of stone during the building of Seti II's tomb and 1,960 tonnes (2,160 T.) during the building of Siptah's.[50]

Paneb directed his surplus energy at those he felt had wronged him or that he just wanted out of the way. Although he had a fair claim to his father's position given his relative youth and experience, his uncle Amenakht was by custom in line for the job. Paneb handled the matter by bribing the new vizier, presenting him five servants from his recently deceased father's household, who were themselves contested property. To silence his uncle's family and enforce his claim as rightful heir, he took to lurking around Neferhotep's tomb, throwing stones at relatives who dared come there to make offerings. At night, Paneb was wont to climb atop the village wall and prowl the periphery, hurling stones at men gathered below, his colleagues in one capacity or another, as they sat drinking beer. The men of the left- and right-hand gangs were no doubt proud of their work and between them, under two different foremen, a degree of competition was to be expected. But Paneb upped the ante, antagonizing foreman Hay on several occasions, telling him 'I will get you to the desert, and I will kill you.'[51] That Paneb's wife, Wa'bet, was related to Hay may have had something to do with his animosity, but his threats raised controversy if not disputes among the inhabitants of Deir al-Medina.

The first thing Seth did after murdering his brother Osiris was try to seduce his wife, their sister Isis. Highly sexed, he was sometimes equated with Baba, god of the erection, as noted in the Coffin Texts: 'My phallus is Baba. I am Seth.' His penis was said to emit fire and men suffering from impotence could turn to him for help, as could whoever hoped for sexual gratification in this life and kingdom come.[52] The follower of Seth was accordingly described as 'beloved of women through the greatness . . . the greatness of his loving them'. In a characteristic demonstration of Paneb's greatness, 'he stripped Yeyeymewaw of her garment, threw her atop the wall, and violated her.'[53] The verb used here and elsewhere for the sex act, *nik*, is still operational in Arabic and in French, having entered the language through Moroccan slang. Like 'to fuck', *nik* leaves us uncertain as to whether or not the act was consensual. Also like fuck, *nik* was commonly used in insults, some of which involved a donkey, another animal associated with Seth ('a donkey will nik him', or 'nik his wife'). Although we do not know the time of day of Paneb and Yeyeymewaw's coupling, doing it on the wall was infra dig. People had sex in private, or in as much privacy as possible in a village where everyone lived in one another's lap. According to Herodotus, the Egyptians believed 'that things unseemly should be performed in private, but things not unseemly should be done in the open'.[54] Urinating, incidentally, belonged to the latter category and Herodotus tells us that women did it standing up, and men sitting down.

In choosing his partners, the follower of Seth did not care if a woman was married; then again, she might not have cared much either. 'I carried the basket, and another man nik-ed [my wife],' complained a cuckolded labourer in a tone of resignation.[55] Marriage was more a legal than religious matter, made by agreement between individuals and their families and celebrated throughout the first year. Adultery by either party was cause for divorce, also by agreement, and people remarried frequently. While polygamy was legal it was not commonly practised (except by pharaohs), though there is evidence that some men had more than one wife, or perhaps kept a mistress. Women were equal under the law and had the right to own property. Owing to their husbands' frequent absence and numerous responsibilities, the women of Deir al-Medina maintained a considerable degree of independence, and some may have been literate. Some worked in nearby temples, and others managed small businesses.[56] Paneb's wife chose to ignore her husband's indiscretions, but their first son, Apahte (meaning 'great of strength', one of Seth's epithets), was outraged. 'I cannot bear with him,' Apahte said, testifying to his father's liaisons with several colleagues' wives and one of their daughters, with whom Apahte confessed that he too had sex, whether on the same occasion as his father or not is unclear.[57]

Sex is frequently mentioned in a copy of a book of dream interpretations, the oldest on record, found in Qen's library on the same papyrus as the description of the followers of Seth. Brief summaries of the dream content followed by its portent appear under the heading 'if a man sees himself in a dream'. Sex 'in the sun' (in public) is a bad omen, meaning the gods will see one's misdeeds, as was certainly the case with Paneb. Seeing his penis 'growing large' in a dream meant that a man's riches would multiply, whereas seeing it erect meant victory to his enemies. Animals figure in a number of dreams, as might be expected in an agrarian society. Sex with a cow portends 'a happy day in the house'; sex with a pig, that a man will lose his possessions; and with a jerboa, a desert rodent resembling a miniature kangaroo, that a judgement will be passed against him, which seems only fair. Dream sex with women had several contradictory meanings, as might also be expected. Sex with one's mother was a good thing, meaning that family members would be loyal to the dreamer; sex with a sister meant an inheritance was on the way. Straight-up sex with a woman, however, meant 'mourning', and seeing a woman's vagina in a dream boded 'the last extremity of misery'.[58]

If the lyrics of ancient Egyptian love songs are any indication, the sexual urge was openly expressed by men and women alike. 'My desire is not yet quenched by your love, my wanton little jackal cub,' reads one New Kingdom verse, 'My lust for you I cannot forego/ Though I be beaten and driven off/ To dwell in the Delta marshes.' Or from a woman's perspective, 'My lover enkindles my heart by his voice/ Causing yearning for him to seize me.'[59] While there are many talismanic figurines with outsized phalluses, depictions of Egyptians in the act are few; among them, the Turin Erotic Papyrus (twentieth dynasty) found in Deir al-Medina shows exceedingly limber women and hyper-endowed men gleefully demonstrating positions for intercourse. Someone jotted playful dialogue in the margins: 'Look here, come round behind me,' says the woman, 'I make your job a pleasant one.'[60] During long nights camped at the work site, the tomb builders tried their hand at erotica and two examples drawn on ostraca have survived: a dancing girl bent over backwards, her long, dark hair resting on the ground, and a woman's lower torso, etched along the fracture lines of the stone.[61]

Everyone in the village was related, whether by marriage or blood, resulting in mixed loyalties, family squabbles and the impossibility of keeping secrets. Whether between men working in the necropolis all week or the women left at home, the exchange of information was probably a prime entertainment. Amenahkt's complaint to the vizier described Paneb's transgressions over a period of years, but while venting his accumulated rancour, the accusations were certainly true; everyone would have known if they weren't. Paneb was a bully who made people work for him, tending his ox, crafting the things he was commissioned for by outside clients, and helping him build and decorate his tomb, whose lacklustre interior suggests their hearts weren't in it.[62] But his worst offence in societal terms was the violation of his oath as a servant in the Great Place.

Paneb stole blocks from the Tomb of Seti II, whose building he'd supervised, to use for a tomb of his own. He must have had help dismantling them, because one of his assistants ratted. Having entered the pharaoh's burial chamber, Paneb broke open wine amphorae, hoisted himself atop the sarcophagus and got drunk, perhaps in the belief that anyone named after Seth wouldn't mind. On another occasion, he stole the bed out from under the mummy of a fellow tomb builder; on yet another, he took the statue of a goose from the tomb of a daughter of Ramses II, an interesting choice of plunder, since the goose, associated with the god

Amun, had sexual connotations.[63] These infractions, while strictly forbidden, display more bravado and rebellion than the desire for personal gain, since the theft of gold or precious goods is not mentioned. Compared to later raiders, Paneb's thefts were child's play.

Paneb wasn't the only thief in town and women were sometimes accomplices. Although she swore innocence, a woman named Heria was found guilty of stealing workmen's tools and items from a temple when these were recovered from their hiding place in her home. Perjury and tomb or temple theft carried the same heavy sentence, and Heria was likely executed.[64] Following his uncle's complaints, Paneb's crimes too must have caught up with him, and while his fate is unknown, he disappears from the record during Siptah's reign, at the end of the nineteenth dynasty. But Paneb's type, so vividly drawn in the documents found in Deir al-Medina, lived on, as elaborated in a later New Kingdom text:

> The hot-headed man is like a wolf cub in the farmyard.
> And he turns one eye to the other
> For he sets families to argue.
> He goes before all the winds like clouds,
> He changes his hue in the sun;
> He crooks his tail like a baby crocodile,
> He curls himself up to inflict harm,
> His lips are sweet, but his tongue is bitter,
> And fire burns inside him.[65]

Paneb offers a textbook example of the irreverence and discontent felt by those who dared to rob tombs and temples. The quintessential tomb raider, his character is not unfamiliar; indeed, more than one 'follower of Seth' still serves in public office.

Seth's cult enjoyed a heyday in the New Kingdom; Ramses II appealed to the god of the tempest for protection from wind and snow during a foreign expedition, and two nineteenth-dynasty kings (Seti I and II) named themselves after Seth to appropriate his raw power. Military officials of the twentieth dynasty likewise petitioned Seth to aid their campaigns in foreign lands.[66] The first ruler of the twentieth dynasty was named Sethnakhte ('Seth is victorious'), probably a grandson of Ramses II. A text announcing his reign described the previous half-century of internecine strife and institutional decay, promising better days:

> [Before Sethnakhte] the land of Egypt was cast adrift, every man being a law unto himself, and they had no leaders for many years, empty years when . . . each joined with his neighbour in plundering their goods and they treated the gods like people and no one dedicated offerings in the temples . . . But the gods turned themselves to peace so as to put the land in its proper state – they established their son Sethnakhte . . . upon their great throne . . . he brought order to the entire land – he slew the rebels – he cleansed the great throne of Egypt.[67]

Sethnakhte died two or three years later having cleansed nothing. His son and successor, Ramses III, was the first of a series of twentieth-dynasty pharaohs calling themselves Ramses, harking back to the glory years of Ramses II (a proven redhead). But far from restoring order, during the 32 years of Ramses III's rule and the shorter reigns of his successors, the palace's hold on power weakened and tomb and temple theft escalated like a run on a defaulting bank. Ramses III built the last (and best preserved) of the magnificent Theban temples. The twentieth dynasty witnessed the disintegration of a society intoxicated with gold and greatness, as an empire that had endured since time out of mind neared its end.

In later centuries when Egypt was subjugated to foreigners, Seth was condemned as an 'enemy of the gods', his temples defaced and abandoned. Ceremonies performed to 'overthrow Seth and his gang' involved a waxen image that was stamped on with the left foot and chopped into pieces, while reciting a spell that reads, in part: 'Robber! Lord of Lies, king of deceit, gang-leader of criminals . . . [he] who creates rebellion; lord of looting, who rejoices at greed, master thief, who [solicits] theft, who gives offence.'[68] Seth's vilification as exemplified in this ritual may reflect the hatred of intruders who pillaged Egypt at will. But in the course of a millennial career, the god of thieves and disruptors was far more revered than despised, both by pharaohs and their nemesis, the tomb raiders.

In the annals of Egyptian art, largely religious in nature, there are few departures from accepted themes and styles. The decoration of tombs, temples and funerary equipment was based on templates that determined how gods and people were portrayed. Most of the surviving exceptions treating non-religious topics were made in and recovered from Deir al-Medina. The so-called 'satirical papyri and ostraca' feature familiar scenes but with animals provocatively cast in human roles. Perhaps the best-known example is a wily fox herding goats while playing a double flute, the archetypal pied piper. Elsewhere, a donkey judge wields his crook and staff while animal captives cower before him; hordes of militant mice storm a fortress guarded by scared cats who raise their paws in surrender; the leader of a flock of ducks attacks a cat and a cat servant fans his mistress mouse.[69]

Whether or not these drawings correspond to an otherwise lost oral tradition, they were likely viewed in their time as cartoonish social commentary, tinged with ridicule and disdain. Egypt's history offers ample proof of the constancy of certain behaviours, including the greed and self-absorption of the privileged and the frustration of those obliged to put up with them. As befits the world's oldest, best-documented autocracy, Egypt boasts the world's first recorded strikes, a series of sit-ins organized by the tomb builders protesting against palace officials' repeated failure to deliver their payment in supplies. 'We are in extreme destitution . . . lacking in every staple . . . a load of stone is not light! . . . truly we are already dying, we are no longer alive,' wrote a Tomb scribe during the reign of Ramses III (c. 1156 BC).[70] 'The company . . . has leeched my blood . . . I'm saying, save me, hunger has consumed my guts.' Thus spoke a striking employee of Petrojet, Egypt, in 2012.[71]

The sociopolitical conditions of Ramses III's rule were ominous. During the fifth and eleventh years of his reign, Egypt suffered incursions from both the Libyans in the west and sea peoples arriving from the eastern Mediterranean. His nineteenth-dynasty predecessors had likewise dealt with Libyan attacks and waves of Libyan refugees owing to drought in that region. Despite Ramses III's many building projects in Thebes, jobs were scarce and religious festivals lengthened to appease the people and give them something to eat. The builders were busy with the tombs Ramses III ordered for five of his sons, but construction works depleted the grain stores. Shortages, compounded by administrative corruption, including the diversion of recycled temple offerings slated for tomb workers to the tables of favoured officials, left the inhabitants of Deir al-Medina hungry for weeks on end. Like his predecessors, Ramses III lived in the northern Nile Delta. Tellingly, his temple, with a royal residence for his visits to Upper Egypt, was fortified with battlements and ramparts.

When the tomb builders decided to strike in the 29th year of Ramses III's reign, they didn't just lay down their tools; they set precedents, marching the short distance to the pharaoh's residence to voice their grievance in person. Denied entry and presumably chased off, they demonstrated at the temple of Thutmose III, further north. 'If we arrived here, it is because of hunger and because of thirst,' the workmen claimed, their actions detailed by the Tomb scribe in a papyrus recovered in Deir al-Medina. The vizier and his subordinates tried putting them off, saying that the 'white house' (the treasury) was depleted even though they had plenty of grain themselves. The workers bargained but got only half of what they were due, so they brought their wives and children to protest until their demands were met. At one point a workman betrayed two of his fellows, saying they stole blocks from the tomb of Ramses II, to gain traction with the authorities and food for his family. Rations continued to be delayed and sporadic strikes occurred throughout the few remaining years of Ramses III's reign. The tomb builders eventually had their day in court, but only after having bribed two fan-bearers to get their case before a magistrate.[72]

The deference towards authority figures born with kingship and the divine nature of pharaoh endures to the present day; Egyptians seldom challenge their leaders openly. Over the course of over 1,500 years, only three pharaohs are known to have met their deaths at an assassin's hands: one in the Old Kingdom, Teti (2629–2623 BC), murdered by a bodyguard; in the Middle Kingdom, Amenemhat I (1994–1964 BC), killed by his attendants; and in the New Kingdom, Ramses III (1185–1153 BC), victim of a palace conspiracy organized by his wives. Others implicated in the coup included a chamberlain, chief of archers, overseer of the white house, priests and scribes from the house of life (royal library). Recent CT scans of Ramses III's mummy show that his throat was slit from behind and one of his big toes hacked off, perhaps by a second assailant.[73] The language used to record the event was aimed at obfuscation, owing to the unspeakable severity of the crime and the attendant scandal. The news that reached Thebes was that 'the falcon has flown up to heaven,' alerting the tomb builders that Ramses III's burial was imminent.[74] His son and successor, Ramses IV, sentenced the conspirators: some had their nose, ears and lips cut off, others were punished by 'leaving them alone', that is, being allowed to take their own lives.[75]

Undaunted by his father's fate, Ramses IV hatched grandiose plans for temple building. In the first year of his reign, he launched expeditions to the Eastern Desert to quarry stone and gold, the largest involving 9,000 men, mostly conscripted labourers, in addition to an armed guard, scribes, horses, chariots and provisions for all. Nine hundred people died in this coffer-draining endeavour. Having survived a coup designed to derail his father's line of succession, Ramses IV's overconfidence helped hasten its end. He ruled for six years, leaving his projects unachieved.[76] His son Ramses V died after five years of rule, at age forty, the earliest known victim of smallpox.[77] At the outset of Ramses VI's reign, Thebes was in disarray, with disenfranchised mercenaries, bedouin bandits and gangs of dispossessed locals roaming unchallenged, creating favourable conditions for tomb-raiding and placing the necropolis guard, the Medjay, on edge.

In times of strife people look to their leaders, and when they're found wanting, they look to their gods. Disillusionment grew as New Kingdom rulers claiming to do the will of official deities acted with impunity on their own behalf. The dramatic religious reforms introduced by Amenhotep IV (Akhenaton; 1360–1343 BC) came at a time when change and revitalization was overdue. Akhenaton rejected top god Amun-Ra and his coterie of powerful priests, in favour of Aten, the visible sun, raising a new capital, Amarna (400 kilometres/250 mi. north of Thebes), and breaking with architectural conventions in temple design and decoration. However revolutionary his acts, Akhenaton was still an absolute autocrat, and a relentlessly demanding one judging by the amount of building accomplished during his seventeen-year reign. His wish to strike 'a new deal between king and god', however short-lived, foreshadowed the attempts of average Egyptians to establish more direct lines of communications with their deities.[78] Individuals sought to forge intimate, as opposed to state-mediated, relationships with their god of choice, as evidenced by the proliferation of acts of personal piety, including shrines in homes and votive offerings placed in the forecourts of temples.

To settle personal and legal disputes without the middlemen, people began consulting divine oracles using a peculiar practice derived from the procession of the gods' shrines that featured in religious festivals. While the carriers shouldered the heavy litter, the weight sometimes shifted in transit, causing them to swerve or dip. Priests interpreted these random movements as signs favouring the legitimacy of their rulers; the verb 'to nod' was used to signal the god's approval. Oracles of the Theban Triad (Amun, his wife Mut and son Khonsu) helped determine the outcome of political affairs throughout the late New Kingdom. Consulting the oracles started out as a divine privilege that was eventually extended to average people. During religious festivals and on appointed days, the shrine of divine patrons like deified pharaoh Amenhotep I, founder of Deir al-Medina, was carried out for consultation. Ostraca were laid on the ground, each bearing a possible answer to people's questions, and at some point the god either nodded towards or recoiled from one or the other, or else a list might be read and a response elicited by one of its items. Questions often regarded mundane issues like property disputes or the prospect of jobs or windfalls, and the god could be enlisted to identify thieves or find missing objects.[79]

This process bears a striking resemblance to the most commercially successful of oracles, the Ouija board, originally marketed in 1891 as 'the wonderful talking board'. Having posed a question, participants place their fingertips on a planchette, moving it involuntarily towards the letters of the alphabet or numbers one through to nine, or the words 'yes' and 'no' marked on the board. Born of America's late nineteenth-century obsession with spiritualism in the wake of the Civil War, the Ouija board's popularity surged after the First World War. In 1967, in the heat of the Summer of Love and anti-Vietnam War protests, it sold 2 million copies.[80] The 300 per cent sales increase it enjoyed in 2014 was perhaps less a reflection of tumultuous times than the canny marketing of a film about a diabolical Ouija board that persecutes kids who dabble with it.[81] But it's fair to say that susceptibility to omens and oracles is not unrelated to the real or perceived vulnerability felt by those who rely on them.

The most common ancient Egyptian term for oracle was derived from the word 'wonder' and it's a wonder people were willing to overlook the fact that although they could now question their deities directly, the answers were still determined by the authorities, in this case the interpreter priests.[82] Ordinary people consulted oracles regularly in the later New Kingdom, and even the pharaoh was eventually obliged to submit his decisions to the oracle for approval. That the priesthood gained traction in this scenario suggests the rise of a theocracy, but this assumes that priests were religious in anything but job title.[83] Priests sometimes doubled as magistrates, arbitrating local affairs under the fig leaf of divine neutrality afforded by the oracle. Many high priests of Amun kept their position longer than the pharaohs they served; their reliable presence in Thebes enhanced their power and presented opportunities to flex it in ways that were hard to resist. The corruption that had discredited royal institutions lent power to the oracle, which in turn became a vehicle for whitewashing priestly corruption. The oracle decided appointments to the priesthood and nodded assent in more delicate matters that predictably served the priests' interests.

Halfway through the twentieth dynasty, during the rule of Ramses IX (1123–1104 BC), Egypt faced economic disaster brought on by man-made and natural crises. Some fifty years before, the Nile had delivered a devastating flood, causing enough damage to warrant the assembly of 3,000 men to repair Luxor Temple. After that came severe drought. As the annual flood diminished, the amount of cultivable land was reduced; the drop of 1 metre (3 ft) below the normal flood level cut the crop yield by half. Temple storehouses were emptied, and people obliged to survive from harvest to harvest. Under Ramses IX, one of the more frequent questions that tomb builders asked the oracle was if they'd be paid their rations so they could eat. Repelling the Libyan incursions during the eighth and fifteenth years of Ramses IX's reign placed additional stress on financially and administratively fragile palace and temple institutions. But an empire has no greater foe than famine; the climate change that brought extended droughts in the previous millennium contributed to the downfall of the Old Kingdom, the age of the pyramid builders. After 130 years of unrest, however, the old order was re-established and maintained throughout the Middle Kingdom. This time, with the need for food compounded by hunger for power and gold, chaos won the upper hand.

Anyone who has spent time in the desert has known a silence so profound that one can almost hear the sun's rays hitting the ground. Sound was the tomb raider's enemy; airborne it might easily reach the Medjay in their outposts along the mountains, or the priests performing rituals at royal tombs. The tomb doors were visible but sealed so that any disturbance would be obvious. Tunnelling into them was tough going; a group of eight men might take a week to clear pits and shafts to penetrate a burial chamber. The utmost stealth was required so the raiders worked after dark. It helped that the necropolis had grown crowded; sometimes they could tunnel from one tomb straight into another. Once they'd gathered the loot, they took it to a secluded place and lit a fire, burning the wooden coffins or statues coated in gold or silver and recovering the pools of molten metal from the cinders once they had hardened in the night-cooled sand. These were scrupulously measured using a stone counterweight and divided among the gang members, as was whatever else the tomb had surrendered.

Whereas the wealth of the early New Kingdom had come from foreign tributes and booty that entered the economy from the top, the tomb-raiding of the late New Kingdom 'released a surge of wealth into society from, as it were, the bottom'.[84] Theft altered the market, halving the value of precious metals against grain and changing the bartering rates for commodities. In the raid-based economy that coalesced in the reign of Ramses IX, thieves and their accomplices had the most tradable goods, while the go-betweens (traders, shopkeepers and travelling salesmen) profited from inflated prices placed on items purchased with stolen goods. The black market became a feature of daily life, where booty was bartered for basic needs, like food, clothes and parties replete with honeyed wine, but also, ironically, for the equipment people desired for their own burials.

Much of our knowledge of the stolen goods that flooded the market comes from a series of papyrus documents unique in the annals of antiquity, translated, correlated and interpreted by British Egyptologist T. Eric Peet (1882–1934) in his opus *The Great Tomb-Robberies of the Twentieth Egyptian Dynasty* (1930).[85] The papyri contain what amount to the court transcripts of investigations into tomb and temple theft that occurred during the reigns of Ramses IX and Ramses XI, including the depositions of witnesses and the accused, the tombs they robbed, the things they stole, the bribes they paid and evidence of a fencing network extending all the way north to Memphis. We hear the raiders speak, justifying their crimes in startlingly familiar terms: 'This inner coffin is ours; it belonged to our great men. We were hungry; we set out . . . to search for this piece of bread so as to profit from it,' claimed one of the suspects.[86]

The circumstances surrounding the acquisition and analysis of these papyri, mostly purchased in the mid- to late 1800s and later sold or gifted to wealthy collectors or museums, offer an example of the flukes of fate that sometimes accompany archaeological discoveries. Scores of papyri were rescued from the sands enveloping Deir al-Medina by Egyptian raiders who must have wondered what the foreigners planned to do with them. Purchased on a whim, ancient documents languished in sundry collections for decades, awaiting integration into the growing body of Egyptological knowledge. Peet was peeved when he asked if he could get photos of a papyrus in the vast holdings of Pierpont Morgan and was told 'it might be several years before it was unpacked.'[87] Raiders and their fences scattered artefacts across Egypt, typically without recording their exact provenance so as to avoid detection by the authorities, but Western collectors scattered them around the world, further complicating the matter of their study. Fortunately, the ancients were exacting in their documentation.

A papyrus first translated by Černý and re-examined by Peet, the so-called Papyrus Ambras, is dated year six of Ramses XI (c. 1088 BC). It relates how two clay vessels full of documents that were probably stolen from the archive of Ramses III's temple during the unrest that occurred there twenty years earlier had been 'found by people of the land' and returned to the temple, where they were duly inventoried.[88] One of the jars contained documents 'concerning the thieves' and the trials that took place during the reign of Ramses IX, that is, some of the very same papyri that Peet was examining more than 2,000 years later. As much as it must have thrilled him to identify the documents at hand as the former occupants of that ancient clay jar, Peet was vexed by lacunae and the fragmentary nature of some of the papyri. A year after his death, in 1935, the missing upper half of one of the documents he examined (Amherst Papyrus) cropped up among the souvenirs King

Leopold II of Belgium had acquired in Egypt, stuffed inside a statuette by a local broker to sweeten the deal. In a strange case of historical symmetry, the Amherst Papyrus, in which twentieth-dynasty thieves confessed their crimes, had apparently been torn in two by nineteenth-century raiders to divvy up their shares.[89]

The earliest trials recorded in the papyri Peet studied were held in year sixteen of Ramses IX's reign (c. 1107 BC), when the army was busy with the Libyans, grain was scarce and gangs of raiders from every walk of life were having a field day. The court process involved the vizier and a group of high officials who acted as prosecutor, judge and jury, in addition to scribes who recorded the proceedings. Suspects were rounded up, often with their wives, and questioned one by one. All were required to swear an oath to tell the truth on pain of mutilation or of being 'placed on the stake' or banished to a faraway place to work in mines or quarries. Interrogations involved torture regardless of gender, including the bastinado (foot whipping). A stout stick was used for more general beatings. Suspects were also placed in wooden hand- or ankle-cuffs that were tightened or twisted, shedding fresh light on the etymology of the expression, 'he twisted my arm'. The cases of those deemed guilty were referred to the pharaoh for sentencing. Egyptians did not take bloodshed lightly; impalement was reserved for the greatest of crimes, among which tomb-raiding ranked highly.

For the sake of concision, scribes pared the proceedings down to laconic, oft-repeated phrases such as 'he/she was examined with the stick' and said, 'stop, I will tell you!' or, in the case of those proclaiming innocence, 'far be it from me [to have stolen anything]!' Sometimes conflicting witnesses were made to confront one another, and one of them backed down. Some witnesses implicated others in the crimes of which they were accused, like the woman who was questioned about the silver her husband had swiped and said she never saw any silver in her house, and that the court should try asking his mistress.[90] Members of the raiding gangs were often related, people who knew and might trust one another. Some were experts, with knowledge of tomb construction and locations. We can imagine them comparing notes about the habits of the police, identifying those easily fooled or bribed, discussing how heavy objects were best handled, relating past mishaps or tales of eleventh-hour escapes from detection or disaster. But whatever code of honour or friendship the thieves may have shared was forgotten when their lives were literally at stake. In the course of interrogations, whether in hope of a lighter sentence or simply to stop the beatings, raiders readily submitted the names of their partners and anyone else implicated in the crime.

As for the trials' aim, the delivery of justice was incidental; the main objective was the recovery of stolen goods that were confiscated by the state. The trials also served as proxy battles between high officials, who used them to legitimize themselves as upholders of the law while settling scores through blame-laying, a tactic still popular among politicians. Such was the case in year sixteen of Ramses IX, when Paser, the mayor of east bank Thebes, claimed there had been thefts in the Great Place, which was under the jurisdiction of his west bank counterpart and rival, Pawero, chief of the necropolis police. Pawero immediately went on the offensive, also denouncing the thefts to the vizier, who personally inspected the ten tombs of 'the blessed ones of days gone by' that Paser had mentioned, accompanied by the royal butler. Three had been violated, including the resting place of Sobekamsef, a seventeenth-dynasty pharaoh, and those of two lesser personages.[91] One of the perpetrators described opening the outer and inner coffins of Sobekamsef's four-hundred-year-old tomb, and finding the pharaoh

> equipped like a warrior. A large number of sacred-eye amulets and gold was at his neck, and his headpiece of gold was on him. The noble mummy of this king was all covered with gold and his inner coffins were bedizened with gold and silver inside and outside with inlays of all kinds of precious stones. We appropriated the gold we found on this noble mummy of this god . . . We set fire to [the] inner coffins. We stole their outfit . . . consisting of objects of gold, silver and bronze and divided them up among ourselves.[92]

Grave Matters

The take from this tomb was 160 *debens* of pure gold, 14.5 kilograms (32 lb), the largest amount on record, but a small indication of the quantities of finely wrought treasures that were unearthed over time and melted down for barter.

Among the suspects Pawero had rounded up were two carpenters and three masons, tomb builders gone bad, in addition to a farmer and a water-carrier. All were expeditiously questioned and beaten, and duly confessed. 'Their trial and their doom was set down in writing and a dispatch was sent to Pharaoh.'[93] That same night, probably on Pawero's prompting, necropolis staff crossed the river to celebrate what they considered their vindication, since most of the tombs were found intact. Paser took exception to their taunting, saying 'You have rejoiced over me at the very door of my house. What do you mean by it?'[94] He reminded them that the robberies that were discovered were no small crime, and threatened to take the matter directly to the pharaoh. But Pawero's manoeuvring with the vizier and his direct authority over the necropolis workers left Paser humiliated and obliged to back down. The investigations meanwhile called attention to the sorry state of the necropolis, and rather than exonerating the officials responsible for its safekeeping, only heightened suspicions that they were aiding and abetting theft.

One of the tombs that the vizier and royal butler inspected belonged to Queen Isis, a wife of Ramses III, and according to their report it was unmolested. But a year later (year seventeen, Ramses

Earring, *c.* 1295–1186 BC, New Kingdom, Ramesside, gold, lapis lazuli.
Beaded penannular earring, *c.* 1550–1425 BC, New Kingdom reign of Thutmose III, Dra' Abu el-Naga' (Thebes), Carnarvon/Carter excavations (1914), gold, lapis lazuli.

87

ix) the queen's tomb was found ransacked and it seems likely that the vizier, in collusion with Pawero, had agreed to overlook its violation, whether in exchange for 'something' or simply to discredit Paser. All eight of the thieves accused of robbing Queen Isis were necropolis staff, and now Pawero was in the hot seat, obliged to find the stolen goods post-haste. A total of 4.3 kilograms (9 lb) of gold, 7 kilograms (15 lb) of silver and 63 garments were found in possession of the thieves. Within two weeks, still more was recovered from the individuals with whom the raiders had done business.[95]

Lists of recipients of the stolen goods illustrate their ubiquity in the local market, alongside the authorities' alacrity in recovering the goods when it was a matter of enriching the state. Among those who received a portion, whether in exchange for assisting the thieves, or keeping quiet, or in a bartering arrangement, were the chief treasury guard of the Temple of Amun, the chief of the Medjay and a necropolis policeman, two priests, five scribes, a temple weaver, an oil boiler, a coppersmith, several gardeners, a herdsman, a chief stable man and a groom, a washer-man, two fishermen, a sandal-maker, a porter, a servant, a baker, a woman of Thebes and a beekeeper, who was relieved of the 'coloured cloth and a whiplash' he'd acquired in exchange for honey. The raiders also revealed the names of fourteen traders who helped launder the loot, converting precious metals into livestock and other less conspicuous commodities in exchange for a hefty percentage. Some of the traders worked for institutions as far afield as the Fayoum, the Delta and Memphis, and all were obliged to reveal their clients so that they too might surrender the hot goods. These included numerous priests, a doctor of the temple of Amun, travelling merchants, local shopkeepers, a brewer, a sailor, a soldier, a barber and 'the cripple Kenben, who lives in the chapel of [a god]'.[96]

In the end, the treasures that had been buried with Queen Isis for eternity instead touched the lives of around one hundred people. Unsurprisingly, the authorities' recovery efforts, as recorded in the documents they authored, were highly efficient. But the trials for which we have records tell only part of the story. Given the opportunities for theft and a culture of bribery, plus the personal relations between people implicated in robbing and dispersing the goods, the authorities could not hope to recover everything that was stolen, and much remained in circulation. So it was that theft propped up an economy where the preternatural value placed on burial goods as tickets to paradise had only quickened need and greed. That ancient Egypt had enjoyed long eras of relative peace and stability suggests that people were generally content with the system and willing to defer to their rulers, or else fearful of outright rebellion. But 'beneath this bland, law-abiding exterior lurked a predatory instinct directed towards property rather than persons.'[97] Raiding redressed the inequity of the social order, but institutionalized theft drove a wedge into society, leaving space for dissent and aggression.

The second series of trials for which documents have survived was held during the reign of Ramses XI, a king of whom we know little. He was the end of the line, ruling nominally for thirty years as the priests gradually usurped royal power. In addition to marauding Libyans and severe food shortages, the palace had to contend with a dispute between two high officials that sent Egypt spiralling into civil war, with Thebes as its epicentre. The control of scant food supplies probably fed the rivalry between Amenhotep, the high priest in charge of the vast landholdings and wealth of the Domain of Amun, and Panehsy, the governor of the Nubian provinces and overseer of pharaoh's granaries. As the conflict escalated, Ramses XI sided with Amenhotep, sending one of his generals to defend him. Panehsy sent the Nubian troops in his purview to occupy the funerary temple of Ramses III, and likely did his best to prevent Amenhotep from distributing rations. Amid the turmoil, treasures were disappearing from tombs and temples like towels from a five-star hotel. Once again, tomb-raiding became a cause célèbre as two powerful men locked horns in a politically motivated crackdown on theft. Amenhotep conducted trials of suspected thieves, while governor Panehsy arrested three and had them executed to demonstrate his zeal for law and order.[98]

When Ramses XI took the side of the high priest, Panehsy was branded a public enemy and retreated to Nubia. Amenhotep submitted his formal thanks to the god Amun-Ra for '[attacking] the one who attacked me' and seized the opportunity to announce a new era of moral rectitude, the so-called 'repeating of births', with year one corresponding to year nineteen of Ramses XI's reign.[99] Tomb and temple theft provided the perfect axe for the priests to grind in their rhetorical renaissance. More than a crime epidemic, raiding had become an affair of state. Witness testimonies documented in the trials of tomb and temple robbers were often headed 'examination of the great foes' or 'the great criminals'. The ancients understood how sensationalizing an issue distracts from the need to address its root cause, and the proceedings were known to the public. But it's a reasonable assumption that tomb-raiding, by then commonplace, was no longer shocking, nor were the thieves likely viewed as a lethal threat, especially compared to the officials prosecuting crimes in which they were complicit, even while steering Egypt into famine and war.

The contentiousness issuing from the halls of power is echoed in the testimonies of suspected raiders recorded in the new era. Where goods equivalent to years' and sometimes decades' worth of average salaries were involved, there was bound to be thuggery, and some of the situations the raiders related would not be out of place in a mafia film. In the first year of the repeating of births, the court commanded a herdsman named Bukhaaf to name those he was with 'when you were about that business . . . and the god caught you and brought and placed you in the hand of Pharaoh'.[100] Bukhaaf prevaricated, relating how he'd been cheated by some of his own men, who visited their hidden stash behind his back and removed some of the goods that had not yet been apportioned. Before he could complain further, a beating brought him to the point, which was that he and his twelve-member gang had made away with a trove including a silver inner coffin and the shroud of gold and silver covering the mummy of a queen.

It seems that some of Bukhaaf's men turned on him to maximize their profits. The wife of a raider who was either dead or missing and had received her husband's share told the court how she was muscled by members of the breakaway gang, including her own brother. 'I took the share of my husband and put it in my storeroom and I took one *deben* of silver and bought grain with it,' she said, suggesting that food was a priority. A few days later her brother and three other men came to her home and insisted she relinquish her husband's cut: 900 grams (32 oz) of silver, 180 grams (6 oz) of gold and two jewelled seals, one of lapis lazuli the other of turquoise, set in 60 grams (2 oz) of gold.

> They said to me: give up the treasure. But I said to them with an air of boldness, my brother will not let me be interfered with. So said I, and [my brother] gave me a blow with a spear on one of my arms and I fell. I got up and entered the storeroom and I brought [the goods] and handed it over to him.[101]

Among those questioned were two trumpeters of the Temple of Amun, whose day job was heralding the arrivals and departures of pharaoh when he came to call. Amenkau maintained that Perpethew had falsely implicated him in the theft, saying 'Far be it from me!'

> Perpethew the trumpeter is an enemy of mine. I quarrelled with him and I said to him, you will be put to death for this theft which you committed in the necropolis. He said to me: If I go [to the stake], I will take you with me.[102]

Having stuck to his story throughout five days of beating, Amenkau was freed, as were several other suspects who maintained their innocence despite much arm-twisting. Then as now, the death sentence only worked as a deterrent to crime for people who were disinclined to break the law in the first place. A carpenter from Deir al-Medina suspected of participating in the theft denied his guilt, saying, 'I saw the punishment which was done to the thieves in [an earlier] time. Is it then likely I should go and seek out the death when I know it?'[103]

One of the confessed thieves told how Perpethew enlisted him in raiding the stash behind Bukhaaf's back. When Bukhaaf came to his home to demand the loot, his father resisted, saying, 'As for the noose . . . which [you] have laid upon the neck of the lad, you have come to take away his share, and yet his punishment will overtake him tomorrow.' Unimpressed, one of Bukhaaf's men responded in a manner suggesting that age was no guarantee of respect in such situations. 'Oh doddering old man, evil be his old age; if you are killed and thrown into the water, who will look for you?'[104] Murder was not out of the question to get rid of witnesses, as one raider confessed, 'I have killed the native of the area of the tomb along with the little servant who had been with us, so he would not keep us out.'[105]

Robbing tombs in the dead of night involved considerable daring but temples were now also considered fair game, and their doors, plated with precious metals, made for an easy haul. More than 108 kilograms (238 lb) of copper fastenings were harvested from one door, 99 kilograms (218 lb) from another.[106] Thieves scraped away the gold and silver sheathing, a *deben* here, a *deben* there, when needed, 'somewhat like a modern ATM'.[107] In one case (investigated by Amenhotep), a priest and a scribe helped steal 35 kilograms (77 lb) of precious metals (389 *debens*) from a temple on Thebes' west bank.[108] When a temple official discovered his employees stripping a door, instead of punishing them he made them give him an ox, thus sparing the trouble and exposure of trading gold. Yet another scribe overheard their plotting and demanded a cut as hush money.[109] Trial depositions show how temples were virtually dismantled by priests and scribes who stole entire wooden doors and floorboards from the Ramesseum. The imported cedar used for temple furnishings was prized, as it could be recycled to make coffins and other items for people's tombs. The gilded wood statues of deities, gold-coated portable shrines and palanquins used for religious processions were brazenly lifted, without a care for the gods' wrath. Such profit-driven sacrilege could only be accomplished with the participation of temple insiders who knew enough about the institution's routines to figure they could get away with it.

One temple scribe was paid to acquire a cedar shrine for a client and there were likely other cases of theft on commission.[110]

The food shortages of Ramses XI's reign alluded to in depositions encouraged both theft and betrayal. 'I was sitting hungry under the sycamores,' a woman testified, when she saw men trading the copper pole fittings of palanquins and reported them to a local official.[111] Another woman, questioned about a quantity of silver found in her possession, claimed she got it 'in exchange for barley in the year of the hyenas when there was famine'.[112] This vernacular expression for troubled times offers insight into the zeitgeist. The striped hyena, native to North Africa, was viewed with fear and loathing; depictions of pharaohs hunting hyena for sport connote the vanquishing of evil, and upholding of a just order.[113] Naming a year after an animal known as both a predator of small animals and a scavenger of larger animals' kills was a neat way of summing up the prevailing social dynamic.

The line of succession in the final years of the twentieth dynasty is still debated by Egyptologists. General Piankh (who was sent to settle matters between Amenhotep and Panehsy) and General Herihor, both of whom held the additional title of high priest, may have governed for several years, possibly while Ramses XI was still alive, though who came first and what exactly they accomplished is uncertain. What is clear is that the Domain of Amun was now in charge of Upper Egypt, ruling through the medium of the oracle. Although one of the priesthood's most sacred functions was securing the afterlife of the royals through temple ritual and the safekeeping of their tombs, it rose to power on a rampant wave of corruption and raiding. Whether to reaffirm their religious duty or to scrape the bottom of the barrel, the priests of Amun launched a thorough inspection of the necropolis. Their desultory findings were unsurprising. Tomb after royal tomb had been violated, their outsized coffins shattered and mummies rifled for their precious amulets. The scribes of the Tomb who handled the matter were perhaps dismayed to find the body of Amenhotep I, the patron of their home town, Deir al-Medina, hacked to pieces, at a time when the villagers still consulted his oracle for advice on how to live their lives.

The unfinished tomb of Ramses XI (who was buried in Lower Egypt) was converted into a workshop for mummy restoration and the old kings were pieced together, rewrapped and labelled by priests and necropolis workers. One of the restorers added his own name to the wrappings of Ramses II, the way people leave graffiti on ancient monuments. In the course of the work, the gold sheathing of royal coffins was meticulously scraped away while leaving identifying inscriptions intact, and the gold, along with anything else of value, was confiscated. High priest Pinudjem I (r. 1049–1026 BC) expropriated the five-hundred-year-old coffin of a pharaoh for his own resting place, regilding and encrusting it with faience and carnelian inlay; other items recovered during the restoration turned up in tombs of later high priests. Shorn of royal trappings, 'the broken kings, in all their plundered finery, [were reduced] to the skin and bone of sacred relics.'[114]

Documents known as the Late Ramesside Letters indicate how restorations had turned into a refinancing operation. Part of the correspondence was between Piankh, who had mounted a campaign to Nubia to oust renegade former governor Panehsy, and the scribe of the Tomb, Djutmose, whom Piankh left in charge of necropolis affairs. Among Piankh's instructions was to 'go and do for me a commission which you have never yet done ... Uncover a tomb among the foremost tombs and preserve its seal until I return.' The scribe responded, 'we are executing [your] commissions,' noting that he looked forward to the assistance of a necropolis inspector, who would guide them in their search for burials. Piankh's minions were expected to spy for him, and their report that necropolis police had been complaining about him and his actions prompted an order to 'get to the bottom of it' and, if necessary, 'place them in two baskets and throw them in [the Nile],' and to do it without letting 'anybody in the land find out'.[115]

Djutmose, and later his son Butahamun, scoured the desert for the burial places of royals and nobles, sometimes marching for days to reach tombs whose approximate locations were apparently known. The search for tombs lasted years, and Butehamun would continue the work until his death (c. 1056 BC). The fruits of these labours initially helped fund Piankh's excursion to Nubia, which coincidentally failed; Egypt's last province was lost, and the Nubians would eventually rise up against their former overlords to establish their own dynasty of pharaohs. The items recovered during the restorations meanwhile kept the priests aloft at a time when the state was essentially bankrupt. Following a logic that still holds currency as exemplified by the arch-raiders of Wall Street, the priests decided that since so much had already been stolen, the best solution was to steal some more. Not only had tomb-raiding helped shift the balance of power from palace to temple, state-sanctioned raiding constituted history's first bailout.

Rather than returning the royal mummies to their original resting places, the priests adopted an unorthodox tactic to discharge their religious obligations, grouping clusters of royals in a single tomb. Although easier to guard than many separate tombs scattered about the desert, downgrading the kings from a suite to a dormitory was a radical break with tradition. The oracle was consulted on the matter and gave a nod to the new, top-secret arrangement. High-profile New Kingdom pharaohs received priority, as indicated by the docket information accompanying the royal mummies. Ramses II had this written in ink on his wrappings:

> Day of bringing the Osiris king Ramses II life! Prosperity! Health! To renew him and to bury him in the tomb of the Osiris king Seti I – Life! Prosperity! Health! by the high priest of Pinudjem.[116]

Ramses II's sojourn in the tomb of his father, Seti I, was temporary. It seems the priests took Seti I from his magnificent alabaster sarcophagus and moved him, along with his son, and his father, Ramses I, to the tomb of a seventeenth-dynasty queen, high in the cliffs overlooking the necropolis. A century later (c. 918 BC), these three kings were relocated again, accompanied by a coterie of other legendary rulers, queens and courtiers, to the tomb of high priest

Pindjum II (later known as the Royal Cache, DB320) in Deir al-Bahari, north of the Valley of the Kings. All this tomb-hopping, in addition to the creation of a second royal dormitory (whose occupants included Merenptah and Ramses III, IV, V and VI) suggests that the priests were hard-pressed to stay a step ahead of prospective thieves.[117] In the end, they succeeded and these caches of royal mummies rested undisturbed in the Theban necropolis for nearly 3,000 years. Yet despite the priests' best efforts, not all the tombs of notables were found and subjected to restorations and/or regrouping. They missed Tutankhamun's, for one, while the tombs of Piankh and of Herihor, which would likely have contained treasures recovered from earlier royal burials, have yet to be discovered.[118]

The first king of the 21st dynasty, Smendes, ruled Lower Egypt while his relatives, the high priests of Amun, governed Upper Egypt from their Theban stronghold. Smendes made Tanis his capital in the Nile Delta, where he and his successors were buried instead of Thebes. The Place of Truth, the grandest of all necropoli, was relegated to history. Their services no longer required, the tomb builders abandoned their five-hundred-year-old village with its chequered past, its lineages of matchless artisans and scheming thieves. Families moved for greater safety to locations within the enclosure wall of Ramses III's temple; some acquired land and took to farming. The desert reclaimed Deir al-Medina, and the 'footprints on the sands of time' that the tomb builders left behind would take 3,000 years to be discerned.[119] At least some of their gods survived, as the Greeks and Romans who later ruled Egypt absorbed Egyptian deities into their pantheons. Ptolemy IV (r. 222–205 BC) used the site of the tomb builders' temple to raise one to Hathor, goddess of fertility, and Maat, goddess of cosmic order. Roman citizens who travelled to Thebes to visit its forsaken monuments could look upon them through a tunnel of time as long as that from which we now view the Coliseum. By the fifth century AD, the language inscribed on tomb and temple walls was unreadable and all but forgotten. All that remained of Thebes' riches was the inextinguishable memory of pharaoh's gold.

Massive *mastaba* (κ1), Beit Khallaf (Upper Egypt), 3rd dynasty, reign of Djoser.

Hatshepsut's temple, West Bank, Luxor, 2018.

Cloisonné pectoral pendant, 1279–1213 BC, New Kingdom reign of Ramses II, Auguste Mariette excavation at the Serapeum (Saqqara, 1852), gold, lapis lazuli, turquoise and carnelian.

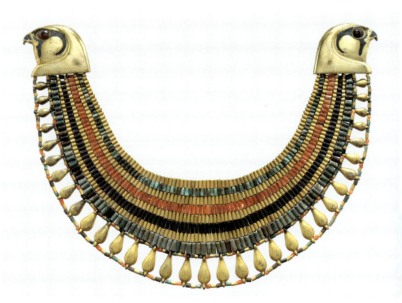

Broad collar of Senebtisi, c. 1850–1775 BC, Middle Kingdom, Tomb of Senwosret, MMA excavations (1906–7), faience, gold, carnelian, turquoise.

Necklace with a heart scarab of Hatnefer, c. 1492–1473 BC, New Kingdom reign of Thutmose III, Sheikh Abd el-Qurna (Thebes), MMA excavations (1935–6), serpentinite, gold.

Aegis with the head of Sekhmet, c. 945–715 BC, Third Intermediate Period, gold.

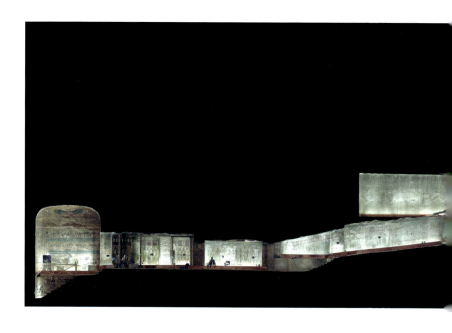

Tax defaulters being beaten (upper register), winnowing of the fields below, Tomb of Menena (TT69), 18th-dynasty overseer of the fields.

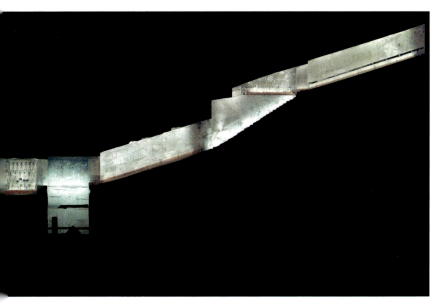

Three-dimensional rendering of the tomb of Seti I, recorded with the FARO LiDAR Scanner, 2016.

Artisans on scaffolds finishing statues belonging to Thutmose III, Tomb of Rekhmire (a governor and vizier during Thumose III's reign, TT100), Theban necropolis, 18th dynasty.

Stela depicting the god Seth and Apahte, Paneb's son, Deir al-Medina, 19th dynasty, reign of Seti II.

(*left*) Sekhmet, relief in the temple of Khnum, Esna.
(*right*) Paneb and his wife Wa'bet, depicted in Paneb's tomb (TT211).

Alaa Awad, *Cat and Mouse*, 2012, acrylic, detail of a now lost mural reprising scenes from satirical papyri and ostracon, painted on the wall of the American University in Cairo, Mohamed Mahmoud Street (near Tahrir Square), during a period of unrest.

Winged Isis pectoral, 538–519 BC, Napatan Period, Tomb of Amaninatakelebte, from Nuri (Sudan), pyramid 10, excavated by the Harvard University–Boston Museum of Fine Arts Expedition (1916), gold.

Valley of the Kings, with the Nile viewed from the top of Gebel El-Qurn mountain, West Bank, Luxor, November 2004.

THREE

THE SEEKERS

Verily thy fortune is in Cairo. Go thither and seek it.
– 'TALE OF THE RUINED MAN WHO BECAME RICH AGAIN
THROUGH A DREAM', *THE THOUSAND AND ONE NIGHTS*
(351ST–352ND NIGHT)

Tomb-raiding in late antiquity is not well documented, though there was little reason for it to stop. The practice of mummification and the burial of costly goods lasted well into the Roman Period, adding to the store of underground wealth. With the spread of Christianity in the first century, tombs and temples felt the pious wrath of the newly converted, their inscriptions diligently battered to erase the pagan gods. The Copts (Egyptian Christians) nonetheless associated ancient monuments with treasure, as would the Muslims who joined them in AD 639. Our story resumes with Egypt under Arab rule, when tomb-raiding was transformed into a respectable, taxpaying profession. The Arabs were a pragmatic bunch, treating ancient treasures like any other resource, but they weren't exactly down to earth. Islamic culture was imbued with the desert-dweller's intimacy with nature and wonderment at its powers, now channelled towards the worship of an omnipresent god. Revelling in the diversity they encountered through contact with ancient civilizations, the Arabs transformed their assimilated knowledge and wealth into an idiosyncratic urbanity, brilliantly manifested in architecture, the arts and sciences, including the sciences of the occult. In Egypt under Islamic rule, treasure hunting was irrevocably linked with magic, the stuff of *The Thousand and One Nights*.

The Arab army that invaded Egypt in AD 639 knew the country was wealthy because its grain had fattened the Roman and later Byzantine empires. The bulk of the 4,000 troops who arrived on foot, camel and horseback originated from the settled communities of the Hejaz (Saudi Arabia), some of whom had long traded with Egypt. The commander of the Arab forces, ʿAmr ibn al-ʿĀṣ, a former merchant, had accompanied caravans to Egypt and correctly calculated both its strategic value as a base for further conquest and the ease with which it could be taken. The renowned port city of Alexandria offered the Arabs a naval advantage for expanding their influence and provisioning their growing territories.[1] Alexandria's grandeur may have faded but its legendary status remained. The lighthouse with its 'burning mirror' built by Ptolemy II (r. 280–247 BC) was one of the ancient world's wonders, believed to incinerate enemy ships at a distance with its glare.[2] The weary conquerors found comforts in the city to which they were unaccustomed, but while some took up residence in the

Great Pyramid of Khufu during Nile flood season, Cairo, c. 1867–99, photograph by Félix Bonfils.

Philips Galle, engraving after Maarten van Heemskerck, 'Lighthouse of Alexandria', 1572.

seaside villas of the Alexandrian elite, they were soon ordered to abandon them. To avoid the contagion of Byzantine decadence and keep his men on their battle-ready toes, ʿAmr ibn al-ʿĀṣ chose to settle south of the Nile Delta, near the Roman fort of Babylon by the river, which as ever facilitated the movement of grain. The garrison tent-town they called Fustat (encampment) was the embryo of what would one day be known as Cairo.

Islam was born of austerity. Mohammed, its founder, was orphaned soon after birth (AD 570) and as a youth he worked in the caravans that plied the Arabian Desert. He was forty when he experienced his first revelation, in a mountain cave of the Hejaz. His announcement of a god, whose 99 names or attributes emphasized the power of oneness, attracted tribal adherents willing to unite and test their fortunes in battle under the green banner of Islam. Mohammed's efforts also attracted the ire of the contentedly pagan tribes who precipitated his exile from his home in

Mecca to the oasis of Medina in 622. While planning and executing raids on his opponents, Mohammed built a headquarters, a small mud-brick enclosure with a portico of palm trunk columns and frond-roofed rooms set around an open courtyard. Ten years later, he died and was buried there, having converted Arabia and amassed an army. For Mohammed and his fellows, life was circumscribed by the desert and near absence of water. While wealthier merchants may have had larger mud-brick dwellings and more domesticated animals, their possessions were few and purely functional. Excess was absent from their lives; the only things the Arabs possessed in abundance were dates and sand.

Imagine, then, the amazement of the desert-bred warriors when they overcame the far larger Persian forces at the Battle of Qadisiya (Iraq) in 636, and found the standard the defeated troops had left behind: 3.5 metres (11 ft) of panther skins, encrusted with rubies and pearls. The booty recovered the following year from the palaces of the Persian capital Ctesiphon on the banks of the Tigris was breathtaking: chests of jewels, large and mysterious gold-wrought objects, stacks of silver and gold ingots and the fabulous 'Spring of Chosroes', a silk tapestry embroidered with gold and strewn with pearls that measured 1 kilometre square (240 ac.). These trophies were sent forthwith to the modest mud-brick residence of the Caliph Umar, in Medina, who must have wondered where to put them.[3] The road from austerity to extravagance would prove short.

From their foothold in Lower Egypt, the Arabs pushed into Upper Egypt and in 651 reached the Nubian capital of Dongola, where the so-called Church of the Granite Columns was relieved of quantities of precious metals; Egypt's churches were likewise gradually stripped of their wealth. The phantasmagorical treasury of the Visigoth kings of Toledo (Spain) fell to the Arabs in AD 711, with its piles of gemstones, loads of gold and silver ingots, 170 jewel-studded gold crowns, 1,000 royal sabres and masses of golden ecclesiastical paraphernalia. Between booty and taxes the Arabs were soon in possession of most of the world's supply of gold.[4] But another boon awaited them.

The accidental was as influential in shaping the Arabs' trajectory as Egypt's strategic conquest. Alongside the cumulative burials of former ruling elites that yielded precious goods, the long-standing practice of securing valuables in walls or gardens resulted in serendipitous finds. With Egypt the Arabs acquired pharaonic, Greek and Roman antiquity and all the tangible and intangible treasures that went with it. For the Egyptians, Arab rule changed little at first; their old overlords had been replaced with new ones; they still paid taxes and their grain was directed to faraway ports they'd never see.

But for the Arabs, like magic, Egypt changed everything. Some of the original occupiers were likely familiar with the mausoleums of the Nabataeans (dating from 100 BC to AD 100) in the northwestern desert of the Arabian Peninsula. Resembling the monuments of the Nabataean capital of Petra (Jordan), they were carved into limestone outcroppings, so perfectly proportioned and precisely cut it was as if they'd emerged from the rock mass, fully formed.[5] But nothing Egypt's newcomers had experienced could have prepared them for the scale, splendour and strangeness of pharaonic buildings. We are too saturated with Egyptian imagery and inured to monumentalism to imagine their impact when first seen up close by unsullied eyes. Perhaps the last Western testimonies to that effect were recorded by Maxime Du Camp and Gustave Flaubert, in 1849 on a trip to Egypt, coincidentally to experiment with photography. Exploring the Giza Plateau on horseback, Du Camp and Flaubert encountered the Sphinx, which the Arabs called 'the father of terror'. 'I am pale,' wrote Du Camp, 'my legs trembling. I cannot remember ever having been moved so deeply.' Flaubert was similarly rattled: '[The Sphinx] fixes us with a terrifying stare ... I am afraid of becoming giddy, and try to control my emotions.'[6]

Such emotions shaped Islamic popular culture and the Arabs' approach to science and literature. Awe of a past by which they might measure their own achievements combined with optimism towards a promising future inflamed the collective imagination. Egypt was a land of plenty, thanks to its fecund Nile-fed fields, but more than this, it was a land of marvels. Of the thirty wonders of the world noted in medieval Islamic texts, twenty were in Egypt, with the pyramids at the top of the list.[7] By the twelfth century, descriptions of marvellous places, buildings, creatures and natural phenomena (*mirabilia*) had coalesced into a literary genre (*ʿajaʾib*).[8]

The Arabs developed a nuanced rapport with the remnants of past civilizations that fell to their lot, as expressed in the prolific works of medieval Islamic scholars. Visits to the monuments scattered throughout the land were encouraged as edifying educational adventures, and their architecture and iconography inspired both far-fetched speculation and serious study. The language of the hieroglyphs, whose original meaning had been lost, was subjected to new, albeit largely inaccurate, interpretations. The pyramids were measured, and attempts made to fathom their age, and how their massive blocks were laid so 'that not even a thread could be drawn between [them]'.[9] Profuse admiration for the skill and knowledge behind ancient achievements was leavened with the recognition that pharaoh, as portrayed in the Qur'an, was a tyrant and a pagan to boot. Overall, the ancient Egyptians were perceived as a strange but instructive people, their ruins a lesson in history and an admonishment to arrogance, for even the greatest of men's creations must surely pale before Allah's.

The Qu'ran, viewed as an unimpeachable historical source, spoke of pharaoh's riches, relating the story of Qarun of the tribe of Moses, who possessed 'treasures whose keys alone would burden a band of strong men'.[10] Narratives involving well-known figures likewise set precedents for hunting Egypt's treasures. According to historian Ibn Abd al-Hakam (d. 871), having secured Egypt, army commander ʿAmr ibn al-ʿĀṣ acquired tons of gold following his decree that all treasures be rendered to him. Some stories carried a note of caution, like that concerning Egypt's Umayyad governor Abdel Aziz ibn Marwan (685–705), who was said to have spared no expense in treasure hunts that rendered nothing and cost a thousand men their lives.[11] Abbasid Caliph al-Mamun (813–833) reportedly tried to force his way into the pyramid of Cheops during a visit in 832. After a protracted effort using fire and vinegar to weaken the stone, followed by an assault with battering rams and iron tools, the crew gained entry only to find a quantity of gold amounting to exactly the cost of the project.[12] Far from discouraging treasure hunts, stories such as these only added to the conviction that, given the potential gains, the game was worth the candle.

Historian al-Masudi (896–956) cited Egypt's reputation for riches in his history of the world, *Fields of Gold*. Born in Baghdad, he lived in Cairo, where there were 'wondrous reports of buried hoards and . . . of what [they] would contain from the treasure houses of the kings who deposited them in the earth, and the other civilizations that dwelt in this region'.[13] This sort of claim was common among Islamic scholars, including the eleventh-century historian who wrote that Egypt was 'the land with the most treasures, wonders, and ancient monuments'.[14] Such endorsements were surplus to requirements, since physical proofs of ancient wealth were everywhere in the form of spectacular buildings in greater or lesser states of disrepair. Native Egyptians' stories, beliefs and practices regarding buried treasure surely influenced the notion that ready wealth was there for the taking, a conviction that grew firmer with time. Syrian historian and geographer Ibn al-Wardi (d. 1349) maintained 'that most of [Egypt] bears buried gold; it is even said that there is no place which is not full of buried treasures'.[15] Medieval treasure lore is full of stories about stumbling upon riches, but separating fact from oral history, received wisdom and pure fiction is as difficult now as it was then. What is certain is that the belief in hidden treasure as a relatively accessible and inexhaustible source of wealth led to an obsessive search for it.

The success of the Islamic enterprise helps account for the enthusiasm surrounding the availability of treasures. Egypt's star was rising, as evidenced in the building outside of Fustat. When the central power shifted hands from the Damascus-based Umayyad dynasty to the Abbasids, Baghdad became the seat of their caliphate (766), designed not on a square or rectangular grid but in concentric circles. To advertise the Abbasid accession, Egypt's new governor built Al-'Askar ('the cantonment') just north of Fustat, a grandly appointed administrative centre that reflected the new prosperity. In the course of conquest, the Abbasids began investing in young Turkish slaves, training them to serve as the caliph's bodyguard and in other official positions. The so-called Mamluks ('the owned') would later rule Egypt but Ahmad ibn Tulun, born in Baghdad, was the first to wrest control from his former owners. After acting as Egypt's governor for a decade, he declared himself its autonomous ruler in 878. To signal his independence, he built al-Qata'i' ('the wards') just north of Al-'Askar, centred on Egypt's largest mosque.

Happenstance helped finance Ibn Tulun's building, according to his biographer who wrote that during a hunting trip the hoof of one of his servant's horses sank into the ground. When it was pulled out, the area caved in, revealing a treasure worth a million dinars that Ibn Tulun used to build Egypt's first hospital and distribute alms.[16] Whether or not the story is apocryphal, Ibn Tulun had enough faith in buried treasure to formalize its recovery. Under his rule (868–83), treasure hunting was organized like a craft guild, its members called 'the lords of the places of seeking' (*ashab al-matalib*) or simply 'the seekers' (*mutalibun*). A state-appointed eunuch supervised their activities and a trusted official accompanied the seekers on their forays to ensure they surrendered a fifth of their haul.[17] The seekers combed the land for treasures, exploring sites on the Giza Plateau, along the Nile banks, in the Eastern and Western deserts, in ancient cemeteries and temple precincts. The fruits of their labours helped finance both Ibn Tulun's largesse, including meals served to the public in the town square (*midan*) and the outlandish expenditures of his son and successor.

Ibn Tulun was a pious, unostentatious leader, but his son Khumarawai liked living big, transforming the public square into a private garden where tree trunks were sheathed in copper and outfitted with pipes that turned them into fountains. On the request of his favourite concubine, one of his palace rooms was plated in gold and featured larger-than-life-sized statues of himself and his consort placing crowns on each other's heads. Khumarawai was fond of lions, which were kept in cages equipped with running water, a royal amenity in those days. He suffered from insomnia for which his physician prescribed massage, but Khumarawai disliked being touched by strangers, so he dug a pool in his garden and filled it with mercury where he might float on a mattress of inflated animal skins, dozing in the reflected moonlight, or perhaps undone by the fumes.[18] However inventively deployed, Khumarawai's wealth paled beside that of the Fatimid caliphs who subsequently ruled Egypt (969-1171) and purportedly profited from the proceeds of treasure hunts.

A disagreement over who should succeed the Prophet, after his death in 632, resulted in a schism, with Sunni Muslims supporting one of the Prophet's earliest followers, and the Shi'a Muslims favouring his closest male relative, who was also married to Muhammad's daughter Fatima. The Sunni won the argument. The Islamic expansion proceeded under Sunni leadership, until the Shi'a Fatimids, intent on replacing the Abbasid Caliphate as rulers of the empire, began their campaigns. Having established cities in what is now Tunisia, after several failed attempts they took Egypt, their greatest triumph. The fourth Fatimid caliph, al-Mùiz (r. 953-75), was enamoured of astrology, and his Egyptian capital, propitiously founded with Mars in the ascendant, was named for that planet, *al-Qahira* in Arabic, 'the conqueror'. Like the ancient Egyptians, the Fatimids understood the power of spectacle, and spared no expense to win the favour of a wary (largely Sunni) population, celebrating Muslim and Christian holidays, as well as traditional Nile feasts. On the first and fifteenth nights of certain Islamic months, a bonfire blazed from atop the pyramid of Cheops, and barges lit with flaming torches illumined the Nile.

The new royal city was just north of Fustat, its enclosure wall fitted with grand entries, including the northern gate of Bab al-Futuh (Gate of Conquests) and the southern one, Bab Zuwayla, named for a Berber tribe in the Fatimid army. Next to a central *midan* large enough to hold 10,000 horsemen, a mosque was built called Al-Azhar ('the most resplendent'). The palaces flanking the *midan* were 'lofty and splendid structures having marvelous plantings and tamed waters', with names like 'the camphor audience hall' and 'the chamber of the diadems'.[19] While forging an empire encompassing North Africa, Sicily and Syria, the Fatimid caliphs made an art of luxury, producing lifestyle accessories that advertised their wealth and refinement: gold-brocaded garments; jewels of filigree, cloisonné and minuscule droplets of gold; masterpieces of ceramic lustreware; sparkling rock crystal ewers and carafes that sent prisms dancing across their banquet tables; chandeliers of metalwork pierced in intricate arabesques that cast nets of shadow and light. More than opulence the Fatimids loved complexity, and their aesthetic, fusing Byzantine, Coptic, Persian, Mesopotamian and North African influences, was tinged with the metaphysical.

The enthusiasm for scientific inquiry that the Fatimids shared with their Abbasid rivals was owed in part to the confidence that accompanied conquest, which was viewed as a sign of Allah's favour that extended to all worthy endeavours. 'Seek knowledge, even in China,' said the Prophet, who likewise relayed Allah's command to 'Read!' in the Qur'an (Sura 19).[20] Abbasid caliph al-Mamun sent emissaries to Constantinople and elsewhere to acquire manuscripts (Euclid's *Elements*, c. 300 BC, was among the first) and Baghdad's House of Wisdom was staffed with teams of Christian and Muslim translators. Ancient texts concerning anything deemed of practical value were duly translated, as foreign learning was embraced, tested and built upon, with scholars taking strides towards the future while serving the present. In his investigations of alchemical processes in Baghdad, Jabir ibn Hayyan (722–815) formulated the basics of chemistry, devising methods for fabricating cheap ink and ceramic glazes, for refining metals and waterproofing cloth.[21] Ibn Musa al-Khwarizmi (d. 850) developed algebra as a means of efficiently settling property and inheritance disputes. Hydraulics was used not only for fancy fountains in royal gardens but for the construction of underground irrigation canals and dams. An illuminated copy of Dioscorides' *De materia medica* (AD 50) was translated, corrected and greatly expanded, with new pharmacopoeia added by scholars in North Africa but also in Islamic Spain, where the science of agronomy

The Seekers

Al-Azhar mosque, Cairo, early 20th century.

developed to improve crop productivity.[22] Physicians identified physiological mechanisms, including the lungs' purification of the blood, centuries before their Western counterparts.

Arabic became the lingua franca for scholars communicating across a far-flung empire.[23] The Chinese art of paper-making from cotton or linen rags, which the Arabs encountered in the eighth century in Central Asia, transformed manuscript production, making books (formerly made from parchment) cheaper and more accessible.[24] The exchange of ideas was further accelerated by airmail: carrier pigeons with relay towers at intervals covering hundreds of kilometres. Just as the Arabs preserved Greek texts that might otherwise have been lost to the West, so in Europe, works of Islamic science were translated into Latin and therefore escaped the destruction of Baghdad at the hands of the Mongols (1258). 'Upon this tenuous and almost miraculous line of transmission, the scientific achievements of the modern world are based.'[25]

The florescence of medieval science, however driven by pragmatism, was shaded with esoteric yearnings. The Arabs called Aristotle 'the foremost teacher' but their admiration for the Greek's attachment to reason was tempered with the belief that divine revelation and intuition were legitimate tools for acquiring knowledge.[26] Astronomers did practical things like calculating the direction of Mecca (to which the five-times-daily prayers were addressed) and the progression of the Islamic lunar months, the distances of ships at sea and the height and position of lighthouses. But they also practised astrology, referencing *Altagest* (*The Greatest*) written by Alexandrian astronomer Ptolemy (c. AD 85–165), translated into Arabic in the early ninth century and subsequently much revised.[27] Astrology was a popular method of divination that proved integral to treasure hunting, and the sixth Fatimid caliph, al-Hakim (r. 996–1021), took a shine to both.

Eleven years old when he came to power, wilful and erratic, al-Hakim is remembered for his disruptive decrees, like banning certain popular foods, or requiring that all businesses operate exclusively at night. But when he was barely twenty, al-Hakim founded a *dar al-Hikma* ('House of Wisdom') along the lines of the eponymous institution established by the Abbasids in Baghdad, a library and centre of learning akin to the ancient Egyptians' 'house of life'. Under al-Hakim's patronage, Ibn Haytham composed his *Treatise on Optics*, designing the camera obscura, and providing the mechanical basis for the later invention of photography. In the observatory that al-Hakim built on the cliffs overlooking Cairo, astronomer Ibn Yunus compiled astonishingly accurate tables of planetary motion, to within nine digits after the decimal point. Devoted to his studies of the planets, al-Hakim reportedly dressed in a monk's woollen garb for seven years, during which time he never bathed, 'worshipped' Mars for three years and 'then returned to his adoration of Saturn'.[28] One night in 1021, while out riding Moon, his favourite donkey, al-Hakim vanished, and was never seen again, dead or alive.

Treasure was said to have financed the building of al-Hakim's mosque, Al-Anwar ('the most radiant'), but Fatimid historian Ibn Hammad claimed that al-Hakim's treasure hunts were profitable enough to subsidize subsequent caliphs' expenses, including the salaries of civil servants and soldiers. 'They drew their resources from the treasures which al-Hakim extracted from the soils of Egypt which had been deposited in antiquity in the temples, tombs and great towns,' he wrote, noting that, 'astrologers aided them in their quest.'[29] Accounts such as this, alongside al-Hakim's stargazing and the aura of the supernatural that accompanied his disappearance, help account for subsequent legends portraying him as a champion treasure hunter. The popular 'Epic of al-Hakim' was recited in public as an entertainment in the thirteenth and fourteenth centuries, alongside stories from *The Thousand and One Nights*. In the epic, al-Hakim orders an observatory built to alert him to a particular Saturn conjunction when the magical conditions would be met for acquiring all of Egypt's riches.[30]

Gold aside, the Nile was Egypt's greatest treasure, the ultimate arbiter of its fortunes. Measured at the height of the flood season (August), a rise of 16 cubits (7.3 metres/24 ft) meant an ample grain harvest could be expected for the coming year.[31] In August 1023, during the reign of al-Hakim's son, al-Zahir (r. 1021–36), the Nile rose just over 14 cubits, and two days later it receded dramatically, an unprecedented event that sparked fear and public prayer gatherings pleading for divine intercession. When bakeries hiked up the price of bread and wheat-sellers began hoarding in anticipation of the coming shortage, the authorities' first response was to round them up and beat them. When that didn't work, al-Zahir obliged the wealthy to contribute portions of their grain stores to keep the people from starving or rioting.[32] Although the 1024 flood level was adequate, promising a return to normal the following year, the situation deteriorated and the inhabitants of the capital, mostly concentrated in Fustat, were forced to eat grass. Palace servants went hungry, as did the ranks of the infantry. Ramadan, the month of fasting, was nonetheless observed and when it ended, the palace held its traditional banquet for courtiers and the city's elite, who stripped the buffet bare, stuffing their pockets with food.[33]

Cairo was fully recovered and there was no unseemly banquet-raiding in 1047, when Nasir Khusraw, Persian poet and scholar, attended the post-Ramadan palace feast held by caliph al-Mustansir (r. 1036–94). Khusraw, who spent several years in Egypt (c. 1047–50), described passing through a dozen adjacent pavilions, 'one more dazzling than the last'. In the inner hall, silver stairs led to the caliph's golden dais, running the length of the room, spread with 'carpets and pillows of Byzantine brocade'. The menu included desserts of decorative confections, 'thousands of images and statuettes' and 'an orange tree, every branch and leaf of which had been executed in sugar'.[34] The *dolce vita* extended to Cairo's inhabitants, who Khusraw said were 'very rich'.[35] Khusraw was present for celebrations surrounding the birth of the caliph's son, writing that 'the city and bazaars ... were so decorated with gold, jewels, coins, gold spun cloth and embroidery, that there was no room to sit.'[36] In the markets of Fustat, shopkeepers supplied bags for customers and a donkey taxi service was available to take them home. People wore clothes made of fabrics dyed in colours whose trade names are redolent of the Fatimid quotidian: 'pearl', 'cloud', 'silver', 'lead', 'soot', 'pepper', 'sky blue', 'pistachio', 'emerald', 'pomegranate', 'ruby', 'apricot', 'bitter orange', 'sandalwood', 'saffron', 'safflower' and 'sandgrouse'.[37] In keeping with a consumer protection decree, merchants caught cheating had to circulate the streets on camel-back, calling out, 'I deserve this punishment ... [as does] whoever tells a lie.'[38]

Professional treasure hunters were meanwhile thriving. Khusraw reports that in 1049 the eunuch seeker-in chief, Umdat al-Dawla, 'possessed a great estate and vast wealth' while noting that '[the seekers] expend great effort and much money on their expeditions in the mountains, rocks and valleys. Many of them find great buried treasures but others spend great sums and find nothing.'[39] Perhaps the seekers were able to absorb their losses but like everyone in Egypt they would be affected by the events of the coming decades. Owing to internal and external pressures, Egypt, particularly Cairo, was about to crash. Fatimid administration was weakening; the position of vizier changed hands 27 times in seven years (1060-67). The troops were restless, with rival factions at each other's throats. A series of feeble Nile floods beginning in 1065 sparked unrest due to exorbitant bread prices. 'We face anarchy and hunger,' wrote a woman of Cairo in 1069. The crisis peaked in 1070 when people were eating horses and donkeys before turning to their pets; even the caliph had only three mounts left in his stable. Members of the wealthy Jewish community left the country, and poorer inhabitants of Fustat abandoned their homes to forage in the countryside.[40]

Unable to defend their eastern territories, the Fatimids lost Syria to the (Sunni) Seljuk Turks in 1076. Two mortal threats now fixed their eyes on Egypt: the crusading Franks in Palestine, and the Nur al-Din, Turkish ruler of northern Syria and the Crusaders' fiercest enemy. Nur al-Din sent his best general to defeat the Crusaders, a Kurd named Shirkuh, who brought a nephew along for the campaign, named Salah al-Din (Saladin; 1138-1193). Having rid Egypt of the Franks, Shirkuh died after an otherwise triumphal banquet, leaving Saladin vizier. The sickly Fatimid caliph was next, followed by Nur al-Din, struck down by angina in Damascus. Saladin promptly claimed the title of sultan of Egypt and Syria and founded the Ayyubid dynasty (1171-1260). On his orders, the Fatimid palaces were pillaged, their riches redirected towards the building of Sunni schools.

The House of Wisdom that by some accounts held more than half a million books, including thousands on the occult sciences, was dismantled. The palace's occupants were evicted, and male relatives of the caliph assigned residences far from the women of their families so as to stamp out their bloodline.[41] While there is no direct proof that the crises surrounding the Fatimids' demise caused a surge of treasure hunting, it's not unlikely; famine, unrest and invasion encouraged raiding in the past. Fear and uncertainty may help explain why interest in magic and divination seems to have widened in the twelfth century, when the occult dimension of treasure hunting, involving a range of magical tools, coincidentally grew more pronounced.[42]

Egyptian scholar al-Idrisi (d. 1251) was an Arab aristocrat, a descendant of the Prophet. Born in Dendera, site of a temple complex dedicated to Hathor, he studied pharaonic ruins all his life. In his treatise on the pyramids of Giza (*Lights of the Translunar Bodies: On Uncovering the Secrets of the Pyramids*) he presented precise outer trigonometric measurements and detailed descriptions of the masonry. Al-Idrisi dated the pyramids to the antediluvian era but there was much discussion about whether they were built before or after the Great Flood, which figures in the Qur'an. Some said they were there before Adam (whose name means 'human' in Arabic), others that they were the granaries of the Hebrew prophet Joseph. One twelfth-century scholar concluded that the pyramids were 20,000 years old, based on calculations concerning the star Altair of the constellation Aquila.[43] That they were ancient almost beyond imagining was without question; al-Idrisi cited a contemporary poem about how everything on Earth fears time 'except the pyramids, of which Time is afraid'.[44] Medieval scholars' attempts to date the monuments were a way of coming to terms with the breadth of antiquity so they might incorporate its histories into their own, which, Allah willing, might likewise stretch across millennia.

Al-Idrisi tried to separate facts from legend but the line is blurred when the subjects in question are ancient and marvellous. Considering the labour and wealth that went into them, it was commonly believed that the pyramids concealed both material riches and valuable knowledge, and that their purpose was to preserve these treasures from a prophesied catastrophe.[45] It was also said the pyramids served as talismans protecting Egypt against a cataclysmic flood that would mark the end of the world. Al-Masudi tells how, digging near the pyramids in 932, treasure hunters found statues, gemstones and mummy masks ('faces of gold and silver'), one of the more credible stories associating the area with ancient finds.[46] In the *Sun of Gnosis*, attributed to al-Buni (born in Algeria, lived in Egypt, c. 1225), the author boasted of seeing what the pyramids hid himself:

> By my life, they contain rich knowledge. Underneath the large pyramid exist thirty-six treasures ... hidden there before the deluge of Noah. I deciphered the seals, entered one of the treasures, and took out a book, in which I have found the pure [teaching of] alchemy.[47]

Like the pyramids, the Sphinx was believed to guard treasures and act as a protector, holding back the tide of sands that at times covered all but its head. Al-Idrisi said it was an idol to the sun, because the first rays of dawn landed squarely between its eyes.[48] Its face still bore pigment, 'a red varnish, as bright as if freshly put on',[49] lending colour to a thirteenth-century story. It seems a man who squandered his inheritance chanced upon instructions to improve his situation by burning incense at the Sphinx while reciting a spell seven times. To reward him, it stuck out a gold dinar on its tongue, like a PEZ dispenser.[50] The Sphinx came alive again to assist two poor and startled travellers, according to a fourteenth-century story. The 'father of terror' had a reputation for beneficence; in hard times, people petitioned it with prayers and fumigations.[51]

As for the temples, some claimed they were alchemical laboratories and repositories of ancient knowledge. The science of alchemy (al-kimya') practised in medieval Egypt largely followed Greek traditions, including Aristotle's theory that earth, air, fire and water are the basic elements of all matter. The ancient Egyptians were considered masters of alchemy, able to transpose matter and concoct miraculous elixirs. According to Baghdadi book-trader Ibn al-Nadim (d. 995), Egypt was 'the Babel of Sorcerers' with 'underground libraries [in temples] containing scientific works written on hides ... as well as on plates of gold, copper and stone'.[52] Hieroglyphs were thought to hold both alchemical secrets and directions to hidden treasure. It was said that some Coptic monks could read them and that Upper Egyptian Dhu al-Nun al-Misri (d. 861) apprenticed with a monk to learn how. Studying the ruins of his home town, Akhmim (former cult centre of the fertility god, Min), al-Misri mastered 'the sciences of the *birba* (temple)', learning how to make diamonds and to travel great distances in a single night.[53] A fourteenth-century story has him assisting the seekers, deciphering a tablet inscribed with 'the greatest name of god', one that grants superhuman powers and is known only to the elect.[54]

In *The Lights of Translunar Bodies*, al-Idrisi said that a seeker-in-chief gave him a book 'on the sciences of hidden treasure' with directions on how to find them.[55] He also relates the eerie tale of treasure hunters who entered a pyramid and lost one of their crew in the process. After three days of searching, they were about

Abu Simbel Temple interior, lithograph by Louis Haghe after David Roberts, 1836.

to give up, when his head sprouted from a wall of the structure, his face red with the strain of shouting something in what they presumed to be an ancient language. The terrified treasure hunters fled the scene and hastened to find a Coptic monk to translate what turned out to be a frenzied warning. 'This is the fate of those who violate the sanctity of kings in their homes!' the trapped man cried, an admonishment that appears to be the moral of the story.[56] Treasure-hunting manuals like the one al-Idrisi received often highlight the physical dangers seekers faced; they could be buried alive in collapsing rubble, drowned in rising groundwaters or suffocated by noxious fumes. Such accidents were typically blamed on jinn, the otherworldly beings believed to guard treasures, and stories about treasure-hunting mishaps reinforced those beliefs. It's possible the seekers circulated the stories as a scare tactic to keep amateurs away from their hunting grounds, or that scholars like al-Idrisi, who deplored the destruction of monuments by treasure hunters, related them to discourage vandalism.[57] But whether or not they had an agenda, everyone who transmitted these accounts saw the supernatural as a genuine force to be reckoned with.

The Arabs' belief in jinn dates to pre-Islamic times, when they were associated with a particular place in nature like a tree or a spring and believed to cause desert phenomena like whirlwinds and mirages. Their name derives from the Arabic *janna*, to cover, hide or veil.[58] Although invisible, jinn are shape-shifters who may inhabit animals, preferably wild ones but also donkeys, cats and dogs; animals are understandably more sensitive to their presence than humans. Like ancient Egyptian demons, jinn could cause illness, infertility and madness; the mentally deranged are said to be 'touched by the jinn' (*majnun*) and people wore amulets to ward off these and other misfortunes. Jinn are mentioned frequently in the Qur'an, and while made from fire as opposed to the clay used for humans, they are subject to Allah's will.[59] Like people, the jinn eat and drink, are male and female, have sex, produce children, and can be killed or die. But their special powers distinguish them.

Trans-dimensional beings that can travel great distances in the blink of an eye and materialize objects at will, jinn can access whatever is hidden from mere humans. Their powers were admired, as evidenced in medieval *grimoires*, books of magic containing spells for flying, invisibility or walking on water, things the jinn could do in a flash.[60] The ability to command the jinn was advantageous to the seekers, to reveal treasure locations and keep the nasty ones from interfering with the hunt. Belief held that with great treasures came great 'impediments and repellents' including guardian jinn known as 'the dwellers' (*'ummar*), but also deadly booby traps and talismans installed by the treasure's original owner.[61] The seekers fought fire with fire, turning magical practices into tools as essential to their kit as a torch and pickaxe.

The word 'magic' (*sihr*) denoted everything from sleight of hand to subtle poetry, to invocations to god, the planets or jinn for assistance in shaping events.[62] Drawing from ancient traditions that underscored the interactions between the material and supernal worlds, medieval magic incorporated pre-Islamic beliefs. The prophets Solomon and Idris (associated with the Greek god Hermes and ancient Egyptian Thoth) were cited as the originators of occult knowledge, as were sources in India and North Africa.[63] Everything in nature was believed to hold a seed of the wondrous. Tenth-century 'stone books' described the magical virtues of minerals and rocks; the healing properties of plants and how to activate them were the topic of in-depth studies. The medicinal and metaphysical were interwoven in treatises that came with designs to engrave on rings that conferred nature's powers on the wearer.[64]

The world was seen in both magical and scientifically knowable terms, as illustrated by a protective spell written in many medieval manuscripts. Believed to ensure the book's long life, the phrase 'O Buttercup' referenced a member of a poisonous plant family (*ranunculacae*) known to repel insects attracted to fish glue and starch paste used in manuscript production.[65] In the absence of the plant itself, its name was deemed sufficient to produce the desired effect, like depictions of food in ancient Egyptian tombs that provided nourishment when the real thing was unavailable.

The occult sciences flourished in medieval Egypt and authors of occult texts were respected; many held multiple credentials as

The Seekers

Albert Letchford, illustration of an encounter with a jinn, in 'Ma'aruf the Cobbler and his Wife Fatimah', frontispiece to Richard F. Burton, trans., and Leonard C. Smithers, ed., *The Book of the Thousand Nights and a Night*, vol. VIII (1897).

mathematicians, physicians, historians, geographers, thinkers, musicians and poets. While the future was technically Allah's domain and some occult practices infringed on his territory, no one was ever burned at the stake. Divination was used more for making decisions than for prophesying. The 'method of choices' (*tariq al-istikharat*), the Arabic term for bibliomancy, typically involved opening a Qur'an at random with the understanding that Allah guided the questioner towards the best response.[66] Many kinds of divination pre-dated Islam, like reading the patterns of birds in flight, or hydromancy, based on the ripples appearing on water.[67] Dream interpretation, practised by the ancient Egyptians and throughout late antiquity, remained popular with the Arabs, though like other divinatory techniques it was revised and augmented. The astrology-based forecasting of weather patterns employed by the Byzantines, for example, was elaborated by Baghdad-born polymath al-Kindi (d. 970) who also authored a handy bibliomantic manual with 144 popular questions and twelve answers each, to randomly choose from.[68]

Pythagoras was credited with inventing the science of letters (*'ilm al-huruf*), a form of divination using letters assigned numerical values. A complicated Islamic offshoot (*jafr*) focused on the letters of Allah's 99 names. The most perplexing letter-number divination, *za'irja*, developed in the thirteenth century, involved diagrams of concentric circles representing elements of astrology, poetry and astronomy that were manipulated to arrive at a phrase that itself required interpretation. A later historian remarked that the only one who could use *za'irja* accurately was 'the Mahdi (prophet) expected at the end of time'.[69] Magical writing comprising letters, numbers and symbols figured in the amulets and talismans commonly used as personal protections against the evil eye (a force activated by envy), and in some cases to command the jinn.[70] A student of al-Buni, reputed master of *huruf*, praised him in suggestive terms: 'I swear by god his utterances are like pearls of Egyptian gold. They are treasures, the mystery of which is a blessed talisman for one who has deciphered them and understands.'[71]

Geomancy, 'the science of sand' (*'ilm al-raml*), originated with the Arabs and at its most simplistic involved interpreting hollows in the sandy ground.[72] Some geomancers used a 'dust board' where numbers and figures could be drawn in sand spread on a smooth surface to create geomantic tables, derived from random marks made by the questioner. Others devised more sophisticated instruments, finely wrought mechanical devices like control panels with knobs turning notched dials labelled with compass points, star positions, houses of the Moon and areas of concern – 'the house of soul and life' or 'property and wages' – and houses dedicated to family members, sex, power, glory and death.[73] When al-Idrisi said that the book the chief seeker gave him contained 'the sciences on the treasures', he referred to practices such as astrology, geomancy and letter magic that were pressed into service for the hunt.[74]

Public appetite for buried treasure encouraged practitioners of the occult sciences to adapt to meet the demand, and techniques traditionally used for locating mineral deposits or underground water were bent to the task of 'opening treasures' (*fath al-kunuz*).[75] A text by al-Kindi ('Letter on the Matter of Buried Things') described a method for pinpointing treasure using astrology as a cosmic GPS. Once a general area was chosen, the casting of charts began, with the first one advising whether the hunch was worth pursuing. Further charts and calculations gave a longitude, latitude and approximate depth of the treasure.[76] Not everyone could carry this off. Prospecting treasure sites required experts whose services were presumably a line item on the seeker's budget. Similarly, while treasure hunters were prepared to plough through soil, potsherds, rubble, bones, animal dung and alluvial clay by ordinary means, disarming protective seals, booby traps and maleficent jinn called for specialized magic, 'the invalidation of obstacles' (*tabtil al-mawani*), involving incantations and fumigations.[77] Since water was often found near treasures (at sites near the river, canals, wells or when excavations reached the water table) there was a method for removing it, 'the drying of waters'. Should hindrances such as chains or padlocks be encountered, al-Buni offered spells that began with invocations to Allah, one of whose names, coincidentally, is 'he who opens'.[78]

Along with jinn, the most lethal obstacles were the mechanical contraptions said to guard treasures, including sword-bearing statues with motion detectors that slashed unsuspecting intruders to ribbons. Automation was the latest thing in medieval technology, a modern marvel in its day. The late tenth- or early eleventh-century *Book of Mirabilia* mentions 'moving statues' created by 'the priests of Egypt', though there's no proof they existed at that time.[79] Later Alexandrians had, however, built wondrous machines, inspired perhaps by those described in myth and legend. According to Homer, Hephaestus, god of the forge, made 'twenty tripods with wheels of gold they might go of their own selves to the assemblies of the gods, and come back again'.[80] Hephaestus also created Talos, the mountain-moving man of bronze, a proto-cyborg whose metallic body had a 'blood-red vein' in one ankle.[81] Automation was the goal of mechanical engineering's founders, beginning with the son of an Alexandrian barber, Ctesibius (fl. 270 BC), who invented hydraulic and compressed air devices, including a water organ that played itself by using the weight of water to force air through the pipes. Philo (aka 'the Mechanic', d. 220 BC) described the properties of air, water and vacuums and provided instructions for building pneumatic machines. Heron (first century AD) invented the aeolipile, the first steam-powered engine, where a sphere connected to a boiler by an axial shaft was made to spin by steam escaping through canted nozzles.[82]

This foundational work was reprised and developed in the ninth century by the Banu Musa ('sons of Moses') as described in their *Book of Ingenious Devices* (ninth century). Three brothers working in Baghdad's House of Wisdom, the Banu Musa built automated fountains that altered the patterns and frequency of spray through calibrated variations in air and water pressure. They were likely the first to employ the crankshaft, which converts linear into rotary motion and vice versa, but Badiʿ al-Zaman al-Jazari (1136–1206) refined it and developed other pivotal mechanisms in his automatons.[83] Born in Cizre in Anatolia, al-Jazari was court engineer to the Turkmen rulers of eastern Anatolia, building machines that pumped and delivered water. But his signature inventions, described and illustrated in his *Book of Knowledge of Ingenious Devices* (1206), were designed to astonish. A water clock he devised was housed in a life-size replica of an elephant with a mahout behind its head and a turbaned scribe in the palanquin. A tub floating in a water tank in the elephant's belly was perforated to sink at a controlled rate, tugging on a rope connected to pulleys that moved the scribe to indicate the hour.[84] Hitting bottom, the tub unleashed a series of interdependent actions that made it resurface, and begin its descent anew. Still more ingenious were the automatons that al-Jazari presented in *mises en scène* that entertained the king and court while putting his experimental technologies to work.

Al-Jazari programmed his automatons to perform for extended periods, using 'feedback control and closed-loop systems, and various types of automatic switching to close and open valves, or change flow directions'.[85] An automated boat with a crew of oarsmen rowed while servant girls played flute at thirty-minute intervals for seven and a half hours. Another set of automatons, constructed within a scaled-down, two-storey palace, poured drinks. It involved a servant on a dais, four lady attendants and a male dancer on one level of the miniature palace, and a lance-bearing horseman on the top. When activated, the women played music, the dancer twirled and the horseman directed his lance at a member of the audience, causing the servant girl to fill a wine goblet and extend it to the indicated guest.[86] On a more sober note, al-Jazari designed machines for use during blood-letting treatments that measured the blood while amusing the (presumably royal) patients with automatons that popped out of a series of doors at intervals corresponding with the units of accumulating blood.[87]

It has been suggested that al-Jazari's book was produced 'to delight the eye and entertain the mind rather than give guidance to a working technician'.[88] But whether or not his inventions were replicated, the book was known and admired in scholarly circles throughout the Islamic world.[89] Like modern technological advancements, automation appears to have entered the popular imagination and re-emerged in treasure lore as science fiction. The sword-wielding statues that menaced treasure hunters were technically plausible, even if their presence as underground security systems was not. But in a world where the applied, natural and occult sciences were overlapping fields of enquiry, illumined by wonderment and trust in divine guidance, the marvellous was absorbed and domesticated. This is not to say it was less affecting, only that the extraordinary was at home everywhere.

The marvellous was literally digested, as evidenced by the market for ancient mummies, or more precisely for the resins used in mummification present in the corpse. It was a fairly wild conjecture on behalf of the ancients that their mummified bodies would deliver them, new and improved, to eternity. But one wonders what they would have made of the fact that people ate them to prolong their own lives, a practice that lasted centuries. The demand for mummies that arose from the belief in their medicinal qualities provided a means for treasure hunters to monetize goods that were less valuable than precious metals but had the virtue of widespread availability. The Persian word *mummia*, adopted by the Arabs, referred to natural bitumen obtained from several sources including the Dead Sea. Pliny (AD 24–79) reported that *mummia*/bitumen was used to treat illnesses, with the Babylonian variety particularly indicated for skin ailments, everything from itchiness to leprosy. While modern research suggests that bitumen can improve some skin disorders, there is no clinical proof of its efficacy in treating the many ailments for which it was prescribed.[90] Mixed with wine, bitumen was taken for cough and dysentery; mixed with vinegar, to thin the blood and treat rheumatism; and mixed with flour, to make plasters for staunching blood and healing wounds. Flavius Josephus (AD 37–100) remarked how bitumen was not only a reliable remedy, but helpful for caulking leaky ships.[91]

Dioscorides (d. AD 90) repeated Pliny's prescriptions for bitumen in *De materia medica* and these were followed by Arab physicians as early as the eighth century.[92] Like Strabo (d. AD 27) before him, Dioscorides also noted that Egyptians used *asphaltum* (the broader Greek term for bitumen, and substances like it) as an ingredient for embalming their dead. Bitumen was in fact used in mummification in the late New Kingdom but in far smaller quantities than other similarly dark resins, oils and beeswax (*mum* in Arabic).[93] Nevertheless, the meaning of the word *mummia* migrated from bitumen (the natural substance and similar ones with which it was conflated) to the embalmed body, where it was believed to be found in large amounts. Eleventh-century Persian physician and alchemist Ibn Sina (Avicenna; 980–1037) considered *mummia* a panacea, good for healing abscesses and fractures, concussions, paralysis, diseases of the throat, lungs, heart, stomach, liver and spleen, and as an antidote for poisons. Greek and Islamic sources regarding *mummia* meanwhile found their way west. The association with medicinal bitumen was forgotten; *mummia* meant mummified flesh, ideally that of ancient Egyptians, and it was used as commonly as aspirin. King Francis I of France (r. 1515–47) was said to never leave home without it; Francis Bacon (1561–1626) affirmed its 'great force in staunching blood', and seventeenth-century European herbalists kept the medical tradition alive.[94]

As early as the twelfth century, Jewish traders in Alexandria were exporting mummies wholesale to Europe.[95] Physician and historian ʿAbd al-Latif al-Baghdadi (b. Baghdad; 1162–1231) described the Egyptian market:

> As for that which is inside bodies and heads which is called mummia, there is a lot of it. The people of the countryside bring it to the city and it is sold for very little. I bought three heads full of it for half a dirham. The seller showed me a sack full of this, with the breast and belly with a filling of this mummia, and I saw that it was inside the bones, which absorbed it until they became part of it. I also saw on the back of the head traces of the shroud and the imprint of its fabric inscribed upon it, like drawing on wax if you stamped it on cloth. This mummia is black, like tar, and I saw that if the summer temperature gets very hot, it runs and sticks on whatever comes near it, and thrown into fire it boils and produces a smell of tar; it is most likely pitch and myrrh.[96]

Al-Baghdadi studied the works of the physician Galen (AD 129–210), who recommended Egypt as ideal for learning anatomy owing to its abundance of ancient corpses.[97] At a time when post-mortem dissection was forbidden, al-Baghdadi followed Galen's advice and made significant contributions to the understanding of the human body, including the articulation of the jawbone, the sacrum and the coccyx. Observant, questioning and insatiably curious, al-Baghdadi was the epitome of medieval Islamic erudition. He mastered the minutiae of Arabic grammar as a youth in Baghdad, while committing the Qur'an, works of philology and jurisprudence and thousands of verses of poetry to memory, feats of mental prowess considered requisite achievements for scholars in his day. In Mosul and Damascus he advanced his knowledge in several fields and in the early 1190s he arrived in Cairo, where, in 1200, another

Apothecary vessel (albarello) with inscription (MUMIA), 18th century.

devastating bout of famine aided his anatomical observations, enabling him to examine thousands of fresh, emaciated corpses.

In his *Account of Egypt*, al-Baghdadi writes that 'the year swept in like a monster, bent on destroying all the resources of life.'[98] When the Nile flood arrived at just over twelve paltry cubits, the hoarding of wheat began. Although Sultan al-Adil (Saladin's brother and successor) and his high-ranking officials helped feed the poor, in 1201 he and his troops were needed in Syria where the Crusades wore on, and the provisioning of his campaign exhausted the grain store. Al-Baghdadi described the 'rising tide of hunger', estimating 110,000 deaths in Cairo, and as many if not more in the district of Fustat, a perhaps exaggerated number, but the famine death toll was possibly augmented by tainted water.[99] The 'grievous pestilence and mortality' was not confined to the capital. Travellers told al-Baghdadi that the countryside was like 'a field sown with the limbs of the dead'.[100] Fustat, once 'choked with bustling crowds', became a ghost town, he wrote, 'so deserted . . . that one crosses [it] with terror'.[101] Women sold their daughters as servants and prostituted themselves. Most disturbingly, cannibalism became commonplace.

'When first the poor began to feed on human flesh . . . everyone expressed the utmost horror and aversion,' al-Baghdadi wrote, but soon 'these sensations were worn out by the force of example and the calls of hunger.' Rather than a last resort, human flesh 'was reckoned among the first delicacies of the table, and was dressed in many different ways'. He saw a woman attacked and robbed of a 'roasted child' in the marketplace where she'd purchased it, and no one batted an eye. Alarmed by a sentiment with which we are now all too familiar, al-Baghdadi observed that 'the effect of custom is so powerful it can divest the most prodigious crimes of their horror, by presenting them repeatedly to the senses, and reducing them to the . . . most trivial occurrences.'[102] The 1201 flood level of fifteen cubits would have been dangerously low, he remarked, were it not for the much-reduced population, further decimated by the earthquake of 1202.[103] Radiating from northeastern Syria, it struck Egypt's capital in the early morning of 20 May, and was 'so violent, that men leaped from their beds in the utmost consternation and began to call upon the Almighty'.[104] The mounds of skeletal remains thrown outside Cairo's walls grew higher.

The treasure hunters al-Baghdadi encountered were not vaunted members of the seekers' guild, but desperados, '[men] who have no other means of support than searching the burial places and taking whatever they find'. This included the linen mummy wrappings that were fashioned into second-hand garments or else sold in bulk to paper-makers 'who use them in the making of paper for the grocers'.[105] Yet, despite years of depredation resulting from political upheaval and a slew of natural disasters, amid 'piles of refuse and detritus', the markets and riverine port of Fustat were running full tilt again by the 1240s. According to Andalusian traveller Ibn Sàid, the horrors of decades past were forgotten; near the mosque of ʿAmr Ibn al-ʿAs, 'vendors sold cakes and tarts' and 'children carrying water containers [made] the rounds of the eaters.'[106]

As war machines go, it was hard to beat the Mongols, who at their thirteenth-century peak counted everywhere from Hungary to China as their turf, a globe-gripping reach that only the British would one day surpass. The Mongols slammed through Baghdad in 1258, tearing the Abbasid capital to bloody shreds. Cairo would have been next if not for the Mamluk troops who met them in battle at Ain Jalut (Palestine) in 1260, and delivered a crushing defeat. Derailing the Mongol expansion would have sufficed to win the fealty of everyone lying trembling in their path but the Mamluks also finished off the last Crusaders with the Siege of Acre in 1291. Sons of shamanistic nomads enslaved by Islamic rulers who trained them to ride, fight and lead, the Mamluk 'oligarchy of lost children' now held the Islamic world in the palm of their calloused hands.[107]

Their ascendance was owed to the shift towards armies composed of slave troops that was initiated by the Abbasids. Saladin and his successors favoured Kipchaks from the Eurasian Steppes, the so-called *bahri* (river) Mamluks, named after their barracks

The Seekers

Jan Swart van Groningen, 'Three Mamluks with Lances on Horseback', 1526, etching.

on the Nile Island near Cairo. Only non-Muslims could be purchased as slaves but only Muslims could exercise military authority, so at manhood they were freed, welcomed to the faith and granted a substantial salary. In the absence of blood relatives Mamluks were loyal only to their owner/employer, but there were multiple owners, emirs (commanders) who could lead up to a thousand men in battle, prompting fierce group rivalries that eventually resulted in the emergence of a Mamluk meritocracy. The Mamluk sultans were the leaders of the most powerful factions, consensually drawn from the ranks of the emirs, based as much on accomplishment and seniority as intrigue and assassination. Technically, Mamluk status could not be inherited, though exceptions were made for many a ruthless sultan.

Under Mamluk rule (1250–1517), Cairo replaced Baghdad as the mind of the Islamic empire. Whatever misgivings Egyptians may have had as subjects of a rambunctious militia given to murderous feuds and horseback rampages through Cairo's narrow streets, they were safe from external threats. Trade flourished and the building of magnificent Mamluk residences, mosques and mausoleums created jobs while expanding the city in every direction. At a time when London's population was 60,000, and Paris's 80,000, Cairo's was at least 200,000 and by some estimates three times more. 'Like the waves of the sea, it surges with her throngs of folk,' wrote peripatetic historian Ibn Battuta in 1325, 'yet for all the capacity of her station and her power to sustain, [Cairo] can scarce hold their number.' Twenty years later, the city was relieved of overcrowding, when the Black Death killed at least a third of its inhabitants.[108]

Creeping west from Central Asia, the plague reached the Black Sea in 1338 and was carried by merchant ships to Alexandria in 1347, arriving in Cairo in 1348.[109] Islamic physicians knew of the first pandemic (Justinianic Plague, sixth to ninth century) and followed Hippocrates' and Galen's theory of miasmatic transmission (by bad air). Between 1348 and 1517, Egypt suffered twenty countrywide plague outbreaks, sometimes accompanied by famine owing to the dearth of farm labour. Recurring epidemics generated treatises and chronicles, some strictly medical, others addressing religious issues arising from the Black Death, arguing for and against prevailing Islamic tenets. These held that the plague issued directly from Allah and was therefore not contagious; that the faithful should neither flee nor enter a plague-stricken area; and that plague was a punishment to the infidel, but a mercy to the pious Muslim, who dies a martyr and enters paradise direct. Characteristically, these treatises presented accurate clinical observations and deductions, combined with ideological bias and a dose of magical practices for treating the disease.[110]

The Black Death left a melancholy mark on historian Ibn Khaldun (1332–1406), who watched its march across North Africa when a child. 'The entire inhabited world changed,' he wrote, 'It was as if the voice of existence in the world had called out for oblivion and restriction, and the world responded to its call.'[111] Born in Tunis and destined for travel, scholarship and prestige in the courts of conquerors, Ibn Khaldun settled in Cairo in 1383, under Sultan al-Zahir Barquq (Barquq meaning 'plum' in Arabic), the first of a dynasty of Circassian Mamluks, also called *burji* (tower) Mamluks, referencing their garrison in the citadel. The carnage resulting from factional disputes during the reigns of the river Mamluks intensified under their successors, with ghoulish massacres and public punishments, as if the plague had robbed all but the most torturous deaths of meaning. Enemies and criminals were hacked in two, or heavily chained and hung alive on iron hooks on Bab Zuwayla, the southern city gate, where chopped heads were likewise displayed.

Ibn Khaldun had nothing but praise for his Mamluk patrons and protectors, lauding them for reinvigorating a decadent, urbanized culture that had strayed too far from its desert origins. '[The Mamluks] embrace Islam with determination . . . while retaining their nomadic virtues . . . unmarred by the habits of civilization, their youthful strength unshattered by the excess of luxury.'[112] Wealth, in Ibn Khaldun's opinion, eroded virtue, but so did unchecked power, which didn't seem to bother him as much. His remark that Egypt was famed throughout North Africa for its prosperity, 'greater than anywhere else', reflected nicely on its rulers and his description of Cairo offered an indication of its resilience in the face of adversity:

> [It is] the metropolis of the world, the garden of the universe, assemblage of all the nations, the ant-hill of the human species, the portico of Islam, the throne of royalty, a city embellished

with palaces and arcades ... with dervish monasteries and with schools, and lighted by the moon and stars of erudition.[113]

In contrast, Ibn Khaldun's student, Egyptian historian al-Maqrizi who was born and died in Cairo (1364–1406), thought his city had gone nowhere but downhill since the Fatimids and characterized the Mamluks as 'more lustful than monkeys, more ravenous than rats, and more harmful than wolves'.[114]

Ibn Khaldun described the Egyptians as lighthearted, the grasshopper to Aesop's ant. They kept no stores of food, shopping daily for their needs, which included social interaction. A gregarious nature contributed to the success of Cairo's markets, he suggested, and assisted the recovery of commerce in the wake of the Black Death.[115] But having spent time with North African Berbers and Arab tribesmen whose way of life he admired, Ibn Khaldun maintained that city folk could never match up. 'Sedentary life constitutes the last stage of civilization,' he wrote, 'and the last stage of evil and of remoteness from the good.'[116] Among the most feckless of urbanites Ibn Khaldun placed treasure hunters, 'weak-minded persons in cities [who] hope to discover property under the surface of the earth and to make some profit from it'.[117] Some were indigent, unwilling to do an honest day's work, unable to succeed in business, farming or the crafts, and prone to resorting to 'unnatural' and 'devious' ways of making a living. Others were rich and spoiled, '[accustomed] to ever-increasing luxury ... their only way out is to wish that at one stroke, without any effort, they might find sufficient money to pay for their habits'.[118]

Ibn Khaldun was not the first to notice that treasure hunting attracted the rich and poor alike. Al-Baghdadi portrayed treasure hunters as poverty-stricken wretches, but also mentioned a wealthy judge who unearthed gilded mummies on the Giza Plateau.[119] Another thirteenth-century writer lamented how treasure hunting's appeal was so widespread, it cut across classes.[120] Islamic jurist Ibn al-Hajj (d. 1337) called it an illness, incompatible with the teachings of Islam. As an index of its popularity, he noted how private and public buildings were demolished in its pursuit and suggested that treasure hunting served as a subterfuge for vengeance on a neighbour, or as an underhand means of freeing up desired plots of land. If someone wanted to destroy another's property, al-Hajj reported, all they had to do was produce a seemingly old document saying that treasure lay beneath it and allow that document to fall into the right hands.[121]

Like the ancient Egyptian authors of wisdom texts who saw tomb-raiding as a form of anarchy, to Ibn Khaldun treasure hunting signalled a morally lax and decaying society. The fact that the occult sciences were implicated in the process only heightened his conviction:

> They believe that all the property of the nations of the past was stored underground and sealed with magic talismans. These seals, they believe, can be broken only by those who may chance upon the (necessary) knowledge and can offer the proper incense, prayers and sacrifices to break them. They circulate stories to this effect that sound like idle talk. Those who don't know the right spells, find the place empty or full of worms, or else the riches are there but guards stand over them with drawn swords. Or the earth shakes, so that he believes he will be swallowed up, and similar nonsense.[122]

Ibn Khaldun acknowledged that the ancient Egyptians and Greeks buried their wealth and that Egyptians had always hunted treasure, noting how a tax was levied on treasure hunters, and that 'stupid and deluded persons' who engage in such pursuits deserved to pay it.[123] Yet, however scornful of treasure-related magic, Ibn Khaldun did not dismiss magic altogether, far from it. 'No intelligent person doubts the reality of sorcery,' he wrote, referring to aspects of the occult sciences frowned on, if not forbidden, by Islamic law.[124] Alchemy was the worst infraction in his opinion, but while he rejected the possibility of turning metals into gold, he thought scorpions, bees and snakes could spontaneously generate, and said that this had been observed.[125] He approved of letter magic and numerology, which made it possible 'to be active in the world of nature' and 'influence created things'.[126] He was fascinated with divination and wrote extensively on astrology, geomancy, the reading of entrails and catoptromancy, a form of divination involving mirrors and moonlight. While attempting to foretell or alter God's will was impermissible, Ibn Khaldun believed divination could serve as a vehicle for the spiritually inclined to enhance their receptivity to higher truths.[127] Using it for material gain was another matter.

Ibn Khaldun thought that casual applications of otherwise valid practices degraded them and weakened society. In other words, magic had become too popular. Commercial demand, driven in part by treasure hunting, was in fact strong enough to require regulation, the same as any other commodity sold at market.[128] While furnishing their households or buying food for dinner, Cairo's shoppers could also purchase magical amulets or consult astrologers and experts in other types of divination.[129] Market inspectors were on hand to keep everyone honest, equipped with manuals listing rules for commercial transactions and their purveyors, including practitioners of the occult sciences. Magicians' premises might, for example, be moved from side streets to main ones, so as to police them with greater ease.[130] Security guards patrolled the markets, ejecting drunkards and other undesirables, including thieves. Theft was so common that there were magical rituals to prevent it, or failing that, to identify the crooks and locate stolen property. Some thieves were called 'burrowers', because they bored through the walls of people's houses to rob them.[131] Craftier burglars determined whether or not their victims were at home by attaching a candle to a turtle's back and slipping it inside the house. If the four-legged flashlight failed to elicit exclamations of surprise, the coast was clear.[132]

Yet another class of thieves exploited the gullibility of prospective treasure hunters, ensnaring them with confidence tricks. A tenth-century text warned that some treasure hunters were frauds and al-Baghdadi mentioned how the wealthy were often lured into paying real money for faked hunts.[133] But Syrian scholar al-Jawbari produced what amounts to an investigative report on treasure-related con-jobs, *The Book of Charlatans* (c. 1264), designed to expose the tactics of tricksters of all kinds. There were phoney sheikhs and monks, quack druggists, dentists ('those who extract worms from teeth') and, most insidiously, doctors, who alternately improved and sabotaged a patient's health, '[turning] him into a nice little pumpkin patch that they can crop'.[134] In al-Jawbari's day, trickery was viewed as a kind of magic, the 'science of artifice or wiles' (*'ilm al-hiyal*), and his characterization of its practitioners has stood the test of time.[135] Then as now, con artists needed to inspire trust, possess talents for dissembling, persuasion and a shrewd understanding of human nature. They had to be good talkers; eloquence is a trait admired by Arabic speakers, who enjoy a clever turn of phrase. Patience was and remains a virtue, since treasure-hunting scams usually involved what is known as the long con. According to al-Jawbari, people were willingly bamboozled by anyone saying they knew where to find treasure, '[falling] for them out of that greed for money that plays havoc with men's minds [and makes them] slaves to its influence'.[136]

In one scenario, preparations involved finding a cave or abandoned tomb, digging a hole, planting a gilded iron key along with a plaque inscribed with unreadable text, and coating everything in sandarac, a fragrant resin. A parchment was meanwhile treated to look weathered, and directions to the designated place written on it. The con man then looked for his mark, showing the parchment around and asking people if they knew the place it mentioned, arousing curiosity and setting the rumour mill awhirl. When someone took the bait and wanted in, he feigned reluctance and made them swear not to cheat or hurt him, 'for I am a stranger, with no one to take his part, who presents himself at god's door and at yours.' At the appropriate moment he remarked how dearly that parchment had cost him, and asked his new partner to contribute, 'as his generosity and manliness dictate'.[137]

Having chosen the mark, the con man made him wait, to lend the hunt authenticity, for success could only be obtained under certain astrological conditions. At last, they proceeded to the spot indicated on the forged parchment, where the discovery of the golden key and inscribed plaque (that provided further instructions) caused much excitement. It was like the classic three-card monte, where the card sharp lets the players choose the winning card once or twice before he starts fleecing them. Cash outlays were needed to procure the necessary tools for the hunt, including magical accessories. If some of the pricey aromatics used for fumigations were unavailable, the con man happily embarked on a trip to find them, never to return. In some cases, the mark was told to purchase a gold statuette to pinpoint the location of a treasure so great, 'loaded camels couldn't carry off all the prize'. Once the statuette was produced, the swindler made off with it. 'Wise up to these things!' warned al-Jawbari.[138]

Since treasure hunting was believed to incur supernatural dangers, fake booby traps were installed at the site to fulfil expectations. The 'fire trap' involved a water-skin inflated with air, its mouth stuffed with wadding soaked in flammable resins and sulphur and sealed with a thin film of wax. As they entered the cave, the con man melted the seal of the skin with his taper, or perhaps left a bit of burning wick. 'Go ahead,' he told his companions, 'I'm right behind you.' When the unwitting mark stepped on the inflated skin, it expelled air that ignited the wadding and produced a startling burst of flame. Al-Jawbari described an 'artificial snake with eyes filled with mercury', fitted with a similar device that made fire spurt from the ersatz serpent's mouth.[139]

Schooled in group dynamics, the scammer sometimes discussed the prospect of finding treasure with a number of interested people. He then confided in each of them that he would attempt this adventure with him alone, and secured their vow of silence, lest someone learn of their plans. Knowing they'd talk, he set his marks against one another, sparking competition as to who would actually participate in the hunt. Having extracted fees from them all, 'each according to his means', he had to deliver. But before they set out, he arranged that they be ambushed by his cronies, en route. The dupes ran, leaving the con man to face the alleged assailants. Days later he re-emerged in public, complaining how badly he'd been beaten. 'This increases the people's trust in him even more,' noted al-Jawbari, 'wise up to these things!'[140] But people did not wise up; on the contrary, the hunt for treasure, real or not, seems only to have gained momentum. Ibn Khaldun, writing a century after al-Jawbari, felt that tricksters and treasure hunters were so pernicious they should all have their hands cut off.[141]

Amputation was the punishment for fraudsters in 1424, who had been discovered boiling the exhumed corpses of the recent dead in a cauldron to sell as *mummia*. First they were flogged, then hung (handless) by the back of their necks on an iron hook, 'while the whole of Cairo walked around them, until at last they were sent to jail'.[142] During an outbreak of the plague in the later 1400s, when a man was caught stealing mummies and their shrouds, the Mamluk sultan ordered the skin of his face to be flayed.[143] Punishing desperation with gratuitous cruelty is never a sign of strength; having failed to learn that savagery was better for conquest than for governance, the Mamluks began to falter. 'They were responsible for much disorder in Egypt,' wrote al-Maqrizi, 'They attacked the inhabitants, slaughtered them, pillaged their wealth and carried off their wives.' The Mamluks were even worse than the Europeans, he maintained, which considering the atrocities of the Crusades was saying something.[144] War with the Ottoman Turks, intent on folding Mamluk territories into their empire, was waged from 1485 to 1491 on several fronts, halting trade and ending in a short-lived truce. Egypt's sporadic bouts of plague and famine depleted resources and further destabilized the Mamluk stronghold. Robber gangs on horseback ransacked Cairo's markets at will, and for every fraudster forced to face the law, there were plenty who escaped it.[145] Before long, the city known as 'the mother of the world' was relegated to the status of a provincial capital under Ottoman rule.

On 14 April 1517 the last Mamluk sultan, Tuman Bey, dressed in rags, bound in chains and seated atop a camel, was paraded through Cairo to Bab Zuwayla, where he was hanged, surrounded by Ottoman soldiers. The rope broke twice before successfully throttling him, a *fait divers* recreated in a shadow play performed that summer on the Nile island of Roda. Egypt's new Ottoman ruler, Selim the Grim, so-called for the determination with which he dispatched his rivals, was in the audience. The spectacle of Tuman Bey's ignominious end tickled him so much he awarded the play's producer 200 dinars and invited him to Istanbul for a command performance.[146]

Like the inhabitants of other medieval cities, the people of Cairo enjoyed a good show. Street theatre was bawdy and comical; shadow plays likewise enacted social and political farce. Physicality was celebrated by acrobats, tightrope walkers, jugglers, contortionists, wrestlers and stick-fighters.[147] There were professional farters, only the most talented of whom could compete with ambient noise in the narrow streets or marketplaces where such entertainments took place. Snake charmers, illusionists and fire-walkers (who reportedly coated the soles of their feet in frog fat, orange peel and talc) awed an audience willing to suspend disbelief, as did storytellers, practised in the art of eliciting incredulous gasps and the laughter of recognition. Ibn Khaldun, in his dour way, disapproved of such distractions, saying that excessive entertainment reflected a society's decline, and there's truth to that, as twenty-first-century binge-watchers in their cogent moments might concede. Storytellers provided a service as integral to medieval society as it is to ours, albeit in the street, for tips.[148]

The interlocking narratives of *The Thousand and One Nights*, part of the standard repertoire of Cairene storytellers, sometimes featured kings and queens in sumptuous palaces but more frequently were set in Cairo neighbourhoods and animated by people like the ones in the storyteller's audience. *The Thousand and One Nights* are rich in the sociological and topographical detail that grounded the medieval reader or listener in the familiar while setting them up for fantastical events and denouements. Ordinary characters (cobblers, tailors, blacksmiths, goldsmiths, servants, fishermen, water-carriers, carpenters, porters, barbers, butchers, bean-sellers, Christians, Jews, merchants, hucksters, burglars, beggars, policemen, prostitutes, school children, mothers and often disgruntled wives) encounter the extraordinary in plots turning on dreams of wealth, romance, adventure and their magical fulfilment, and on the power of fate to deliver justice when least expected. *Thousand and One Nights* scholar Robert Irwin likens them to science fiction, replete as they are with 'fantastic voyages, distortion of time and space, alien beings, strange technologies, alternative societies, post-apocalypse societies and imaginary histories'.[149] Yet the most typical plot-driver employing these themes was treasure hunting that, however embellished with occult interventions, synchronicities and heroic ordeals, was but a pickaxe away from lived-in reality.

The origins of *The Thousand and One Nights* are as labyrinthine as their plot-lines; 'no one knows where they began or when they will end,' writes Irwin.[150] While often assumed to be written versions of oral tradition, the *Nights* are 'a cultural amphibian', both oral and literary in origin, a shape-shifting compilation with echoes of ancient Egyptian, Greek, Roman and Persian narratives.[151] The earliest reference dates to the ninth century, a fifteen-line fragment of a manuscript entitled *Book of the Tale of the Thousand and One Nights* that names Sheherazade and promises the reader 'examples of the excellence and shortcomings, the cunning and stupidity, the generosity and avarice, and the courage and cowardice that are in man, instinctive or acquired'. Al-Masudi (tenth century) mentions a book called *A Thousand Entertaining Tales*, and a character named Sheherazade. The title *The Thousand and One Nights* appears for the first time in twelfth-century documents in the Geniza archive.[152] In short, the *Nights* emerged from the same cultural context as treatises on the occult and applied sciences, on pharaonic monuments and the treasures they were believed to hide, at a time when treasure hunters, taxpaying or otherwise, searched for treasure.

Almost every aspect of treasure hunting as related by medieval scholars is present in *The Thousand and One Nights*, including spells for deactivating booby traps and jinn and the use of astrology, dream interpretation and other methods for divining locations, usually in Egypt or some faraway land. That the magicians in fictional hunts often came from North Africa is owed to the fact that authors of some well-known occult treatises were born there. 'Aladdin or the Wonderful Lamp', Hollywood's favourite *Night*, involves a geomantic table, North African magicians, magical invocations and a magical device that places a jinn at the protagonist's command. Treasure-hunting con men appear in the 'Tale of the Sharpers with the Money-Changer and the Ass', one of several tales featuring tricksters, whose guile was much admired. In 'Judar and His Brothers' there are more North African magicians, spells to remove water and disarm automatons and magical saddlebags that produce endless quantities of choice foods and wines, reminiscent of the depictions of offerings in ancient Egyptian tombs that did likewise. In 'Maruf the Cobbler' the protagonist's plough strikes an immovable obstacle, a flagstone opening to a staircase leading to rooms full of riches, and a casket with a golden ring 'inscribed with talismans that looked like ants' tracks' that produced an obedient jinn when rubbed.[153]

Many of the treasure tropes present in *The Thousand and One Nights* appear in a recently translated compilation, *Tales of the Marvellous and News of the Strange*, whose tenth-century origin in Egypt or Syria is more literary than oral, related to the genre of *mirabilia* (*'aja'ib*). Rather than scholarly accounts of natural or man-made wonders, *Tales of the Marvellous* were 'a very early and impressive example of pulp fiction', with treasure hunters and their supernatural adventures occupying the ground lately held by detectives investigating murder.[154] A page-turner entitled 'The Story of the Four Hidden Treasures' describes four different quests. The narrator of the first one is released from prison to entertain a prince with the story of how he squandered his inheritance, took to the road, met a man with a book of instructions for finding treasures and joined him in his search. Along the way they encounter automatons, including a statue 'with revolving eyes' and another who helpfully smashes a padlocked door, enabling them to pass through, only to be greeted by a choking 'cloud of vapour' that takes several days to clear. When they finally enter the chamber, they find a ship that carries them 'at great speed in pitch darkness five hundred cubits under the mountain'. Eventually they reach the treasure, 'a golden box, a ring and a knife', which causes them 'to faint with pleasure'.[155]

The second quest involves a shipload of one hundred treasure hunters, 'skilled men ... with suitable picks, axes and other tools', who dally with mermaids as delightful as humans but with rougher skin, and who eat fruits 'softer than butter, sweeter than honey'. It's not all a cakewalk; one of the men is mauled by a bronze lion, another is sliced in two by a mechanical swordsman. Their leader rallies them, saying: 'if a man's time is up he will die in his bed!' They soldier on, near exhaustion. Cue the automatons that emit 'tuneful sounds that captivate the heart' and herald their arrival at a mega-palace with an enormous door made of solid, jewel-studded gold. The shrouded corpse of Shaddad the Great, legendary king and pyramid-builder, lies inside on a silver couch with a green topaz tablet by its head. The inscription is his Ozymandian message to whoever covets great wealth: 'I conquered a thousand cities ... lived for a thousand years ... but when death came to me nothing of all I had was gathered to any avail ... Take heed, for Time is not to be trusted.' The treasure hunters think it over, then take the loot.[156]

The third quest is conducted by two connoisseurs of the marvellous, one of whom shows the other a stone from China, 'which gleams at night as brightly as dawn' and can only be found in the mouths of sea-serpents, which '[the Chinese] kill, but that sometimes eat them'. This stone is one of seventy the man has acquired, and they are but a part of a fabulous crown which becomes the object of their quest. On their journey, they nearly drown in a tunnel and suffer a jinn attack; they escape by praying to God, who sends a 'huge cloud filled with flames' that obliterates their assailants. They meet 'a man with legs like those of a riding beast, and a human face', descendant of an Indian king who impregnated his mare one drunken night, producing a boy and a girl and eventually a race of satyrs. 'This was a great wonder,' the narrator comments. When the treasure hunters are temporarily blinded by a gigantic pearl and break out in a rash of large blisters, the satyr supplies a healing tree sap. In the end they find the crown, and 'faint with joy'.[157]

The fourth quest begins with a 'golden book with strange writing' that turns up after an earthquake and falls into the hands of the emir. A monk agrees to translate the book, providing he's well paid. They strike a deal; he sets to work, with his patron breathing down his neck. At first, the book yields nothing but platitudes, like 'good deeds are treasures to store up.' At last the book mentions the 'Scented Mountain' as a place for the 'seeker of wonders'. 'Stop right there,' says the emir, who knows a lead when he hears one. The monk happens to be familiar with the Scented Mountain and together they set out to find a place marked by a stone snake with a frog in its mouth and scorpion on its head. A magical staircase materializes before them; a gigantic automaton hurls a bowl at their heads. They traverse chambers within chambers until finding 'more wealth than had ever been seen', and 'almost dying of joy'.[158]

Gold and jewels were the desired outcome of any treasure hunt, but the greatest treasures were books about how to find treasure, a theme reaching back to at least late antiquity, and iterated by medieval scholars in connection with the pyramids, Sphinx and temples. A classic in the genre, 'The Romance of Setna Khaemuas and the Mummies', dates to the third century BC and while not replicated per se in *The Thousand and One Nights* (where mummies are curiously absent), it uses interlocking narratives and treasure-related themes common in medieval literature. The fictional protagonist, Setna, was based on a historical figure, the fourth son of Ramses II, a high priest of Ptah whose interest in ancient monuments is attested by inscriptions he left throughout the Memphis necropolis. Setna also figures in a Ptolemaic Period Book of the Dead, where he discovers a magical manuscript beneath its owner's mummified head, just as he does in the so-called romance, where the 'scroll of Thoth' is the sought-after treasure.[159]

Hidden at the bottom of the Nile within a series of nested chests of ascending value (iron, bronze, Aleppo pinewood, ivory, ebony, silver and finally gold), the scroll enables those who follow its instructions to 'enchant heaven, the earth, the underworld, the mountains and the seas', to understand the speech of animals and

The Seekers

Albert Letchford, illustration of the jinn, in 'Alaeddin; or, The Wonderful Lamp', frontispiece to Richard F. Burton, trans., and Leonard C. Smithers, ed., *The Book of the Thousand Nights and a Night*, vol. x (1897).

to witness the 'fish of the deep, though there were twenty-one divine cubits of water above them'. Danger awaits Setna, when the scroll's mummified owner awakens to challenge him to three rounds of a board game; if he wins he gets the prize. But he loses, and finds himself buried in the ground, feet first, then 'up to his penis', then

Albert Letchford, illustration of 'Judar and His Brethren' from when the water disappears, uncovering the river-bed and the door to the treasure, from Richard F. Burton, trans., and Leonard C. Smithers, ed., *The Book of the Thousand Nights and a Night*, vol. V (1897).

up to his ears. 'After that, Setna was in great difficulty' until 'the amulets of Ptah' obtained from the pharaoh set him free.[160]

A treasure book drives the plot of 'Judar and His Brothers' in *The Thousand and One Nights*, where Judar meets a magician who tells how he (the magician) and his brothers divided a rich inheritance amicably except when it came to a book entitled *Legends of the Ancients*, 'a unique and invaluable work, worth more than its weight in jewels'. Sons of a magician, they ask the master who mentored their father to arbitrate the matter, and he decides that the book will go to the one who proves his worth by finding what amounts to the treasure of all treasures. It consists of a ring that will allow its wearer to rule the world; a sword that can smite armies; a cosmetic case containing kohl that applied to the eyes gives x-ray vision; and a crystal ball that brings any part of the world into view but can also focus the sun's rays to destroy cities. One wonders what good the book was after all that, except to settle a dispute among siblings, but off the brothers go to find the right place, at the right time, and the right person who can access these marvels, namely Judar.[161]

In narratives concerning treasure books, the effort and courage required to obtain them is commensurate with their reward of knowledge regarding the laws of nature, space/time and matter, how to harness them and create heaps of gold. The relative values of wisdom, dominion and wealth were conflated, and whatever the result of the search, a good story was sure to come of it. The Arabic words for 'story' (*hikaya*), 'storyteller' and 'mimic' share the same root, and in medieval fiction the story and its teller merged. Storytellers imitated the voices and mannerisms of characters in stories about storytellers hearing and relating new stories, meta-narratives where freedom or imprisonment, life or death (and tips or not) relied on the power to enthral. As Irwin puts it, 'the story of a quest for treasure turns out to be the story of a quest for a story.'[162] More to the point, treasure-hunting stories inspired more treasure hunts, and vice versa.

Gambling was another form of entertainment in medieval Cairo, betting on horseraces, pigeon races, backgammon and wrestling matches for which astrologers offered predictive odds. Then as now there were cheaters, welshers, gambling-related cons and gambling addicts.[163] Although prohibited by Islam, people bet on almost anything, like how long a man could stand on one leg.[164] But the most elaborate and compulsive of gambles was treasure hunting. The obituary of a certain Sheikh Mohammed ibn Mubarak al-Athari ('the antiquarian'; d. 1403) says 'he was obsessed with treasure hunting, spending all his earnings on the search, but never gained any.'[165] While the needy hunted treasure by whatever means lay at their disposal, less interested as they were in supernatural adventures and ancient artefacts than putting food on the table, to folks like 'the antiquarian', treasure hunting was a kind of game.

The definitions of play in Johan Huizinga's *Homo Ludens* (1938) easily apply to treasure hunting. Play is voluntary, rule-ordered, performed within fixed boundaries and occupies a different 'mental world', a 'certain imagination of reality'. 'Play casts a spell over us,' Huizinga wrote, describing playgrounds as 'forbidden spots, isolated, hedged round, hallowed, within which special rules obtain. All are temporary worlds within the ordinary world, dedicated to the performance of an act apart.'[166] Treasure hunting differs from pure play only in that it involves material gain, like gambling, both of which nonetheless produce the tension and excitement that amounts to fun. Treasure hunting may be compared to computer gaming, with the action taking place directly in the field and the occult providing the virtual reality dimension. Gamers, like treasure hunters, can be richly rewarded for their skills; and a number of computer games coincidentally involve tomb-raiding.[167] Like gaming today, treasure hunting was addictive, able to produce what Huizinga describes as 'the very essence, the primordial quality of play', namely, 'intensity', 'absorption' and 'this power of maddening'.[168] And just as gamers consult the Internet for instructions on how to win, so medieval treasure hunters consulted manuals.

Medieval texts mentioning books with directions to hidden treasures include an early tenth-century treatise cited by al-Idrisi in *Lights of the Translunar Bodies*, where he noted receiving such a book himself. The late tenth-century bookseller Ibn Nadim listed manuscripts in his collection whose titles suggest instructions on how to find treasure. Several texts transmit the story of how the Byzantines and Franks, when leaving Egypt and Syria, buried their treasures and recorded the locations in books that were stored in Constantinople's Hagia Sophia until such time as they might be useful.[169] In his thirteenth-century *Book of Charlatans*, al-Jawbari remarked how con men claimed their forged parchments had been acquired in Constantinople to lend them authenticity. The story remained current three hundred years later, when Leo Africanus (d. 1554) wrote that priests in charge of guarding the secret books in Constantinople were paid with a page from one of them, that they might have 'a chance of well-being'.[170] In short, conventional wisdom held that books about how to find treasure existed and could be bought.

Among the scores of medieval Arabic manuscripts awaiting translation, treasure-related ones may well turn up, but the one most parsed so far is *The Book of Hidden Pearls and Precious Secrets Concerning Signs, Caches and Treasure Troves*.[171] A compilation of treasure-hunting directions garnered from fifteenth- and seventeenth-century Arabic manuscripts, *Hidden Pearls* reproduced the original Arabic texts and a French translation in 1907. The manuscripts excerpted in *Hidden Pearls* were also compilations, culled from various written and possibly oral sources, snatches of magical treatises and stories old, new and perhaps invented. The dialect and terminology suggest Egyptians wrote them, and directions offer topographic clues that were probably identifiable in the past.[172] While most Egyptians were illiterate, the number of educated merchants and artisans that grew throughout the medieval period provided a readership and Cairo was a known storehouse of occult science and treasure-related literature.[173]

The authorship of treasure-hunting manuals remains uncertain, as they were typically unsigned or speciously attributed. Ibn Khaldun was probably not the first to wonder why anyone would take the trouble to carefully hide treasures only to make their locations known.[174] And once they were public, why believe the locations described in the book still held treasure? Likewise, if they were written by experienced treasure hunters who knew where the goods were found, why didn't they take them? The most likely authors were creative individuals with a grasp of the law of supply and demand and an interest if not a professional background in the occult sciences. Treasure hunting and magic were at the forefront of the popular imagination for centuries; to paraphrase John 4:23, 'Cometh the hour, cometh the book.' As for the manuals' veracity, it didn't matter; then as now, people wanted to believe, and to cut out the middlemen. Treasure-hunting manuals were do-it-yourself handbooks, some of which gave advice in other areas, like *The Shining Suns and the Great Secret Treasures* (1326) by a Cairo professor who devoted several chapters to finding treasure, but also offered techniques for taking vengeance and for making oneself loved.[175]

Like travel guides, treasure manuals advised what to bring, what to wear and when to go. Levers, hoes, pickaxes, ropes, baskets, torches, candles and lanterns were necessities, including special wicks soaked in rapeseed oil, goat fat and 'oil of crow' to render flames resistant to blasts of subterranean air.[176] Certain shoes were specified, like apple-wood clogs, crocodile sandals and 'high boots covered with felt soaked in essence of violet'.[177] Propitious times were suggested, like 'when Jupiter is at its highest point in the sky' or 'when Saturn is in the sign of Aquarius', but the best day overall for treasure hunting was Saturday.[178] Like ancient Egyptian Books of the Dead, the manuals warned what to look for and gave the passwords that granted safe passage. But however fanciful the ancients' instructions for reaching the hereafter, they were clearer than the directions in treasure manuals. This is partly due to repeated transmission whereby texts that were esoteric by definition were excerpted, copied and recopied over time. Yet to a predisposed public, the confounding nature of the manuals may have made them more, not less, attractive. Ibn Khaldun tells us that the seventy works of alchemist Jabir Ibn Hayyan he read were 'like puzzles'.[179] Dr Samuel Johnson associated the name of this alchemist, who was known in the West as Geber, with the word 'gibberish', an apt description for many of the instructions found in *The Book of Hidden Pearls*.[180]

Under headings named for Egyptian villages, towns or quarters of Cairo, *Hidden Pearls* offers directions to 417 treasures of greater or lesser magnitude. Many involve finding a trapdoor or flagstone, a sign that the treasure hunter had hit paydirt but also that he'd arrived at the threshold of a metaphysical world that held dangers for the unprepared.[181] Many entries are brief and all are imprecise, for example, 'look at the start of Lake Qarun [in Fayoum] for the first mountain called Abu Qatran. Leave it to your back and march west 2,000 [paces].' Somewhere around there are 'magnificent *mastabas*' with underground burial chambers where the deceased lies 'with his jewels and precious vestments, and has beside him all the riches he possessed'.[182] Elsewhere one is instructed to put the pyramid of Dahshur (Giza) to one's back (without indicating which side of the pyramid) and to 'walk to the first steep slope, then the second, to direct you towards the north.'[183] Other directions are entirely useless, like 'find [in Fustat] the tree growing near the heap of black soil' or 'north of Batanun [Menufiyya province] there's a building in plastered brick,' the material used for nearly all buildings.[184] Some instructions demand an unimaginable degree of blind faith, like the one about finding a field 'planted with five-hundred watermelons' that can be turned into silver and gold if set on fire 'until they are red' and then sprinkled with vinegar.[185]

More suggestive directions concern a Church of Mary in Ahnas el-Medina (near Beni Suef), site of an ancient Egyptian provincial capital. There one must look for 'the image of a knight in a red cloak riding a grey mare, holding a sword pointing towards the ground at a crow that clings to the mare's belly, striking it with its beak'. There is in fact a sixth-century church in Ahnas el-Medina but it is dedicated to St George, whose dragon was apparently lost in translation.[186] Churches were frequent hiding places for treasures, typically beneath an altar, which had to be smashed to reach underground passages. Readers are directed just as often to mosques, where prayer niches (*mihrab*) are the point of penetration. The treasure hunter must rely on dodgy units of measure, for example 'walk east to within the reach of an arrow' or 'dig to the depth of the height of a man', though cubits are sometimes indicated.[187] While a certain amount of shovelling and smashing is usually required, it's never long before a staircase is promised to appear, or a well, or a flagstone marking a trapdoor leading to corridors with doors opening to rooms within treasure-packed rooms.

The manuals contain enticing inventories of the riches that await those armed with the proper knowledge: quantities of silver, gold, jewels and magical devices. A list of items lying in a trove at the bottom of the 'well of bones' (beneath a church) includes a gold casket sitting on a silver throne holding books about 'the science of the past'; rings that place a gigantic jinn at the wearer's service; a silver bird that when worn in a turban grants invisibility; gold plaques bearing inscriptions that make waters recede; a bonnet with a gold-embroidered text that enables the wearer to travel a year's distance in a day; and a necklace of gems that when rubbed on the eyes of the blind restores their sight.[188] All this came, however, with a somewhat daunting caveat:

> If you want to take any of these things, you must have a baboon and immolate it in the center of town, while saying 'Oh you who inhabit this place, here is your offering and your incense!'
> You must then burn incense in order to take whatever you like. If you don't make this offering, it will not only be impossible to touch anything in the church, you will perish before you do. I'm warning you in advance.[189]

The warnings attached to many instructions inject a hint of danger, just enough to make the treasure hunter feel he's bravely facing risks. When entering the 'grotto of the great jinn of Helwan', he's cautioned to 'wait for the emanations to dissipate.'[190] Elsewhere he is advised to steer clear of a column of gold in the centre of an underground room, 'I pray you, my son, for the love of god the adored, do not go near it or you will perish of poison!' Another entry says to watch out for mechanical lions, and provides tips for disabling them. Treacherous companions could be worse than supernatural misadventures, judging by the number of warnings against them:

> Avoid vile people and don't let them fool you. Keep your distance and don't confide your secrets. Frequent people whose character is distinguished, who have good manners and who understand politics and human affairs.[191]

This apparently excluded Egyptians, who are described as 'perfidious, poor and capable of killing you for treason. My son! I entreat you not to trust them!'[192] Further care should be taken in assembling crews of an uneven number of 'calm, pious' men aged forty or over, including, if possible, a blue-eyed blonde wearing a red woollen cap.[193]

Invocations to exterminate jinn are suitably grandiloquent and must be memorized beforehand:

> In the name of the great god whose light pierces every veil, before whose grandeur all heads must bow, before whose majesty the mountains are defeated! He is the one god, the only, eternal alone in the universe, and his oneness possesses power... Tashlush, Tishash, Hitush, Turesh, Matlesh, Tashu... I conjure you, oh beneficent spirits! By the light of the face of god, the generous, and by the power of his great name, to sweep down upon the jinn of this place, and send them far away, to dismiss them, to stop their movements and to suffocate them![194]

In addition to god's great name the reciter must call on a Judaeo-Islamic archangel, and several planets:

> Hasten, oh people of Metatron, you and your helpers, hurry! Oh inhabitants of Mercury the red, hurry! Inhabitants of Venus, hurry! Oh inhabitants of Mars, hurry! Oh inhabitants of Jupiter, hurry! Oh inhabitants of the Sun, descend!... Sweep down upon the jinn and chase them, distance them from this place, so that

we may act freely. Act upon my order. Oh Metatron! Hurry, by the order of god, who, when he wants something, says simply: be – and it is.[195]

Other invocations are plain silly: 'say four times: "Ah! Jah! Houl! The powerful, the merciful, the sage Bakshtush, Anush, Jahrush!" ... you'll succeed, that's all.'[196] Some entries offer examples of talismanic writing (symbols, letters, numbers), to inscribe on pottery shards to make waters recede, or to carve on limes, to prevent dizziness.[197]

When they weren't engraving limes, those keen to find treasure had plenty of other preparatory work to do, like gathering costly ingredients for the fumigations that accompanied spells and invocations. These include amber; bdellium (resin of *Commiphora africana* trees of Ethiopia, Eritrea and sub-Saharan Africa); camphor crystals; cardamom; carob seeds; grapevine leaves; styrax (resin of the taproots of a plant belonging to the celery family); hellebore flowers; kondor (frankincense); sandalwood; sandarac (resin of the cypress-like *Tetraclinis articulata* native to northwest Africa); sweet myrrh; and *Oxalis corniculata*, the creeping woodsorrel, also known as sleeping beauty. Recipes call for the reader to roll the ingredients into pills and leave them to dry in the shade. Quantities are not specified, yet combinations are important, as per one instruction: 'above all, don't forget the rosemary, or you will not be excused!'[198] Tracking down fumigation materials must have been an adventure in itself, especially when it came to things like pig bristles, gazelle hooves, monkey nails, buffalo horn, tortoise shell, rabbit droppings, snake fangs, vulture feathers, ostrich eggs, goat hairs, camel hump bone and camel fur, which one must pluck oneself.[199] Aside from the aforementioned baboon, animals (some edible, all black) were occasionally sacrificed to provide blood to smear on doors to magically open them.[200]

If one thing is clear from the manuals, it's that treasure hunting involved a lot of shopping. Only the well-to-do would have had the leisure time and money to attempt to follow the instructions. It's possible that some people read the manuals purely for entertainment, yet given the prevailing beliefs and potential rewards, investing in treasure hunting was entirely reasonable and arguably less frivolous than other wistful, acquisitive behaviours. Nowadays women seeking eternal youth and vaginal elasticity turn to the Internet, spending substantial sums on 'jade eggs to harness the power of energy work'; remedies consisting of 'herbs, adaptogens, phytonutrients and vitamins'; and bottles embedded with amethyst crystals that infuse their contents with 'spiritual support', enabling the drinker to 'tap into [her] intuition'.[201] For those with surplus wealth, this sort of online shopping is a kind of treasure hunt. Likewise, it seems possible that by the end of the medieval period, treasure hunting was, for some, an expression of a lifestyle, a game for the adventurous, refined and *sportif*, a way to get outdoors, dirty your hands, bond with your fellows and, who knows, maybe even find something valuable.

Treasure hunting with its occult trappings continued into the twentieth century, as indicated by Ahmed Kamal, secretary-interpreter of Egypt's nascent Antiquities Service, and assistant curator of the Egyptian Museum, in his preface to *The Book of Hidden Pearls* (1907).

> Still today, hardly a month goes by without some Moroccan or professional magician reciting incantations or burning incense before a scene engraved on a temple wall or an isolated tomb, and attacking it with a pick or a stick of dynamite to extract the treasure he believes is hidden there. They find nothing, yet persevere, and when the money they need to continue the work runs out, they join with other credulous people to cover the expenses of the operation.[202]

Kamal noted that 'the current book is one of many of its kind, aimed at discovering treasure hidden in the past,' and condemned them all for leading to the destruction of priceless monuments. 'We can say without exaggeration', he wrote, that books like this 'ruined more monuments than war or the passage of the centuries'.[203] So why would the Antiquities Service decide to put *Hidden Pearls* back into circulation, with a French translation no less? Kamal credited his boss, Gaston Maspero, with the idea that:

> The day that this book, instead of being a priceless rarity, is readily available for purchase for a few francs, the naive will cease to have faith in the instructions it provides, and will be persuaded that the treasures described in it have already been found: Egypt's antiquities would therefore have a better chance of survival.[204]

Talk about naive. Given the appeal of Egypt's treasures and the lore surrounding them, Maspero's counter-intuitive rationale was doomed to failure. All he succeeded in doing was to prolong the book's influence and widen its audience.

In 1931, British Egyptologist Gerald Avery Wainwright, chief inspector of the Antiquities Service in Middle Egypt, wrote:

> I was constantly consumed with applications for permission to dig for buried treasure, and had plenty of opportunity to observe the methods employed. They were those described in the old Arabic treatise which has been published and translated into French by Ahmed Bey Kamal . . . It is a book much studied today, even by educated people.[205]

And so it remains.

FOUR

DEN OF THEBES

I recall a poet's saying:
I shall sleep not to see
My country being bought and sold.
– NAGUIB SOROUR (1932–1978), 'DRINK DELIRIUM'

Egypt entered the nineteenth century quietly indifferent to the passage of time. As the unwitting object of Western desires it was soon, however, drawn into their gyre and introduced to the calculus of progress. While Napoleon's reconnoitre of 1798-1801 failed to result in the hoped-for permanent occupation, it produced documentation of the Egyptians, their storied cities and monuments, that when presented to the world awakened a craving that 'Egyptomania' is too playful a word to describe. Egypt's treasures beckoned from the illustrations in the multiple volumes published in the wake of Napoleon's campaign, and later from the half-tones of photographs and postcards glued into albums and admired in sitting rooms across Europe and North America. Here was the Bible come to life, with the pharaohs' great temples presenting comforting proofs of religious narratives in the midst of a disconcerting technological revolution. In this 'world of new powers and old ideas', the grandiosity of ancient achievements boosted imperialist and industrialist ambitions, warmed by representations of Egyptians as docile and backward.[1] Steamships and steam-driven cotton mills drastically altered Egypt's fate, and a straight line may be drawn from the construction of the Suez Canal (which was completed in 1869) to the British occupation (1882-1952). Yet no modern contrivance had as great an impact on the country's future as the material legacy of its past.

A SHORT HISTORY OF TOMB-RAIDING

Yaqub Sanu (James Sanua), 'Pharaoh after Having Sold the Harvest and the Pyramids at Auction', satirical illustration published in *Abou Naddara Zarqa* (*The Man in the Blue Glasses*), 3 May 1879. Pictured on the right is Khedive Isma'il Pasha.

The hunt for Egypt's treasures went global in the nineteenth century. At first, emissaries of Europe's great heads came to harvest antiquities, large and small, for their patrons. It wasn't easy negotiating the rough terrains, locating prime sites, moving mountains of sand and hauling monoliths to barges to carry them downriver. Egyptians did the heavy lifting, catering to museum agents, antiquities dealers and wealthy foreign adventurers who hunted treasure for sport and celebrity. Under the genteel guise of 'collecting' raiding became a contest, with imperial rivalries playing out on Egypt's treasure-strewn wastelands. In this virtually bottomless pit of antiquities, foreigners fought over them like dogs for a bone, plotting against one another to secure finds, bickering over who had the biggest obelisk. Filling museums became a goal akin to the ancients' effort to build and equip their tombs, only in this case paradise was possession and cultural chest-thumping.

In the early 1800s, the several thousand villages scattered along the Nile banks accounted for the bulk of Egypt's population of 2 to 3 million. Farming remained the main occupation. But whereas outsiders had rarely ventured to Upper Egyptian towns before, their visits began to multiply and Luxor, a sleepy provincial backwater, stood on the verge of a great awakening. On its west bank, near the sand-vanquished site of Deir al-Medina, a community had taken root in and around the Tombs of the Nobles, in an area known as Gurna. The inhabitants' origins are uncertain, but the Gurnawi were said to descend from a tribe of herders called the Horabat and had long been recognized as the most knowledgeable if somewhat formidable guides to ancient sites. 'A ferocious clan,' wrote William G. Browne in 1792, 'differing in person from other Egyptians. Spears of twelve or fourteen feet in length are deadly weapons in their hands.'[2] Browne visited Egypt when the country was still reeling from a devastating outbreak of plague. On arriving at Gurna with his translator, in search of someone to accompany them to the ruins:

> No male inhabitant appeared; but two or three women were standing at the entrance of their dens ... one of the women said in Arabic, 'Are you not afraid of crocodiles?' I replied in the negative. She said, emphatically, 'We are crocodiles' and proceeded to depict her own people as thieves and murderers. In the temple of Medinat Habu we observed a large quantity of blood, and were told by the peasants that the Gurnawi had there murdered a Moroccan and a Greek traveler ... who had strayed thither from mere curiosity, or perhaps with a view to finding treasure.[3]

The blood in the temple was more likely an animal's than any traveller's; the Gurnawi probably cultivated a reputation for hostility to keep trespassers away from homes and hunting grounds. They lived in the tombs, enjoying their cool depths in the long scorching summers, and using them as discreet departure points for burrowing towards potential treasure. Like the tomb builders of Deir al-Medina, the Gurnawi were expert tunnellers and the Theban necropolis was their backyard, a ponderous maze of sand and rock concealing their equivalent of Fort Knox.

Vivant Denon, a member of Napoleon's Scientific and Artistic Commission, portrayed the Gurnawi as recalcitrants:

> We first crossed the village of Kurnu [sic], the ancient Necropolis: on approaching these subterranean abodes, the inhabitants, for the third time, greeted us with several discharges of musketry. This was the only spot in Upper Egypt in which it was refused to acknowledge our government: secure in their sepulchral retreats, like menacing spirits of the dead, they left them only to terrify mankind: guilty of many other crimes, they hid their remorse, and fortified their disobedience in the obscurity of these excavations, which are so numerous that they alone attest the immense population of ancient Thebes.[4]

By 1825, when the British Arabist Edward William Lane visited Luxor, the Gurnawi had adopted a more conciliatory approach to outsiders, owing to their greater frequency and zest for buying. 'In their own interest, [the Gurnawi] now behave with all possible civility, [obtaining] their livelihood chiefly by the sale of antiquities which they procure by ransacking the ancient catacombs.'[5] Lane was struck by the ubiquity of ancient remains, and how they served the Gurnawi's varied needs. 'Their cows, goats and sheep are often seen, for lack of proper pasture, stripping off with their teeth and eating the bandages of cast-out mummies,' he wrote, and 'mummy cases are used for firewood.'[6]

British travel writer and journalist Bayle St John, who toured Upper Egypt in the mid-1840s, called the locals 'poor wretches, who will sit down half-naked and half-fed, upon a stone supposed to cover the aperture of an inexhaustible thesaurus, and yet not pine with desire to possess it'. St John was partly right; people wanted to sell, not possess, treasures. The belief in 'supernatural guardianship' of treasures still held, he noted, remarking that without the 'aid of powerful talismans' the fellahin (farmers/

country folk) did not dare hunt treasure. Only city folk did that, he maintained, echoing Ibn Khaldun, 'ruined debauchees or confirmed sensualists, [who] having sought the assistance of magic [were] frequently crowned with success'. The locals' attitude, wrote St John, was to 'smile with contempt at such greedy citizens' or else 'with violence or feigned stupidity [to] throw obstacles in their paths'. More than jinn, the locals feared the government, who would 'take their pot of gold [and] bring on a beating to force confession of another imaginary pot'.[7]

The first half of Egypt's nineteenth-century governance belonged to Mohammed Ali (r. 1805-49). Son of a tobacco merchant, this hard-nosed strategist translated his appointment as Ottoman governor into de facto independent rule and the establishment of a century-long dynasty.[8] Recognizing France and Britain as Egypt's greatest threats, Mohammed Ali met them in battle on the high ground of modernity. Enlisting foreign expertise (largely French and British) he built an army and arms factories and introduced cotton cultivation that in combination with land reclamation and irrigation schemes greatly augmented Egypt's revenues. Europeans helped develop an education system with engineering, military science and language curricula; Egypt's first publishing house (the Bulaq Press) translated and printed manuals and textbooks. To mitigate the effects of plague and cholera on labour productivity, Mohammed Ali created the world's first international quarantine board and the Middle East's first Western-style school of medicine in 1827.[9]

These efforts were accomplished with the help of the *corvée* and the crippling tax burden placed on Egyptians, twice as high as that paid, for example, in France by the wealthier French population.[10] The fellahin responded with subterfuge, hiding their money or themselves when tax collectors came around and if apprehended, proudly submitting to the lash rather than part with a penny. To prevent their children from being drafted to Mohammed Ali's expansionist campaigns in Syria and Sudan, parents considered cutting off a finger or putting out an eye the lesser evil. Aside from forced labour, taxation and cotton exports, Mohammed Ali relied on the time-honoured use of ancient treasures as currency, in this case as bargaining chips to win the cooperation of foreign governments and consultants. According to Bayle St John, whereas the state had previously commandeered a fifth of all finds, now Egypt's rulers wanted it all.[11] Such policies help account for the defensiveness and rebelliousness of nineteenth-century tomb raiders.

The Egyptians had not forgotten magic; they needed it as much as ever. People wore amulets, made fumigations to dispel the evil eye and consulted practitioner-sheikhs to interpret dreams and find lost things. A much simplified version of *za'irja* still circulated, a table with one hundred squares each holding a letter, that the questioner pointed to at random to form an indicative word. Prayer beads also assisted decision-making, like plucking petals from a flower, but instead of 'he loves me, he loves me not', there were three Allah-related phrases that, depending on which you ended up with, answered yes, no or maybe.[12] Traditional practices remained popular and, as St John remarked, city folk hunted treasure as a hobby with the help of magicians. But professional raiders like the Gurnawi dispensed with the hocus-pocus. Given the burgeoning demand for their services, they had no time for it, and they didn't need astrologers to tell them where to look.

The birth of Egyptology may be dated to 1822, when Champollion succeeded in breaking the code on hieroglyphics. Yet reliable systems of excavating, dating and studying artefacts did not become established practice until nearly the close of the century. In the meantime, so-called archaeological investigation was little more than a prolonged treasure hunt, with countless artefacts spirited away to be studied in the comfort of some stately hall. In 1858 Mohammed Ali's son and third successor, Said Pasha, appointed a Frenchman to oversee a new Antiquities Service and stop the haemorrhaging of antiquities. The Louvre had sent 29-year-old scholar Auguste Mariette (1821–1881) to Egypt in 1850 to search for Coptic manuscripts. Instead, he gambled his funds on a hunch and found one of the most remarkable religious complexes of ancient Memphis, the Serapeum, burial place of enormous mummified and bejewelled bulls. Mariette's new job was to stock Egypt's first museum, at the Nile port of Bulaq in Cairo, a task he pursued enthusiastically, at one point employing 7,000 men to dig at a variety of likely sites.[13] The raiders now had archaeologists to contend with, or practitioners of what passed for archaeology in those days; Mariette was known to use dynamite to expedite the excavation process.

The treasures that Mariette unearthed sparked international public interest at a time when travel was cheaper and faster than ever before, fifteen days from Southampton to Alexandria. In 1869 when Thomas Cook's steamship cruises up the Nile began, the trickle of travellers became a stream of tourists. People flocked to Egypt to experience the past and not only see the antiquities but participate in their discovery. The first popular guide, John Murray's *A Handbook for Travellers to Egypt*, appearing in several editions from 1847, included a section entitled 'Certain Points Requiring Investigation', enlisting travellers to excavate sites and copy reliefs and inscriptions. In 1873 the section was discontinued, since 'Mariette and others had already answered many of the listed questions' and no one was allowed to excavate without Mariette's express permission.[14] Acquiring artefacts remained part of the fun; tourists purchased them from reputable or disreputable sources and sometimes chipped off a bit of tomb or temple frieze themselves. Mariette referred to tourism as 'the eighth plague' but his work did much to promote it.[15] As visitors multiplied so did the demand for ancient souvenirs. The Gurnawi had their hands full, between protecting the locations of treasure-laden tombs and selling their contents piecemeal to the intruders.

Egyptology brought tourism to Egypt, but the extent to which the Bible begat Egyptology is often overlooked. Charles Darwin's *On the Origin of Species* (1859) boldly challenged the Bible-based belief that the world was just 6,000 years old and everything had been created contemporaneously by divine fiat. Whereas Egypt's monuments may have added weight to the argument for a greater age of the human enterprise, they were more commonly looked to for proofs of the Bible's veracity. Like medieval Muslims,

Percy Macquoid, 'Modern iconoclasts at work on the monuments of ancient Egypt', engraving in *The Graphic*, 26 July 1890.

nineteenth-century Christians read Egypt's ruins as warnings against arrogance and divine retribution, as described in the Book of Ezekiel ('And I will make the land of Egypt desolate . . . and I will bring again its captivity').[16] Egypt was seen as a cautionary tale against rapid change, as evidenced in painter John Martin's biblical landscapes, 'ferociously intense panoramas of cosmic rage' that recalled the seething furnaces of modern industry.[17] But where some saw apocalypse, others found ideas. Inspired by Bible verses lauding Egypt's production of fine flax and linen, British Utilitarian John Marshall built the Temple Works mill in Leeds, drawing from the design of the Temple of Horus at Edfu. The mill was 'one monster room', large enough to hold over a thousand workers, heated by basement boilers and illuminated by conical skylights; the rest of the roof was planted with grass for herds of sheep to graze. 'All that mechanical skill can effect is effected,' wrote Charles Dickens, 'that this Egyptian shell might enclose the most advanced productive edifice in the world.'[18]

On the pond's other side, Walt Whitman, like other literate New Yorkers, was fascinated with ancient Egypt, calling its theology 'vast and profound', because it 'respected the principle of life in all things'.[19] Whitman wrote about an exhibition entitled 'Egypt, Land of the Bible', mounted by his friend Henry Abbott (1812–1859), a British physician who had practised in Cairo for twenty years. An amateur collector, Abbott amassed many prizes, including a papyrus that recorded the interrogations of tomb raiders in the reign of Ramses IX. In 1853 when he decided to part with his collection, he brought it to America, where ancient Egypt's rapport with the Bible held as much public interest as it did in England.[20]

Throughout a turbulent century, Egyptology served at times to shore up faith in the Old Testament and at others to reduce it to fable, catalysing debate about the nature of time, history and human origins; never before had public and scholarly concerns dovetailed so neatly. Now idealized, now disdained, the ancients were portrayed as either pious and refined or barbaric and decadent. The Archbishop of Canterbury, Edward White Benson (1826–1896), named the family cat Ra, and his devout daughter confessed her sins to the Sphinx to acknowledge the achievements of a pagan yet spiritual people.[21] Others described the 'bombastic futility' of the Great Pyramid and maintained that the British railway from London to Birmingham was a far superior accomplishment.[22] Controversy inspired merchandising, and a trend for Egypt-themed items: tableware adorned with lotuses and sphinxes; ladies' brooches shaped like winged scarabs; men's coat buttons embossed with a pharaoh's head. In Europe and America, Egyptian cigarettes were all the rage, along with smoking paraphernalia bearing unintentionally prophetic motifs: gold cigarette cases inscribed with scenes from the Egyptian Book of the Dead; cigarette holders featuring Anubis ushering the deceased into the afterlife; and a cigar humidor shaped like a canopic jar, the receptacle for organs extracted from mummified cadavers.[23] Some took accessorizing to the extreme; Alexander, Duke of Hamilton, a trustee of the British Museum who died in 1852, was mummified and buried in the chapel on his estate in an anthropoid coffin purchased from an antiquities dealer in Paris.[24]

Whereas ancient raiders plied their trade to enrich themselves, their nineteenth-century counterparts enriched the world via networks extending to Europe's capitals and beyond, centred on Egyptian agents, men of social standing, with access to wealthy foreigners and their Nile boat captains, and to customs officials in the port of Alexandria. Feeding the supply chain, raiders were the shadow players whose anonymity ensured their freedom to operate. That ended in 1881, when a Gurnawi clan named Abdel Rasul made a jaw-dropping discovery in the Theban necropolis that earned them worldwide notoriety and a place in history as Egypt's pre-eminent tomb-raiding dynasty.

Nineteenth-century collectors treated Egypt's artefacts less as works of art than specimens to be hoarded and classified, '[building up] typological groups of scarabs, rings and amulets, ticking off variants... as though they were collecting stamps or butterflies'.[25]

Aesthetic appreciation came later (early twentieth century), and has never since waned. But not all of Luxor's visitors came for the antiquities; thanks to the relatively warm, dry and crystalline winter weather, many, like Lucie Duff Gordon (1821-1869), came for their health. Born Lucie Austen in Queen's Square in Westminster, her father was a pupil of their next-door neighbour, Jeremy Bentham, social reformist and founder of utilitarianism, whose ideas made a lasting impression. At thirteen, she befriended poet Heinrich Heine, and later translated German historians Leopold von Ranke, Barthold Niebuhr and philosopher Ludwig Feuerbach. Tall and dark-haired, Lucie was described by her mother as 'knowing a great deal . . . in a strange wild way'. At twenty, she married Alexander Duff Gordon, and their house guests included Dickens, Thackeray, Tennyson and Prince Louis Napoléon, who 'dropped in unexpectedly for dinner'. Members of the Chartists, a working-class male suffrage movement, also dined at Lucie's table where toasts were raised to 'liberty, brotherhood and order'. In her early thirties, showing signs of tuberculosis, Lucie tried wintering in European spas, to no avail. She travelled to Egypt in 1862, where she lived the better part of her last seven years, often without husband or children, but never alone. More than the company of visiting Europeans she 'enjoyed the Egyptians', who adored her for her many kindnesses and the interest she took in their lives.[26]

Lucie's published letters scarcely mention antiquities, but she frequently wrote of a close Egyptian friend, Mustafa Agha Ayat (c. 1811-1887), vice-consul for both Britain and America in Luxor, who was known to traffic them, with the Abdel Rasul brothers of Gurna as his procurers.[27] Ayat owned land on the west bank and had a family house 'planted like a swallow's nest against the eaves of the Luxor Temple' where Lucie also lived, in a mud-brick dwelling with a westerly view.[28] Ayat was attentive to all travellers, hiring their guides and captains for the sailboats (*dahabiyya*) that doubled as their living quarters, posting their mail, arranging trips and *fantasias*, parties featuring copious amounts of food, cardamom-scented coffee, music and dancing girls. But he was genuinely fond of Lucie, who gave lessons to his youngest son and arranged for the boy to spend two years in England.[29] Ayat took her everywhere, including parts of town where foreigners did not go. Lucie must have known he sold antiquities, but took no issue with it, and interceded with her influential friends on his behalf more than once. In a letter to her husband, she wrote how Ayat had served as consul for thirty years and was 'old and infirm' and without a salary. He relied instead on 'such presents as the English see fit to make him', she wrote, 'and I have seen enough to know that they are neither large nor always gracefully given'.[30]

Although she visited the tombs and temples, Lucie never dwelt on them in her letters, describing instead the hardships endured by the fellahin, including taxes, conscriptions, unjust imprisonments and land confiscations. She told how Mariette hired the Gurnawi to work on excavations but failed to pay the agreed rate. The workers complained to Ayat, who fronted the monies owed.[31] No background is offered for another incident involving Ayat and Mariette that likely turned on the former's covert antiquities dealings. It seems Mariette 'struck Mustafa and called him a "liar and son of a dog"', unforgivable insults that Mariette denied. She and 'some Americans' complained to their embassies, but while author

G. Pearson, 'The "French House", Luxor' (where Lucie had rooms), illustration in Amelia B. Edwards, *A Thousand Miles up the Nile*, 2nd edn (1888).

Francis Turner Palgrave was apparently sent to Luxor to 'to enquire after the affair', its outcome was left unreported.[32] Lucie had at least some dealings with antiquities, likely with Ayat's help, as alluded to in a letter to her husband, about a 'lion's head' she'd 'sent down to Alexandria' presumably to be shipped to London.[33]

While visiting Ayat's farm in 1866, Lucie met a 'formerly illustrious [tomb] robber' named Sherif, who arrived on a donkey that seemed so much smaller than its sturdy rider, she suggested they trade places. To please her, the strapping fellah shouldered the bewildered animal. Lucie was further impressed by Sherif's tale of taking '1,000 stripes of the *courbash* [hippo-hide whip] on his feet and 100 on his loins at one go', for refusing an official's order to haul his watermelons. Another of Sherif's stories suggests the state of play for members of his purportedly former profession. It was 'a grand romance', wrote Lucie, about a city in the desert two days' journey away, that was impossible to find except by chance, and whose ground was scattered with *anteekahs* (antiquities). Lucie remarked that had Sherif's father found the city, 'he would have seen gold and jewels.' Sherif agreed, saying 'when I was young, men spit on statues or the like, when they turned them up digging, but now it is a fortune to find one.'[34] In other words, the supply of precious metals may have been depleted, but funerary equipment, statuary and papyri remained abundant and were easily sold.

Mustafa outlived his friend and champion; Lucie Duff Gordon died in Cairo on 14 July 1869, at the age of 48. Another Luxor visitor, Scottish physician James Douglas Sr (1800–1886), portrayed the vice consul in less amicable terms. It is uncertain on which of Douglas's six journeys to Egypt (between 1851 and 1865) he first met Ayat, but their acquaintance centred on a shared professional interest in mummies. In an album of photographs produced during the winter of 1860-61, Douglas refers to Ayat as 'one of the institutions of Thebes'. While conceding that 'among the Arabs, he sustains a high character for hospitality and openness,' Douglas described him as 'greedy, grasping and unscrupulous'. Aside from superficial observations about Ayat's 'dark complexion', 'tolerably good English' (he also spoke French and Italian) and 'peculiar fitness and education' he relates how Ayat had travelled as a young man to England and to India 'in the forecastle of a man-of-war' and worked in a British Marine shop, 'first as a servant then as a partner'. Douglas noted that Ayat hoisted the Union Jack and fired his gun in salute when *dahabiyyas* carrying British travellers arrived or departed Luxor. His 'knowledge of the English and of the world particular to that school' came, in Douglas's estimation, 'with a loss of a great part of his religion'.[35]

Douglas was around the same age as Ayat and he too had seen the world. Following his graduation from London's Royal College of Surgeons, Douglas worked on a whaler en route to a Greenland fishery, spent a year doctoring in India and at 23 was appointed director of medical services in a settlement on the Mosquito Coast (Honduras), where he contracted either malaria or yellow fever. Near death, someone put him on a schooner to Boston, where he recovered and set off to visit friends in Quebec. He got as far as Utica in New York, where a farmer impaled himself on a pitchfork and would have died were it not for the surgeon's fortuitous presence. Douglas healed him, winning the gratitude of that small community where he opened a practice, married and might have stayed indefinitely were it not for his run-ins with the law.

Douglas lectured at a local college and kept a dissecting room to improve his understanding of anatomy. Precise knowledge was essential in that pre-anaesthetic era; the swifter and surer the surgeon's knife, the more likely the patient's survival. But dissection was allowed only for the corpses of beggars and convicts, and the medical community's demand exceeded the supply. Those willing to exhume freshly buried bodies (or employ others to do so) were dubbed 'resurrectionists' and harshly penalized if caught. Douglas made the mistake of digging up the servant of a local judge who nonetheless let him off with a warning. But then he carelessly exhumed the body of a well-to-do citizen, whom someone happened to recognize on his autopsy table. Facing imprisonment, Douglas and his wife fled by sleigh to Canada. A distinguished career awaited him, including the founding of Quebec's College of Physicians and Surgeons in 1837, the direction of Quebec's Marine and Emigrant Hospital and the establishment of the Bristol Asylum (later the Beaufort War Hospital), where he instituted progressive therapies using dance and theatre.[36]

That Douglas considered himself nobody's fool is clear from his interactions with Mustafa Ayat. He mistrusted Ayat's gifts of food to visitors arriving by *dahabiyya*. '[Ayat] causes it to be understood that as he received no salary, it is customary to give him a liberal present,' wrote Douglas, and he 'generally fixes' on something belonging to the travellers, who 'find it difficult to resist his attacks'. Douglas had no such compunction; when Ayat sent the usual sheep, he ordered his dragoman to pay for it and make clear that he neither received nor gave presents, to 'put us on a fair footing, then and in the future'. At their second meeting, Ayat broached the subject of antiquities. Douglas said a man had shown him a statue that he liked but was too costly. 'Describe him,' said Ayat, who identified the man and took Douglas directly to his home. The statue Douglas desired was there, 'amid a heap of heads of mummies, pieces of mummy cases, mummy cloth, beads, bronzes, jars and pottery'.[37] Ayat graciously told Douglas to pay whatever he thought fair for the statue, but Douglas insisted the man bring it to his boat where they would settle privately.

Douglas 'became an enthusiastic collector of mummies and all that appertained to them' and in the process he developed a grudging admiration for Ayat's business acumen.[38] As American vice consul, Ayat acquired 'license to explore and excavate and to possess mummies and antiquities, ostensibly for [the Americans]', but, knowing Ayat, Douglas felt their 'share in the spoils would be homeopathic'. The U.S. consul general may have suspected as much when he 'made a *razzia* [raid] on Mustafa's collection', entering his home, and the private quarters of his wife and children (harem), where he found very little since Ayat had hidden the more valuable items in anticipation of such an affront. In an 'amusing instance of Mustafa's rapacity and finesse', Douglas described how Ayat handled a British mummy buyer who insisted he would only buy mummies whose unearthing he personally witnessed. Ayat duly took him riding on the west bank where 'two or three Arabs screaming and making frantic gestures' had made a find at just that moment. Ayat and the prospective buyer descended a pit, where they saw 'two very promising mummy cases'. These were sent to Ayat's house where a deal was struck to unroll one of the mummies and yield all of its precious amulets to the gentleman in exchange for £180. When the only ornament that emerged was 'a gilt-winged scarabeus ... which might have been purchased from an Arab resurrectionist for two shilling', Ayat suggested they unroll the second one at the discounted rate of £73. This one had nothing at all in the wrappings.[39]

The first mummy 'was certainly a very good one', Douglas noted, referring to the quality of the embalmment.[40] With Ayat's help, he acquired at least three attractive ancient Egyptian cadavers, carrying them across the world to Quebec. When Douglas retired to his son's home in the United States, he reportedly sat two of his treasures on the front porch, claiming they would ward off thieves.[41] Another was purchased for a friend, a fine mummy in double cases, even better than the first one Ayat showed to the gentleman, that Douglas bought for just seven sterling.[42] Douglas's friend was Thomas Barnett, a taxidermist and proprietor of the Niagara Falls Museum (est. 1827), a cabinet of curiosities.[43] And so it was that an unnamed Egyptian notable spent 150 years in the company of a two-headed calf, a pair of Sitting Bull's moccasins and the battered barrels daredevils used to go over Niagara Falls, in a room with a view of their rising mists.

Douglas didn't mention the Abdel Rasuls, who likely unearthed the mummies Ayat sold him, but a British writer who visited Luxor a decade later followed the Gurnawi's activities closely and broadcast them worldwide. Born in London to a middle-aged, middle-class couple, Amelia Blanford Edwards (1831–1892) devoured books about Egypt as a child, including Gardner Wilkinson's *Manners and Customs of the Ancient Egyptians* (1837) and *The Thousand and One Nights*. At 24 she published the first of many novels and travel accounts, some of which she illustrated herself and are still in print. She wrote histories of England and France before she was thirty and covered current affairs as a journalist for the *Saturday Review* and *Morning Post*. 'Always radical in politics, religion and social thought', Edwards sometimes dressed like a man and frequented the demi-monde of London and Paris in defiance of her class and gender.[44] At 42 she wintered in Egypt (1873-4) sailing the Nile in the company of a wealthy lady friend, a life-changing adventure that influenced Egyptology, its popularization and, by extension, tourism and the livelihoods of Egypt's nineteenth-century tomb raiders.

Edwards attended several *fantasias* organized by Mustafa Agha Ayat, co-hosted by his eldest son Ahmed, the governor of Luxor, a position his father had finessed for him. Local dignitaries in their immaculate turbans and galabiyyas joined petticoated Victorian women and Englishmen in their crumpled linen suits at round, brass tables set with wooden spoons, tumblers and loaves of bread that doubled as plates. Eating with one's fingers was a revelation for the Westerners. 'We found them exceedingly useful,' wrote Edwards in her popular travelogue, *A Thousand Miles up the Nile* (1877), noting that eating by hand is 'a fine art', whereas 'carving without a knife, is a science.' At one gathering:

> [Ayat] attacked and vanquished the turkey – a solid colossus wearing twenty pounds ... Half rising, he turned back his cuff, poised his wrist, and, driving his forefinger and thumb deep into the breast, brought out a long, stringy, smoking fragment.[45]

This he placed daintily on Edward's plate. Five-course meals and dessert were followed by Turkish coffee, and molasses-soaked tobacco smoked in rose water hubbly-bubblies with amber mouthpieces. Afterwards there were dancing girls (*ghawazi*) that Edwards dismissed as garish but deserved more credit, considering they performed with a lit candle stuck in a bottle balanced on their heads, and could lower themselves to the ground and roll from one side of the carpet to the other without upending it. 'These [dancers] seem to have the power of independent and vigorous motion of all the soft parts of the body,' wrote a male observer.[46]

In her travelogue, Edwards portrays Luxor with relish, evoking the 'donkey boys' on the east bank who solicited business by 'vociferating the names and praises of their beasts':

> 'Hi Lady, Yankee-Doodle donkey! Try Yankee-Doodle!'
> 'Far-away Moses!' yells another, 'good donkey – fast donkey – best donkey in Luxor!'
> 'This Prince of Wales donkey!' shouts a third, hauling forward a decrepit little weak-kneed, moth-eaten looking animal . . . 'First-rate donkey! Splendid donkey! God save the Queen!'[47]

The Prince of Wales himself visited Luxor twice, including while in Egypt for the 1869 Suez Canal inauguration. He too attended a *fantasia* and the serendipitous discovery of a west bank tomb, stage-managed by Mustafa Ayat. Twenty wooden coffins were allegedly recovered from the burial, though it is likely that Ayat had 'salted' it to offer the prince and his entourage the thrill of discovery and gifts to take home without the fuss and muss of the hunt.[48] After an excursion to examine the site, and a tour of the Ptolemaic temple near Deir al-Medina, Ayat arranged a luncheon at the Ramesseum. Everyone rode a donkey and had a boy to attend it; in the case of the Prince of Wales, a young Gurnawi named Ahmed Abdel Rasul.[49]

Ayat exploited the entertainment value of treasure hunting to win the favour of influential patrons and the business of wealthy clients, but every traveller to Luxor savoured the drama of buying antiquities, the encounters with furtive Arabs in temple precincts who produced relics from the folds of their galabiyyas or the 'turbaned officials . . . attended by their secretary or pipe bearer', who 'hinted at genuine treasures to which he alone possessed the key'. The result was a 'roaring trade in *anteekahs*', Amelia Edwards wrote, 'every man, woman and child about the place is bent on selling a bargain,' most of them fake.[50] In that heady atmosphere, travellers were easily convinced of the authenticity of forgeries that were nonetheless skillfully wrought, often from ancient materials like the sycamore wood of mummy cases. Scarabs were manufactured by the thousand and fed to turkeys, whose digestive systems lent them the fine patina of age.

More discerning buyers were shown genuine treasures including papyri, statuary and mummies, and some, like Edwards, secured invitations to be on hand for the opening of tombs. 'Our life here was one long pursuit of the pleasures of the chase,' she wrote, and confessed to doing her 'fair share of antiquities hunting'.[51] She visited Gurna and became acquainted with Ahmed Abdel Rasul, who offered her a baby mummy, 'a little undeveloped infant which had never drawn the breath of life, but which was nevertheless spiced and swathed and laid to rest in a coffin adorned with all the emblems of royalty'.[52] Edwards knew she was transgressing. 'The game, it was true, was prohibited; but we enjoyed it none the less because it was illegal. Perhaps we enjoyed it the more.'[53] But seeing a freshly exhumed mummy, '[looking] startlingly human and pathetic lying at the bottom of its grave in the morning sunlight', and observing her fellow travellers' cavalier attitude towards the ancient dead, she began to have misgivings.[54]

Edwards reported that fifteen mummies were 'successfully insinuated' through customs at Alexandria in the winter of 1873-4 alone. Deriding her contemporaries' desire to 'bring home an ancient Egyptian', she noted how the trade 'in this grim kind of bric-a-brac' was reserved for the wealthy.[55] While babies were sold for £10-12 sterling, adult specimens cost £60-100 sterling, but these were the middling variety, mummies of 'the lesser nobility ... an architect, a sacred scribe, a civil or military official'.[56] Royal mummies were another story, and the Abdel Rasul brothers (Mohammed, Hussein and Ahmed) were their prime purveyors. 'Their goods were too precious or perilous to be parted from except under conditions of absolute secrecy and exorbitant payment,' anywhere from £400 to £800 sterling, according to Edwards.[57] She recounts how her fellow travellers, a Miss Brocklehurst and a Miss Booth, purchased a royal mummy and a papyrus 'at an enormous price' from the Abdel Rasuls, who delivered it to their *dahabiyya*. Finding

G. Pearson, 'Digging for mummies', illustration in Amelia B. Edwards, *A Thousand Miles up the Nile*, 2nd edn (1888).

themselves 'unable to endure the perfume of their ancient Egyptian', the ladies threw it overboard within a week.[58]

Moved by the ruined state of the monuments detailed in her travelogue, Edwards added the insights of Egyptologists she consulted to provide historical context for her readers. She learned all she could and decided to find a way to help preserve Egypt's antiquities, so that the civilization that produced them might be better understood. Her reputation as a best-selling author, combined with her tireless letter writing to solicit donations, resulted in the launch of the Egyptian Exploration Fund (EEF) in 1882, founded with two male partners to sponsor excavations. Many high-profile temple sites were already assigned to French and other missions, but Edwards was undeterred, securing permission to investigate the unexplored mounds of the Delta where, according to the Bible, the Israelites settled for four hundred years.[59] Her supporters ranged from budding Egyptologists and art critic John Ruskin to statesman William Gladstone and sundry clergymen, including the archbishop with the cat named Ra.

While writing *A Thousand Miles up the Nile*, Edwards corresponded with a young Egyptologist named Gaston Maspero (1846–1916), a professor at the Collège de France and the École des Hautes Études. A voracious reader, Maspero knew and admired her novels; Edwards returned the compliment by translating some of his works. Maspero became a powerful ally when he replaced Mariette as director of Egypt's Antiquities Service in 1881, and the

Gaston Maspero in the burial chamber of the Pyramid of Unas, last pharaoh of the 5th dynasty, Saqqara, 1881, drawing by Edouard Boudier from a photograph by Émile Brugsch, in Gaston Maspero, *History of Egypt, Chaldea, Syria, Babylonia, and Assyria*, vol. II (1901).

two stayed in touch until shortly before Edwards' death. In his letters, Maspero was frank about Egyptology's role in propping up the Bible. He related how he'd startled a school chaplain by studying Champollion's *Grammaire égyptienne* and expressing his wish to use archaeology 'to disentangle the history of antiquity', a sinful enterprise according to the chaplain, should God's word be contradicted in the process. Throughout the 1880s the debate raged between those who saw the Bible as a manual for archaeological exploration, and those, like Maspero, who saw it as 'a human document', whose details were at best unreliable. He admitted to adjusting his opinions, 'so as not to incur theological odium' or the rebukes of some colleagues.[60] Edwards must have shared his view of archaeology's purpose, or he would not have ventured to describe it. Yet she was happy to promote the Delta excavations he helped facilitate for the EEF, precisely on the basis of their biblical connotations, a surefire way to gain public support and contributions.

Before long, pioneering archaeologist Flinders Petrie was digging at Tanis, innovating methodologies like sequence dating that would shepherd archaeology from its treasure-addled past into an empirical future. He called Egypt 'a house on fire', so rapid was the destruction owed to 'mindless excavation … and absence of record-keeping'.[61] Petrie paid Egyptian workers for artefacts found on his excavations, so they would not be 'lost', and some of his finds were gifted to the EEF to distribute in exchange for donations. With Petrie in mind, Edwards worked to establish the first chair of Egyptology in England, at London's University College, the only school admitting women at the time.[62] The hundreds of articles she wrote about Egypt enlivened the pages of dozens of magazines. Edwards grew popular enough to fill lecture halls on a 120-stop EEF promotional tour of America (1889–90) where she was billed as 'the most learned woman in the world'.[63] All these accomplishments were greatly advanced by a singular discovery that Edwards had little to do with but that she publicized to further the EEF's cause. Indeed, archaeologists played but a secondary role in the finding of the Royal Cache, where chance and the Abdel Rasuls of Gurna were the main protagonists.

Everyone has heard of the treasures of Tutankhamun. A relatively insignificant pharaoh, his present-day fame is unrivalled except by the likes of the Buddha and Beyoncé. Having spawned an entire industry of kitsch objects bearing the likeness of his funerary mask, the 'boy king' still regularly makes the news. In 2005, his mummy was CT-scanned to determine the cause of his death at age nineteen (possibly infection related to a broken leg). In 2007, computer-generated cranial reconstructions showed us the face beneath the mask, an attractive youth with a wary look as if surprised at all the attention. In 2010, he was DNA-tested to solve the mystery of his lineage (his father was probably Akhenaton and his mother was his father's sister, not Nefertiti). We also learned that he likely suffered from malaria and had a club foot. In 2020, the international press covered the transferral of Tut's treasures from the Egyptian Museum in downtown Cairo to the new Great Egyptian Museum (GEM) near the pyramids, and more ink was spilled on the 'pharaoh's curse' some believe afflicted Howard Carter and the others who opened Tut's tomb. The 'hoopla' surrounding Tut since his 1922 re-entry to the public sphere cannot be explained by media fanfare alone, 'you need an intrinsically magnetic commodity to market in the first place.'[64] In the case of Tut and his tomb, it was gold.

But the Royal Cache (Deir al-Bahari; DB320), officially discovered in 1881 in the Theban necropolis, offered the world something considerably more mind-boggling: not one but forty royal mummies, including those of Amenhotep I, Seti I, Ramses II and III, and Thutmose I, II and III, a pharaonic hall of fame. Here were the conquerors behind the glory of Thebes, not to mention the supposed oppressors of the Israelites; here too were their queens, princesses and royal nurses. The present was all at once populated with characters that had previously lived only in the imagination. To a public with a yen for Egypt, the Royal Cache was a chance to look history straight in its wizened eye. In the case of Ramses II's mummy, according to Gaston Maspero who unwrapped it, 'the expression is unintellectual, perhaps slightly animal; but even under the somewhat grotesque disguise of mummification, there is plainly to be seen an air of sovereign majesty, of resolve, and of pride.'[65] News of the find made headlines in a dozen languages. Preachers wove the Royal Cache into their sermons, declaring that 'the silence of thirty centuries has been broken ... these august personages [have been] brought up afresh before the tribunal of human judgement as to their characters and acts.'[66]

Many mummies were enclosed in striking anthropomorphic coffins, some colossal, though all the old kings were bereft of precious items, having surrendered them to raiders while still in their private tombs.[67] The tomb where they were grouped together belonged to high priest Pinudjem II and his family, the last to be interred there before it was closed. The sheer quantity and strangeness of that family's burial goods, found more or less intact, was cause for wonderment. Amelia Edwards wrote that 'to enumerate all the treasures found in [DB320's innermost] chamber would be to write a supplement to the catalogue of the Boolak [sic] Museum,' including the treasures belonging to Pinudjem II's wife:

> Queen Isi-em-kheb ... was provided with a sumptuous funereal repast, consisting of gazelle haunches, trussed geese, calves' heads, dried grapes, dates, doum-palm nuts and the like, the meats being mummified and bandaged and the whole packed in a large rush hamper, sealed with her husband's unbroken seal. Nor was her sepulchral toilet forgotten. With her were found her ointment bottles, a set of alabaster cups, some goblets of exquisite variegated glass, and a marvelous collection of huge full-dress wigs, curled and frizzed, and enclosed each in a separate basket ... The pet gazelle of [the] Queen [was found] as carefully embalmed as herself.[68]

To the nineteenth-century public, it was as if an ocean of time had surrendered its shipwrecked travellers along with their remarkable trunks. The circumstances surrounding the discovery of the Royal Cache, including the leading role of the mummy-snatching

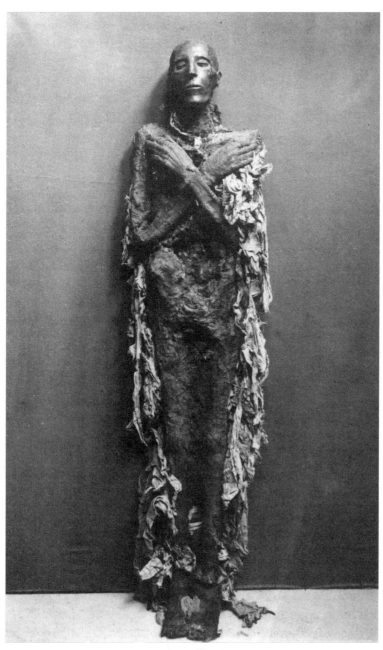

Mummy of Seti I in the Egyptian Museum at Boulaq, 19th century, photograph by Pascal Sebah.

Miniature mummy case inscribed with the name of Soutimes (25 cm long), and various small funerary objects (the small cabinet of Queen Hatasu, and the tiny mummy case in the foreground, each contain a mummified human liver), illustration from Amelia B. Edwards, 'Lying in State in Cairo', in *Harper's New Monthly Magazine*, LXV/386 (July 1882).

Abdel Rasul brothers, inspired reams of purple prose in newspapers and magazines, 'a story more romantic than any told in Egypt since Isis gathered the scattered remains of Osiris'.[69]

In treasure-hunting lore, stories often begin, fablelike, with an animal, the errant donkey whose hoof smashes through the roof of an underground vault, the runaway horse that dumps its rider on the remains of a lost city. It's as if the narrators wished to hide their motivations behind serendipity; they weren't hunting treasure, destiny was hunting them. For Ahmed Abdel Rasul, destiny came disguised as a goat, its tortured bleating luring him to the base of a rock face where he came upon a pit ingeniously hidden in a cleft of the pleated cliff.[70] He would have had to fetch one of his brothers to help haul a palm trunk to throw across the 3 × 2.5 metre (10 × 8 ft) aperture of the shaft, so they could tie a rope around the centre and lower themselves into the dark, a 12-metre (39 ft) drop. At the bottom, they stooped through a stunted door less than 1 metre (3 ft) high to enter a narrow corridor where the light of their candles flickered over several large, fine coffins. A passage opening to the right was narrow but taller, 21 metres (69 ft) long and scattered with burial goods. But the best came last, a staircase leading to a room deep in the bedrock stacked floor to ceiling with coffins, some more than 4 metres (13 ft) tall, in human form with hands folded across their breasts, serene faces and uncannily alert, wide-open eyes. The Abdel Rasul brothers had stumbled upon a royal warehouse, their children's and grandchildren's fortunes secured.

No one knows exactly when the Abdel Rasul family hit the jackpot, but it was years before the authorities caught on. During her trip to Egypt in 1874, Amelia Edwards heard 'whispers ... of a tomb that had been discovered on the western side – a wonderful tomb, rich in all kinds of treasures'. No one had details, but 'there was a solemn secrecy about certain of the Arabs and an air of awakened vigilance about the government officials which savoured of mystery'.[71] In a letter to Edwards, Maspero said he'd caught wind of something big in 1871, while in Paris. 'Having noted how Egyptian antiquities of every description were constantly finding their way to Europe, I came ... to the conclusion that the Arabs had discovered a royal tomb.'[72] In 1875 a Scottish colonel named Patrick Campbell showed Maspero photographs of the first pages of a superb papyrus purchased on the west bank, funerary texts belonging to 21st-dynasty high priest and ruler of Upper Egypt, Pinudjem II (*c.* 980–958 BC). Items meanwhile appeared on the Luxor market inscribed with the same name, including *shabti* statuettes. In 1877, Maspero was shown photographs of yet another papyrus, belonging to Queen Nodjmet, mother of Herihor, the general and High Priest of Amun who governed Upper Egypt sometime before Pinudjem II.[73]

Maspero asked Charles Edwin Wilbour, a former student, to do some snooping in Luxor, to keep an eye out for royal artefacts and help identify their provenance. A lawyer, journalist and the first American trained in Egyptology, Wilbour arrived in January 1881 and within the week attended one of Ayat's *fantasias* and was introduced to an Abdel Rasul brother he did not name, but called 'Mustafa Agha's man for Gurna'.[74] On 9 March, the brother offered Wilbour leather straps he recognized as mummy braces, used to hold the wrapped mummy's shroud in place. This 'curious pair of red Morocco suspenders' was inscribed with the name of Pinudjem II, and 'so fresh, that the mummy must have been opened lately'.[75] Wilbour offered the brothers baksheesh to show him the tomb where they were found but was led in great secrecy to a random tomb that had nothing to do with them. Wilbour nonetheless befriended the Abdel Rasuls, and after coffee one morning made them a sign for their recently expanded homestead which they called 'the white house', the ancient Egyptian name for treasury.[76] Mustafa Ayat and the Abdel Rasuls enlisted Wilbour to translate the inscriptions on some of the artefacts they trafficked, though they'd have done better not to trust him. Ayat had diplomatic immunity and could not be questioned about his dealings, but the Abdel Rasuls were not so lucky. Wilbour shared his information with Maspero, the new director of the Antiquities Service (since Mariette's death in January), who was on his way to Luxor to see to the matter.

An Egyptian parable tells of a man who found a treasure composed exclusively of golden onions. Attempting to load them all into his basket, the handles broke and the golden onions turned into real, tear-inducing ones when they hit the ground. This lesson against greed advises the strategy traditionally adopted by the Gurnawi raiders: to exploit their finds slowly, selling only so much and no more, so as not to draw unwanted attention. Restraint proved hard at a time when their stock was soaring and their needs were many, owing to the financial strain that modernizing efforts (including the building of the Suez Canal) had placed on rural Egyptians. With Mustafa Ayat as their untouchable front man, the Abdel Rasuls got sloppy, but more importantly, they hadn't bargained on archaeologists; for all their specialist knowledge, they couldn't read hieroglyphs. By unwittingly selling objects bearing the same royal names, they practically led the authorities to their door. Maspero arrived in Luxor on 3 April 1881 and ordered the arrest of the Abdel Rasul brothers the next day. He questioned Ahmed and Hussein Abdel Rasul, who stayed silent and were subsequently taken in chains to the jail in the nearby provincial capital of Qena.

Maspero had meanwhile contacted Dawud Pasha, the *mudir* (chief official of the province) in Qena, asking for an official inquiry. Feared and despised by the people, Dawud Pasha was a zealous overlord whose ruthless taxation had reduced many families to penury. He questioned Ahmed and Hussein Abdel Rasul 'with vigour' as Maspero put it, using the bastinado, the same technique that had torn the flesh from the soles of raiders' feet of yore.[77] Dawud promised the brothers amnesty if they confessed to their thefts and revealed the location of the royal tomb. Maspero moreover offered a reward to whoever divulged the tomb's location. The brothers were interrogated for two summer months in a stifling prison, but they didn't talk. The younger one, Hussein, was set free, perhaps as a concession to persuade Ahmed to cooperate. But he remained obdurate, heartened by the support of fellow Gurnawi. 'The notables of Gurna repeatedly gave their solemn word that Ahmed Abdel Rasul was the most loyal and fair-minded Egyptian in the country,' wrote Maspero, 'that he never hunted treasure, and was incapable of trading the most insignificant ancient object imaginable, much less violating a royal tomb.' At last, Ahmed was released, 'his immaculate honor', Maspero writes sarcastically, 'intact'.[78]

When Ahmed came home there was no rejoicing. Instead, a furious family argument erupted over how to escape further punishment while protecting their hunting grounds. Some thought the danger of police action had passed while others feared still worse and wondered if the time had come to disclose the tomb's location. The debate likely widened to include the village elders, members of other Gurnawi families who were stakeholders in the community's dealings with the police, and who had stood up for Ahmed. A decision was taken, and a month after Ahmed's release, his eldest brother, Mohammed Abdel Rasul, mounted his donkey and rode to Qena where he met Dawud Pasha and cut a deal in exchange for the tomb's location. Amelia Edwards described Mohammed as 'a spare sullen, silent fellow, avaricious as Harpagon and extortionate as Shylock'.[79] In other words, he was a close-mouthed, tough negotiator, sterling qualities for a tomb raider. The decision to cooperate with the authorities was only part of an arrangement that worked largely to the Gurnawi's advantage, and whose details later emerged.

That the Abdel Rasuls' knowledge mattered to the authorities may be judged by Dawud Pasha's actions once he had the tomb's location. He telegraphed his direct superior, Egypt's Minister of Interior, who relayed the intelligence to the Khedive Tewfik, Egypt's ruler.[80] Royal burials did not turn up often, and archaeological finds were valuable property. The Khedive ordered several Antiquities Service staff led by Émile Brugsch, assistant curator of the Bulaq Museum, to bring the find to Cairo until Maspero, then abroad, could take over. Accompanying Brugsch on one of the greatest treasure hunts of all time was Ahmed Kamal (1851–1923), Egypt's first Egyptologist, who later translated *The Book of Hidden Pearls*, with his experience of the Royal Cache no doubt close to mind. They left for Luxor by steamer on 2 July 1881. Four days later, Mohammed Abdel Rasul took them to the tomb of the Cache, its entry so organically camouflaged it was visible only when you were about to fall in.

Like the Abdel Rasuls before them, Brugsch and his companions were lowered down the shaft, and crawled through the little door, their excitement mounting at the profusion of objects piled haphazardly against the passage walls. At the corridor's end, they descended the stairs into the chamber filled with mummy cases, 'in such number', Brugsch said, 'as to stagger me'.

Colecting my senses, I made the best examination of them I could by the light of my torch, and at once saw they contained the mummies of royal personages of both sexes. Their gold coverings and polished surfaces so plainly reflected my own excited visage that it seemed as though I was looking into the face of my own ancestors.[81]

Mohammed Abdel Rasul (holding whip), Émile Brugsch and Maspero (reclining) at the mouth of the shaft of the tomb containing the Royal Cache, 1881, photograph by J.H.E. Whitney, reproduced in Edward Wilson, 'Finding Pharaoh', *Century Magazine*, XXXIV/1 (May 1887).

Brugsch and his colleagues expected to find the royal burial of a relatively low-profile king. Instead, wrote Amelia Edwards, they were confronted with 'the remains of heroes who till this moment had survived only as names echoed far down the corridors of Time'.[82] 'I took the situation in quickly,' Brugsch said, 'and hurried to the open air lest I should be overcome.'[83] He recovered fast, knowing that word of the find would race through Luxor, and that ensuring the safe delivery of such a quantity of goods was an angst-ridden task, especially given the propensities of some locals. Setting out to examine the tomb, he took precautions, 'my faithful rifle, full of shells, hung over my shoulder [and] my assistant from Cairo Ahmed Effendi Kamal was the only person I could trust. Any one of the natives would have killed me ... [knowing] I was about to deprive them of a great source of revenue.' Brugsch spent the night of 6 July hiring men to help empty the tomb. 'Early the next morning three hundred Arabs were employed under my direction – each one a thief.'[84]

'Potential thieves' would have been more accurate and still unfair, considering the gruelling labour required to raise hundreds of artefacts from the tomb, especially the mummies in unwieldy cases so heavy some took sixteen men to lift. These were squeezed through the stunted doorway by a hair's breadth, and raised up the shaft, an excruciating manoeuvre performed not once but forty times. The broiling summer heat, combined with the incommodity of the site, its shallow ledge and steep approach, made emptying the tomb a dangerous, punishing enterprise. At the foot of the cliffs everything had to be packed in canvas, wrapped in straw matting then lugged down half a kilometre (1,640 ft) of rough terrain, and another 4 kilometres (2 mi.) over the floodplain to the river. There the contents of the Cache were loaded onto boats, rowed across the Nile and laboriously shifted once more to the museum steamer that would take them to Cairo. All was accomplished in a marathon lasting nearly three days and nights. 'I shall never forget the scenes I witnessed,' said Brugsch, '[watching] the strange line of helpers while they carried across that historical plain the bodies of the very kings who had constructed the temples still standing, and of

Tomb-raiding is a recurring theme in gaming, as illustrated in one of the most popular games set in ancient Egypt, *Assassin's Creed: Origins* (2017) by Ubisoft, whose creators consulted Egyptologists to add detail to its stunning visuals.

Brass geomantic instrument, made by Mohammed ibn Khutlukh al-Mawsili, 1241–2.

Temple of Esna, Upper Egypt, coloured lithograph by Louis Haghe after David Roberts, 1838.

Sandstorm approaching the Sphinx, Cairo, coloured lithograph by Louis Haghe after David Roberts, 1849.

Farrukh ibn 'Abd al-Latif, 'The Elephant Clock', folio from a Book of the Knowledge of Ingenious Mechanical Devices by al-Jazari, 1315, Syria or Iraq, ink, opaque watercolour and gold on paper.

Funerary mask, AD 100–149, Roman Egypt, Tuna al-Gebel, painted cartonnage, gold leaf and glass inlays.

Unknown artist, 'Descent into the mummy pits near Medinet Habu', c. 1890, pen and ink and wash, with an inscription that reads: 'My guide is represented trying to break off a "nice foot" (!) as a memento of this fascinating spot.'

Moving Abu Simbel, 1967, photograph by Per-Olow Anderson.

Demolished Gurna homestead with underground chambers, 2006.

Remains of Gurna, 2021.

Ragab's house, with reused planks sticking out of tunnel entry (left), Nazlat al-Samman, 2010.

Alaa Awad, *Punishment*, June 2013, 5 × 6.5 m mural painted on the wall of the Lycée Français, Mohammed Mahmoud Street (near Tahrir Square), featuring a scene of pitched battles between protesters and security forces in 2011–12.

the very priests who had officiated them.'[85] The workmen probably never forgot it either.

When the steamer carrying the contents of the Royal Cache reached the port of Bulaq in Cairo, it was met with consternation. Customs officials had never seen such a cargo and were uncertain how to process it bureaucratically. After much discussion, the royal mummies were classified and duly taxed as 'dried fish'.[86] Safely arrived in the Bulaq Museum, the artefacts were examined, and the more details emerged, the more there was cause for wonder. As Amelia Edwards explained in an article for *Harper's Magazine* (July 1882), the Cache was assembled by the high priests of Amun to protect their royals' remains from tomb raiders, and though it took nearly three millennia, tomb raiders nonetheless found it.[87] After the unwrappings by Maspero and others, British anatomist Grafton Elliot Smith (1871-1937) conducted forensic examinations of the royal mummies in 1906.[88] His clinical descriptions revealed the ferocity with which the ancient raiders dismembered them before the priests pieced them back together and stowed them in the Cache. Many had torn-open chest cavities, half-crushed skulls and severed limbs. Ramses II's penis was missing; Seti I had been decapitated, although his head was well preserved.

While the mummy cases of Pinudjem II and his wife, the final additions to the Cache, still bore a thick buttery layer of gold, the relative absence of gold and jewels was blamed on thieves, whether ancient or the Abdel Rasuls. That the priests had relieved the royals of their remaining finery when they restored their rifled mummies was not then suspected, and only more recently ascertained.[89] It's possible that the Abdel Rasuls had found and melted down the odd precious item before mining the artefacts that set the authorities on their trail. They certainly stole Ramses I's mummy, as his coffin was found empty. Surrendering the Cache was a blow, but they were far from defeated. As part of Mohammed Abdel Rasul's arrangement with the authorities, they hired him as 'Guardian of the Necropolis for the Egyptian Antiquities Service'.[90] Inviting a fox into this particular henhouse was a calculated move from which all parties stood to profit. Maspero could gain access to the raiders'

Ahmed Kamal and outer coffin of Queen Ahmes Nofretari from the Royal Cache, c. 1881, reproduced in Edward Wilson, 'Finding Pharaoh', *Century Magazine*, XXXIV/1 (May 1887).

knowledge of tomb locations, or at least some of it. And while there is no proof that Dawud Pasha or his minions were in cahoots with the Gurnawi, allowing them to operate in exchange for a piece of the action, the scenario is not implausible. Whatever its tacit clauses, Mohammed's arrangement was in place in 1891, when he led Maspero's successor, Eugène Grébaut, to yet another cache, this time containing 160 mummified priests of Amun (21st dynasty). It seems the Abdel Rasuls still hunted their mountains while taking care to throw the authorities the occasional meaty bone.[91]

On a July morning in 1881 when the treasure of the Royal Cache departed Luxor, families left their homes and fields to line the riverbanks all the way to Qift, 80 kilometres (50 mi.) north, bearing witness as the steamer passed by. Men discharged their rifles; women cast dust on their heads and beat their breasts, their piercing ululations resounding up and down the Nile. Some said they mourned the departure of their ancient kings and queens, but whatever they thought they were losing, they knew who was taking it away. A year later, almost to the day, Egypt's first nationalist revolt began. Despite the cotton boom of the 1860s, when Egyptian farmers filled the supply gap left by America's southern states during the Civil War, the country was bankrupt. Khedive Ismail's massive modernizing efforts, including the construction of the Suez Canal and the refashioning of Cairo as a 'Paris on the Nile', however visionary, were more than the state coffers could bear. In 1875, Ismail was obliged to render Egypt's shares in the Suez Canal to Great Britain, its main debtor.

Outraged by the foreclosure and foreign influence writ large, Colonel Ahmed Orabi, son of a Delta village sheikh, organized his fellow Egyptian conscripts, men who had risen in the ranks thanks to Ismail's military reforms. With 30,000 troops at his back, Orabi challenged the British forces in Alexandria and on 11 July 1882 the Royal Navy responded by bombing the city to bits. Orabi held on until September, when he was captured, court-martialled and exiled to Ceylon. The British now had the Nile-fed lands of Egypt and Sudan as their cotton plantation, the natives as cheap labour and the Suez Canal as their conduit to the world, an imperialist wet dream. As if that weren't enough, Egypt's ancient treasures were theirs to administer largely as they pleased.

The *Illustrated London News* (7 July 1882) remarked how Ahmed Orabi possessed 'that rare quality in a Mussulman [sic], sheer strength of mind'. The condescension directed towards Egyptians, particularly the fellahin, touched tragi-comic depths under British rule, which lasted 72 years. Baedeker's *Egypt, Handbook for Travellers* (1898) compared Egyptians to plants: 'there exists no race of people which possesses so marked and unchanging an individuality as the Egyptians. It is therefore most probable that this unvarying type is a product of the soil itself.' The replication of this passage in Baedeker's *Egypt and the Sudan* (1929) suggests the 'marked and unchanging individuality' of the guide's authors and editors.[92] This edition drew attention to Egyptians' 'particularly strong and massive skulls', and the 'remarkable thickness of their eyelashes', advising travellers to bear in mind that 'the natives ... are mere children, whose demands should excite amusement rather than anger.' Instructions for dealing with horse-drawn cab drivers included '[touching them] with a stick on the right or left arm'.[93]

The '[Luxor] Guides and Donkeys' section of *Egypt, Handbook for Travellers* cagily recommended 'Musa Abd er-Rasul', noting 'he possesses the most through knowledge of the tombs of Gurna, but his honesty is not above suspicion.'[94] That the Abdel Rasuls' exploits contributed to negative perceptions of Arabs was evident in the words delivered from the pulpit of New York's Madison Avenue Church, where the pastor praised Maspero's 'detective process' in tracking down the Royal Cache, which demanded 'getting the truth out of the Arabs, a race with whom lying is a natural gift, brought to its highest perfection by constant exercise'.[95] But the disdainful mistrust went both ways, and while the words of the Gurnawi raiders are undocumented, their actions demonstrate their contempt for the foreigners of the Egyptian Antiquities Service nominally in charge of their territory.

Howard Carter (1874–1939), whose Tut-related fame lay several decades in the future, was seventeen when Percy Newberry, an administrator for the EEF, brought him from London to work as a 'tracer' or draughtsman on his excavations in Middle Egypt. Ten years later, in 1901, Carter was appointed Chief Inspector of the Antiquities for Upper Egypt, in keeping with the wish of Lord Cromer, Egypt's Consul General, to strengthen British control of the country's treasures. Carter brought hands-on experience to the task, including excavating with Flinders Petrie, but while he had no academic credentials, according to his younger successor, Arthur Weigall (1880–1935), Carter was 'a magnificent organizer and policeman'. Weigall romanticized his 'firmness and strength' when dealing with Egyptians, recalling how Carter had punished a local for a minor infraction (begging), charging into his homestead on horseback to collar him, as if he presented some imminent threat. Carter's handling of a villager whose fields encroached on an excavation site was, in Weigall's opinion, 'a delicious scene . . . just one white man administering justice to all that crowd of natives'.[96]

Carter was in Aswan on a tour of duty in November 1901 when he received an urgent summons to Luxor: the tomb of Amenhotep II had been robbed by masked gunmen. Discovered in the Valley of the Kings by Victor Loret in 1898, this tomb (KV35) contained the mummies of eight other kings, including Merenptah, and Ramses IV, V and VI, proof that the first Royal Cache was one of several assembled by anxious ancient priests. Most of the mummies were sent to the Cairo Museum, but Amenhotep's was left in the tomb along with a handsome piece of funerary equipment, a model of a solar boat (pharaoh's conveyance in the afterlife). A padlocked iron gate was installed at the tomb's entrance and guards posted day and night. According to the three night-shift guardians, a posse of thirteen thieves attacked just after sunset on 24 November, and six men restrained them while the others ransacked the tomb. When their work was done the bandits headed for the hills. The guards said they followed them but surrendered the chase when three shots were fired their way. Two guards returned to the tomb

Howard Carter and patron George Herbert (aka Lord Carnarvon) on the threshold of Tut's burial chamber, Valley of the Kings, 1922, photograph by Harry Burton.

and a third went directly to Carter's subordinate, Mansur Effendi, to report the crime. Mansur Effendi promptly gathered his men and found the mummy of Amenhotep II lying rifled on the ground. They searched the hills for the robbers, with no success. The following morning, they hired a spoor-tracker. The guards meanwhile claimed to have recognized two of the masked men as Abdel Rahman Abdel Rasul and Ahmed Abdel Rasul, to whose house the tracks reportedly led. The Gurnawi were arrested and so were the guards.

Carter arrived on 26 November; on the following day he donned his metaphorical deerstalker, and began investigating.[97] The mummy, he observed, had been handled in much the same way as a roasted turkey at a *fantasia*, 'ripped open, but the body not broken ... [the work] evidently, of an expert, as only the places where objects are generally found had been touched'. Carter determined that there had been no jewellery or amulets on the royal mummy in the first place, without speculating as to why they were absent. The disappointed raiders had, however, made off with the solar boat. The police remarked that the tomb's iron gate had been pried open with a lever, but to Carter its broken padlock bespoke a subtler thievery, as it had been cosmetically repaired to appear untouched. Although the police had muddled the dust-covered floor with their boots, Carter spied footprints of a shoeless man that he photographed 'as near to scale as possible'.[98]

Earlier that month Carter had inspected a robbery in a nearby tomb whose iron gate had been similarly forced, and the broken padlock rigged in the same manner. It too bore signs of a barefoot intruder, and Carter had taken pictures. His prime suspect for that raid was Mohammed Abdel Rasul. 'I watched this man whenever possible,' Carter reported, 'he being a well-known tomb plunderer and his house being quite near the tomb.'[99] Carter compared his photographs from both robbed tombs and found they matched the footprints of Mohammed kept on police file. Having arrested Mohammed Abdel Rasul, he turned to his accomplices, and quickly ascertained that the guards, not bandits, had fired three shots that night, to support their fictional alibi of being aggressed while on duty. The guards weren't even there, whether through negligence or complicity with the thieves. Carter ordered a search of the Abdul Rasuls' homestead, a standard, invasive procedure, which stoked people's resentment of the authorities, and for which they were well prepared. The police found nothing of consequence. The case was brought before the local court, but in the absence of conclusive evidence and footprints notwithstanding, Mohammed Abdel Rasul walked.

Necropolis security remained a pressing issue throughout the early 1900s, and Arthur Weigall, appointed chief inspector of Upper Egypt in 1905, waged a virtually one-man war on theft. He built a wall around part of Gurna, and installed iron gates on dozens of opened tombs, knowing they wouldn't stop thieves but that breaching them constituted a crime. If the police, conspicuously lax when it came to penalizing tomb robbery, chose to ignore it, it was on their heads, not his.[100] Weigall was 25 when he came to Luxor. The

Valley of the Kings, Egypt, November 1922.

only son of a British army captain who died in Kandahar the year he was born, he was raised by his mother, a revivalist missionary bringing the Bible to London's slums. Like Carter, he had a talent for drawing and a precocious interest in Egypt that he developed into a body of experience-based knowledge, working with Flinders Petrie and German Egyptologist Friedrich von Bissing. Enamoured of Egypt's monuments, Weigall was disgusted by their neglect, but also by treasure hunting disguised as a scholarly pursuit on behalf of wealthy excavation patrons in search of adventure. 'Grabbing at plums', he called it.[101] He cited the '*Book of the Pearl* [sic]' referring to Ahmed Kamal's 1907 translation of treasure manuals, remarking how the places it indicated had been reduced to rubble 'by the picks and spades of thousands of gold-seekers'.[102] Weigall noted that a local treasure hunter used dynamite, a modern labour-saving technique he'd picked up from foreign excavators, but that he also sacrificed a lamb, to appease the guardian jinn.[103]

In his dealings with the locals, Weigall tried being stern but fair. When a Gurnawi he'd accused of theft threatened to vandalize more monuments if he was arrested, Weigall faced a dilemma.[104] How could he arrest people for stealing what they called their own? 'It is as natural for [Upper Egyptians] to scratch in the sand for antiquities as it is for us to pick flowers by the roadside,' he wrote.[105] Considering the availability and demand, was it any wonder that 'every man, woman, and child makes use of his opportunities to better his fortune?'[106] Weigall knew the Abdel Rasuls, remarking how they'd 'lately had the misfortune of being recognized as thieves and it is one of my duties to point this out to them'.[107] The Gurnawi did not see themselves as thieves, and he could not change their minds, convinced as they were that archaeologists were the richest of men, because all they did was hunt treasure. Weigall received a letter from 'one of the greatest thieves in Thebes' (an Abdel Rasul), then in jail, who not only claimed his innocence, but demanded to be hired as a guardian of the necropolis.[108]

The locals were entitled to doubt that for trained archaeologists, information regarding an artefact's provenance was as valuable as the thing itself, but Weigall expected his peers to know better. Although dealing in antiquities was seen as 'a perfectly honorable business' he objected to it, and blamed museum collecting for driving the market, resulting in further damage to tombs and temples.[109] Weigall documented several monuments where paintings, reliefs and inscriptions had been sold for display in museums, saying the gaping holes they left behind awakened 'black murder in my heart'.[110] Egypt was the best place to learn about Egypt, he insisted, and too much was being carted off without documentation. In Luxor, Weigall was confronted with graver casualties of the antiquities trade, the bodies of a Gurnawi family of five, asphyxiated by poisonous gases issuing from a tunnel they were digging beneath their home.[111] The accident was blamed on jinn. In performing his inspections, along with foul subterranean air, 'evil-smelling' bats were a force to reckon with, hanging from tomb ceilings in such numbers, Weigall wrote,

> that the rock itself seemed to be black; but as we advanced, and the creatures took to their wings, this black covering appeared to peel off the rock ... the roar of wings was now deafening, for the space into which we were driving the bats was very confined ... we therefore crouched down, and ... they came, bumping into us, entangling themselves in our clothes, slapping our faces and hands with their unwholesome wings, and clinging to our fingers.[112]

Such discomfort was rewarded, for Weigall experienced his share of thrilling discoveries. A prodigious writer, his essays, letters and books describe a working life that hovered between the grim and the ecstatic.

Shortly after arriving in Luxor, Weigall was present for the opening of the Tomb of Yuya and Tuya (KV46) in the Valley of the Kings, where Maspero had granted a concession to dig to Theodore Davis (1837–1915), a retired lawyer from Newport in Rhode Island. The tomb of the parents of Queen Tiy, wife of Amenhotep III and mother of heretic king Akhenaton, had been robbed in antiquity but the raiders left a great deal behind. Inside the tomb with Davis

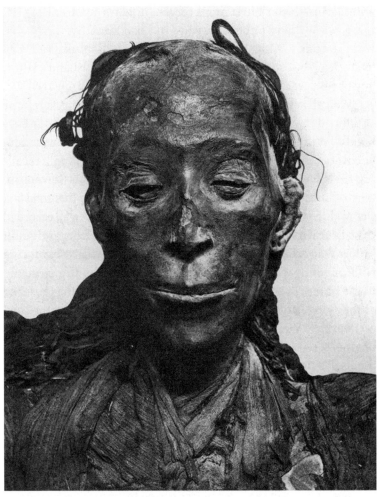

Mummy of Tuya, 1908, photograph by Émile Brugsch.

and Maspero, Weigall 'stood gaping and almost trembling' before the mummies of Tuya, 'her hair still plaited and elaborately dressed', and Yuya, 'his mouth a little open'. He was particularly moved by a pot of embalming resins he mistook for honey, 'as liquid and sticky as the honey one eats for breakfast'.[113] The experience of breaching time's barriers left the men giddy, and they soon climbed back into the sunlight, leaving the others in their party room to descend. These included American painter Joseph Lindon Smith and his wife Corinna, who 'burst into a torrent of tears' upon exiting the tomb, while Davis 'pitched forward in a bad faint'. Writing to his wife, Hortense, Weigall said, 'I'm afraid you will think us all very hysterical,' but she claimed that as she read her husband's letter, 'my cheeks were so crimson, Mamma thought I had a fever!'[114]

Weigall acknowledged the pull of treasure hunting, 'a relic of childhood that remains ... drilled into us by the tales of our boyhood'. '[W]ho has not desired the hidden wealth of Captain Kidd, or coveted the lost treasure of the Incas?' he mused, fondly recalling the novels of H. Rider Haggard and Robert Louis Stevenson, tales of questing and adventure echoing those of *The Thousand and One Nights*.[115] Alert to Egypt's intangible treasures, Weigall recorded the cultural memes he observed that had survived from antiquity: sailors who called out 'Ya Amuni' for protection when crossing the Nile, or young wives placing a scarab in their baths 'to give virtue to the water'. Even the upper class burnt jackal fur in the presence of the dying, 'unknowingly to avert the jackal god Anubis, the Lord of Death'.[116] Weigall heard of several villagers, including twin brothers, who were said to possess the jinn-like power to turn themselves into cats at will. Sensitive to the enchantment of Luxor's west bank, Weigall strolled in the Valley of the Queens after dark with his wife and the Lindon Smiths:

> In the dim light reflected from the brilliant stars, the cliffs and rocky gorges assumed the most wonderful aspect. Their shadows were full of mystery, and the broken pathways seemed to lead to hidden places barred to man's investigation. The hills and the boulders at their feet, took fantastic shape; and one could not well avoid the thought that the spirits of Egypt's dead were at that hour roaming abroad, like us, amidst those illusory scenes.[117]

Weigall and his companions hatched a plan to mount a play there, based on the life of Akhenaton. Weigall wrote the script in blank verse; Hortense was cast in the lead, Corinna Lindon Smith as Queen Tiy and her husband as 'the gods of the underworld'.[118] They spent weeks preparing costumes, sets and lighting, and 'bought all the black worsted Luxor had for a ceremonial wig for Queen Tiy'.[119] Music would be provided by Frederick F. Ogilvie, 'a painter of Anglo-Egyptian fame' who played guitar, and dinner would be served in Medinat Habu after the show. Scheduled for 26 January 1909, an international gaggle of Egyptologists and related dignitaries were invited 'to observe whatever phenomena may take place'.[120] But during dress rehearsal a tremendous hailstorm swept the valley, battering the actors and sets. The performance was cancelled amid rumours that the gods disapproved of such frivolity.

Weigall and his friends were not the only ones susceptible to the intoxication of the ancient. One of Weigall's tasks was to 'stop tourists from worshipping the black lion-headed statue Sekhmet, the goddess of fertility and pestilence, at Karnak'.

> It actually became the custom for English and American ladies to leave their hotels after dinner and to hasten into the presence of the goddess . . . a well-known lady threw herself upon her knees before the statue, and . . . cried out, 'I believe, I believe!' while a friend of hers passionately kissed the stone hand and patted the

Scene from *Burning Sands* (1922, dir. George Melford), reproduced in the eponymous novel by Arthur Weigall (1921).

somewhat ungainly feet ... a kind of ritual was mumbled by an enthusiastic gentleman; while a famous French lady of letters ... made mewing noises.

The 'enthusiastic gentleman' was George Legrain (1865–1917), then savant-in-charge of the Karnak temple complex, whom Maspero reprimanded for behaving like a 'theatrical showman, with the temple for his theatre'.[121] After Weigall's term as chief inspector in Luxor ended in 1911, he actually did work in theatre and cinema, writing screenplays and biographies of the likes of Cleopatra and Alexander the Great, plus a slew of historical romances, all redolent of his time in Egypt. As for the Gurnawi, antiquities inspectors like Weigall came and went, but they remained a constant, pursuing their generational livelihood.

Luxor's east bank was transformed during the New Kingdom by temple building, but now they built hotels, beginning with the relatively modest Luxor Hotel erected on the east bank in 1877, and the grandly colonial Winter Palace (1907). In the early 1900s, an estimated 20,000 travellers, mostly American or English, visited Luxor annually, spending at least a winter week.[122] The First World War short-circuited archaeological activities and tourism, but Tutankhamun's re-emergence in 1922 sparked a recovery, boosted by the 1926 opening of his tomb to the public. The boy-king was the darling of the press, especially in the United States, where his brand was used to sell everything from citrus fruits to face creams, talcum powder ('Lady Tut') and women's low-heeled, ankle-strapped shoes (labelled 'Queen Tut'). In France he was the face of Dentol toothpaste, a laxative and an enamel paint used for cars and bikes, guaranteed to keep them looking young.[123] Thanks to Tut, the antiquities market was booming, and while by this time dealers were ostensibly licensed, subject to inspections and obliged to submit export permissions from the Antiquities Service, artefacts still left the country en masse, with smaller, less sought-after items, or those found in great quantities, made available for direct sale at Cairo's Egyptian Museum.[124]

Tut's discovery awakened widespread interest in Egyptian occultism, beginning with the notion that Howard Carter's patron Lord Carnarvon was cursed for interfering with his resting place, a twentieth-century iteration of the belief that tombs were magically protected. Like medieval scholars before him, British author Paul Brunton (1898–1981) did his part to perpetuate esoteric myth and legend under the guise of history in his travelogue, *The Search for Secret Egypt* (1935), an early example of the thriving 'New Age' genre that ran to many editions and remains in print. Brunton interviewed 'the most famous fakir of modern Egypt, Tahra Bey', who had been 'honoured with the invitations' of kings and of Mussolini, who received him several times.[125] Born in Tanta to a well-off Coptic family and educated as a physician in Istanbul, Tahra Bey had himself buried alive for 28 days, a feat known as 'the resurrection'. In Italy, he entered a lead coffin that was filled

Winter Palace Hotel, Luxor, 1936.

with sand, nailed shut and submerged in a swimming pool. Police stopped 'the demonstration' after an hour. In France Tahra Bey did it again, this time reportedly spending a day and night in the underwater coffin.[126] The *New York Times* called him the 'latest thrill of Paris' in an article heralding his arrival in America under the headline: 'Tahra Bey takes occultism on the vaudeville stage.'[127] 'The world has forced me to commercialize my powers,' the Egyptian lamented, 'to become an *artiste*, when I wanted to be a scientist.'[128]

Brunton was similarly impressed by an 'adept' with 'large, lustrous eyes' he met on a hilltop overlooking the Valley of the Kings. Calling himself Ra Mak-Hotep, he expounded the theory that materialism was the real curse of the pharaohs, a product of their vanity and the opulence of their supernaturally guarded tombs.[129] Tomb raiders and archaeologists intent on acquiring ancient treasures had unwittingly 'released forces upon the world that have endangered it', he said, because each and every far-flung mummy carried 'an etheric link' with the malevolent entities sworn to protect it. His advice was not to 'meddle with tombs whose psychic nature men do not understand', or else be prepared to face the consequences.[130]

The professional meddlers of Gurna may have scoffed at Ra Mak-Hotep's warning, but the 1940s brought consequential circumstances. At the outbreak of the Second World War, around 9,000 Gurnawi lived in clusters of homesteads strung along the hills at the edge of the necropolis. War again halted tourism along with the archaeological digs that employed the locals as unskilled labourers, and many of them left in search of work. The malaria epidemic of the early 1940s likewise hit the community hard, leaving no family untouched, and the British occupiers were blamed for everything, from the war to the mosquitoes. Facing impoverishment, the Gurnawi predictably did their thing. Only this time, an alarming spate of robberies of wall paintings and reliefs provoked a ministerial decree calling for their eviction. Egyptian Egyptologist Ahmed Fakhry reported the damage incurred to the Theban necropolis between 1937 and 1942, writing 'it may

Den of Thebes

Poster announcing Tahra Bey's Paris appearance, 27 June 1927.

be many years – perhaps never – before the full details are made known but the loss is great and irreparable.'[131] Fakhry noted that the Gurnawi were aware of the location of many tombs as yet unknown to the authorities and that in some instances they attempted to conceal the removal of parts of decorated tomb walls by replacing them with material 'similar to one used by restorers'.[132] He also remarked how a guardian who knew that well-preserved portions of walls were targets for theft 'disfigured all the faces' in eight tombs to make them less attractive, a well-meaning effort that caused wholesale destruction.[133]

According to Fakhry, 'the removal of the whole village of Gurna is a long-felt wish which seems to be on the way to fulfillment,' and in 1943, the council of ministers assigned funds to make it happen.[134] Egyptian architect Hassan Fathy (1900–1989) was commissioned to build replacement housing, the village of New Gurna, on the floodplain near the Colossi of Memnon, on farmland protected by dykes. Fathy had studied the mud-brick buildings of ancient Egypt that had stood the test of time, as well as the arches and vaults of traditional Upper Egyptian and Nubian dwellings. He wanted New Gurna, with its covered market and town hall, to be a model for all rural construction, the reaffirmation of an economical, aesthetically pleasing vernacular architecture. Confronted with the prospect of abandoning both home and hunting ground, the Gurnawi were having none of it.

Fathy's choice of labour supervisors helped seal the project's fate. Despite knowing the Abdel Rasuls' reputation for tomb-raiding, he chose 'a man of influential family . . . and well accustomed to engaging labour for the Department of Antiquities', namely Ahmed Abdel Rasul, 'son of eminent sheikh Mohammed Abdel Rasul', descendant of the men who found the Royal Cache.[135] Building began in 1945 but was repeatedly delayed due to creative procrastination and outright sabotage. Sun-baked mud-bricks meant to be moved close to the building site were destroyed when left near a dike that was deliberately breached, causing them to melt away. The Gurnawi's anti-eviction battle proceeded on other fronts; a committee of elders, 'composed entirely of antique dealers, dragomans, ex-guards of antiquities etc.', hired a lawyer, one of whose many arguments was that moving to the floodplain would place his clients 'in danger from wolves'.[136] In the end, New Gurna was never completed, and while several families chose to move there, most stayed on their hillside amid the Nobles' tombs. Fathy recalled how responsible officials referred to 'the peasants [fellahin]' as 'sons of dogs' saying 'the only way to handle them is to build them houses of any sort, and bulldoze the old ones.'[137]

In an historic reversal, Egypt's fellahin were briefly cast as national heroes, thanks to the Free Officers Revolution of 1952.

Festering opposition to the British occupation had erupted in the popular uprising of 1919, nationwide demonstrations supporting Egyptian politicians who won some technical concessions. But it took a military coup to effectively rid the country of both its puppet monarchy (the last of the Mohammed Ali dynasty) and its British overlords. One of the revolution's leaders, Gamal Abdel Nasser (1918–1970), was 38 when he ran unopposed in a presidential referendum where women exercised their right to vote, if not to choose, for the first time. A month later, Nasser nationalized the Suez Canal, driving people nearly mad with pride. Things were looking up for Egyptians, most of whom were farmers living without electricity and doing their best to feed a population of 26 million. Nasser's signature project, the building of the Aswan High Dam, promised to maximize farm output and provide drought insurance, while generating power to light homes and fuel industrialization. The largest civil engineering project of its time, the nearly 4-kilometre-long (2½ mi.) dam was suitably pharaonic,

Hassan Fathy's New Gurna.

and a rising nation rallied to the cause. For five years 30,000 men worked round the clock to build the High Dam, whose volume was estimated at seventeen times that of the Great Pyramid.[138]

Seen as the first native son to rule Egypt since the pharaohs, Nasser was often photographed against a backdrop of ancient monuments, several of which lay directly in the path of the dam's titanic reservoir (Lake Nasser), along with dozens of Nubian villages. Egypt appealed to UNESCO for help to save treasures belonging not only to Egypt, but to the world, and the world responded with funding, equipment and expertise. Launched in 1960, the Nubian Campaign united 52 nations in the name of the universality of art and heritage, a collective act aimed at archaeological recovery on a scale never seen before or since. Phased over twenty years, the campaign documented Nubian culture on the verge of extinction and used advanced engineering to move a select twenty temples, including Abu Simbel, to higher ground. Artefacts collected in the process filled Egypt's superb but little-known Nubian Museum in Aswan (est. 1997) while enriching the collections of participant countries. The dismantling and reassembly of the temples produced captivating imagery, raising Egypt's cultural profile and national optimism to dizzying heights, even while opening the floodgates to mass tourism.[139]

Nasser dreamt of a self-sufficient nation, able to produce whatever it needed, beginning with enough food. But his Robin Hood-esque land redistribution scheme, designed to relieve the old elite of their fiefdoms, benefited only a small portion of Egypt's farmers. Their baksheesh came in the form of Soviet-style propaganda portraying them as patriotic champions. Folkloric entertainment was popularized, dances with men in flowing robes feigning combat with twirling sticks; women balancing enormous clay water jars on their heads. Magazine covers featured ruddy country folk, as did postage stamps, including the 3-millieme stamp of a burly male with a pickaxe on his shoulder and a look that said, 'Lemme at that field.'

While no one was watching, the Aswan High Dam delivered what was easily the most decisive moment in Egypt's long history:

the last Nile flood in 1964, an event whose significance was nearly lost in a deluge of propaganda focused on the dam's trifecta of symbolic virtues: modernity, national unity and the legitimization of the Officers' Revolution. In real life, more than 70 per cent of Egyptians were farmers, bewildered by the disruption of patterns that had guided their way since forever. No more would children wade in the floodwater at the feet of the Colossi of Memnon or lie on their pedestals to take the sun; no more pyramids mirrored in placid seasonal lakes. Nature's crescendo, the swollen river breaking its banks, spreading gifts of rich silt, cleansing the land and refreshing its keepers, all finished, *khalas*. Farmers adapted, digging more canals and planting year-round in an altered landscape throughout a parched and virtually endless summer. For them, the new Egypt must have felt pretty old.

A welcomed outcome of the Officers' Revolution was that Egypt's antiquities were at last in the hands of Egyptian archaeologists and administrators. While foreign missions still excavated, they did so at the state's pleasure, under its sharpened eye, and Egyptian-led excavations grew more common. Damietta-born Zahi Hawass (1947-), the most ardent of post-revolution Egyptologists, obtained his doctorate at the University of Pennsylvania and began his long climb up the bureaucratic pyramid in 1968, as inspector in Middle Egypt. Numerous excavations, TV programmes and manoeuvrings later, Hawass received President Hosni Mubarak's appointment as secretary general of the Supreme Council for Antiquities (2002) and, finally, as Minister of State for Antiquities (2011). An encounter that marked Hawass, in some ways prefiguring his later career, occurred in Gurna in 1974, where he met the reigning patriarch, Sheikh Ali Abdel Rasul (1904-1988).

The only member of his clan who'd ever obtained formal permission to excavate in the Valley of the Kings (c. late 1950s), Sheikh Ali was around seventy, recently married to a twenty-year-old woman, and living in his small, slipshod west bank hotel where he regaled his guests with tales of treasures lost and as yet unfound.[140] Egyptian architect Naguib Amin described him as 'charismatic, quick-witted and entertaining', an insomniac frequently seen

Sheik Ali Abdul Rasoul, Gurna, Upper Egypt, 1946, gelatin silver print, photograph by Paul Strand (printed 1959).

'roaming around all night', perhaps looking for places to dig.[141] Sheikh Ali told Hawass that his grandfather had advised him to explore the tunnel beneath the burial chamber of Seti I, known to run at least 100 metres (328 ft) in the bedrock. The theory was that the burial chamber holding Seti I's sarcophagus was a decoy, and that another one, full of treasure, lay somewhere at the tunnel's end. Around 1960, Sheikh Ali had his chance to explore the tunnel, but having determined it was in fact 136 metres (446 ft) long, his funds ran out, along with his permit.[142] Inspired by Sheikh Ali's story, Hawass later tried his luck at Seti I, but no hidden chamber was found.

A gifted raconteur in his own right, Hawass relates how Sheikh Ali claimed he could 'foretell certain things', predicting he'd one day be a renowned archaeologist, and find a hidden chamber in a royal tomb.[143] Though the latter has not yet come true, it's not for lack of trying. Hawass ensured the first half of the prophecy did, writing frequently for the local press, ratcheting up polemic on the return of antiquities held in foreign collections, authoring many kilograms' worth of coffee-table books, hosting *National Geographic* documentaries and traipsing around the monuments with wealthy tourists for a considerable fee. Hawass never missed an opportunity to promote Egypt's treasures, beginning with himself, and one such occasion arose in connection to a mummy acquired by James Douglas from the Abdel Rasuls via Mustafa Ayat and left mouldering in the Niagara Falls curiosity cabinet since the 1860s.

Thomas Barnett's collection, including nine Egyptian mummies, was relocated in 1958 to a former corset factory near the Falls. The mummy with arms folded across its chest that Douglas had delivered was labelled 'Nefertiti', a showman's claim proved false by a professional peek beneath its linen groin cloth in 1985. In 1991, a visiting Egyptologist remarked the mummy's resemblance to that of Seti I, found in the Royal Cache, and wondered if it might be Seti's father, Ramses I, who was missing from his coffin. The position of the arms suggested a royal personage as did the quality of the mummification. In 1999, when the Michael C. Carlos Museum in Atlanta acquired Barnett's Egyptian collection, the mummy was thoroughly examined. Experts determined it was probably old enough to be Ramses I, and the museum curators graciously offered to send him back to Egypt.[144]

Although the mummy's identity was uncertain, its return was hyped as the homecoming of long-lost pharaoh Ramses I, and Hawass accompanied the mummy on its final transatlantic journey. 'We're not 100 per cent sure it's Ramses I,' he said, 'but we are 100 per cent sure it's a king!' On 26 October 2003 the withered royal was removed from a plane at Cairo International Airport and draped in an Egyptian flag. A military band accompanied a choir of children who circled the coffin singing: 'We are the children of the Nile/Welcome Ramses/Builder of esteemed Egypt!'[145] At least one Egyptologist suspected that the real Ramses I had been thrown overboard by Miss Brocklehurst in 1874, owing to its pungent scent.[146] Still, a royal mummy in the hand is worth two in the Nile and the one bearing the name of Ramses I now lies in the small but exquisite Luxor Museum, surrounded by ancient masterpieces.

Official announcements and press coverage of the mummy's return barely mentioned the Abdel Rasuls' leading role in the Royal Cache saga; Hawass's version of the events of 1881, presented in his online 'Archaeologist Notebook', was a kind of populist Royal Cache lite. The German Émile Brugsch was entirely absent, while Egyptian Ahmed Kamal was the leading authority present and the man to whom Mohammed Abdel Rasul was moved to confess the Cache's whereabouts. 'These people know the secrets of the past,' Hawass wrote of the Abdel Rasuls, explaining that 'the ancient Egyptians had a word for this, *hy*, meaning "he who knows the secret location of the tombs".'[147] Another Egyptologist consulted on the matter had never heard of *hy*, or any other word possessing the ascribed meaning, but while *hy* may not be ancient Egyptian, it is definitely vintage Hawass.

To underline his contention that some people have a nose for treasure, Hawass told a story he claimed that Sheikh Ali had told him, about a cousin, Hussein Abdel Rasul, who was water-boy on Carter's dig in 1922. Excavations had begun ten years earlier, Carter's sponsors were growing antsy and his search was about to end in defeat. On 4 November, as a cool breeze blew and the workmen sang and Carter sat distraught in his tent, young Hussein Abdel Rasul arrived on his donkey as he did each day and dug a shallow hole in the ground to hold the large clay water-jug. But this historic morning, as he brushed away the sand, a limestone block appeared, and lo! It marked the entry to a royal tomb. Thus an Abdel Rasul found Tut, not Carter, because the Abdel Rasuls had *hy*, as it were, in spades.[148]

Despite his affection for the rascally Abdel Rasuls, Zahi Hawass was in charge of Egypt's antiquities in 2006 when it was decided that the Gurnawi's presence was *de trop*. Their building, foraging and open sewage endangered the surrounding tombs, a claim somewhat undermined by the use of bulldozers to destroy their homes and the unceremonious dumping of the rubble at another archaeological site nearby. The historic community's demolition was nonetheless presented as a national triumph in antiquities conservation, a small sacrifice on behalf of the evicted inhabitants for the greater good. Journalists were bused in to watch the action, which began with the customary schoolchildren dressed in pharaonic kitsch singing and beating drums, and officials speechifying at length for the TV cameras. Rows of police stood between the authorities and the erstwhile villagers as the machinery made short work of their homesteads. The pastel-coloured mud-brick facades of a few gutted houses were left standing, a nod to the picturesque.[149]

Yet another New Gurna had been built to accommodate the Gurnawi, 3 kilometres (2 mi.) northeast on a desert elevation, rows of duplexes, smaller than the houses Hassan Fathy had designed, but with modern plumbing. 'Now they can have a hot shower,' said Hawass, who was now free to explore the area, though the 'great finds' he anticipated have yet to be found.[150] The remains of Hassan Fathy's mud-brick New Gurna, now interspersed with modern multistorey red-brick buildings, attracted the attention of UNESCO and the World Monuments Fund (WMF), which placed it on a heritage watch-list in 2010. The WMF website quaintly describes Old Gurna, seat of the Abdel Rasuls' dynasty, as 'a community of amateur archeologists'.[151]

The razing of Gurna in 2006 was part of a larger effort to revamp Luxor for tourism along the lines of an open-air museum. The east bank was torn apart to widen the main thoroughfare along the Nile to make way for more tour buses, and to unearth the so-called 'Avenue of the Sphinxes', the processional pathway that once connected the temples of Luxor and Karnak. The idea was that tourists would pay good money to follow in the footsteps of the ancients, and in the meantime, when the ground was cleared, something sensational might turn up, you never knew.[152] Businesses, homes and gardens, many dating to the late nineteenth and early twentieth centuries, were obliterated, leaving a scar running 2 kilometres (1 mi.) through the town. Luxor merchants and residents were angry but powerless, forced to relinquish their present to accommodate the authorities' vision of a more lucrative distant past.[153]

The long-standing tension between tourism promotion and antiquities management was relieved in 2020, when the ministries assigned to each were merged in a single portfolio. The administrative decision to leverage Egypt's material legacy to maximize tourism revenue, and help fund whatever conservation was deemed appropriate, only formalized existing policy and was otherwise unremarkable. What is instead worth pondering is the vastness of Egypt's treasures. Despite non-stop despoiling that only intensified over time, peaking in the nineteenth and early twentieth centuries, Egyptians today may still dine on the crumbs of their ancients' table. What might we leave on Earth that will last as long and give as much? What modern wonder can compare?

FIVE

A HOUSE OF MANY STORIES

You were appointed as a dam for the destitute
that he might not drown.
But behold, you are a torrent raging against him.
– TALE OF THE ELOQUENT PEASANT (c. 1850 BC)

Buried treasure may be fictional wealth, but the currency of dreams has yet to be devalued, and prospecting the past, however whimsical an occupation, remains a plausible one, especially for the undereducated and unemployed. Observing the methodologies of twenty-first-century tomb raiders, one is as much struck by the arcane beliefs that inform them, as by the canny co-opting of the Internet and social media as expedients. The motivational dynamics of need and greed remain unchanged, as does their historic power to wreak havoc when left unchecked. Recall how the ancients valued order and equilibrium above all else. Yet while sages reminded their rulers of the consequences of blind ambition and their responsibility to punish the wrong and protect the right, they were ignored. That the people might demand payback for injustice was inconceivable; as for accountability, for pharaohs there was no such thing. Extreme privilege such as that enjoyed by the ruling class did not recognize itself; it was a given. With it came entitlement to every wish, no matter the cost to others, without fear of reprisal. If Egypt's history teaches us anything, it's the reason this story sounds so familiar.

In *Anatomy of a Civilization*, Egyptologist Barry Kemp remarked the similarities between ancient Egypt and the world today.

> [I watch] news bulletins of presidential motorcades on thronged boulevards, excited crowds cheering a leader on the balcony of a palace ... public acts of worship and homage performed in strange costumes. I watch, in other words, reenactments of the lives of Bronze Age rulers ... I can, as a member of one of Britain's ancient universities, participate myself in minor manifestations of ancient ceremonial. Or I can go to church. Why do we need such things now (for a real need there certainly is)? ... History is a subversive subject. It undermines our claim to live in an age of reason and progress. Technology streaks ahead ... but institutional man (and sometimes thinking man as well) still struggles to escape from the Bronze Age.[1]

In other words, we are trapped in an archetype. Many societies are organized along the same lines, where the male-dominated, hierarchical format born in families and extended to tribes is enshrined in religion and iterated in bureaucracy and the state, but Egypt offers the most muscular example.

Deference to authority, the feature of patriarchy that allows it to self-perpetuate, enabled Egypt to retain a certain cultural coherence, despite all outward change, for thousands of years. The problem is that humans have complied with this archaic social order for so long we are loath to let go, though it no longer serves any purpose. Gross inequity, armed conflict, human rights abuse, environmental devastation on a global scale and the popularity of political 'strong men' working openly against their citizens' best interests are all proofs of an unhealthy attachment to a failed system. Genuine challenges to the status quo are rare, which is why Egypt's popular uprising in 2011 was so significant. No, it wasn't a revolution in the sense of establishing new norms, but for the first time the people forced the presidential father, pharaoh's imago, to his palsied knees. Egyptians surprised themselves and the world by their spontaneous agreement as to when and how to draw the line, a line that like the horizon has never ceased to recede, no matter how far we travel towards it.

The uprising in January 2011 was a long time coming, sparked by chronic financial hardship and a surfeit of outrage at the punitive, exclusionary tactics characterizing Hosni Mubarak's thirty-year tenure. In the years preceding the mass protests, treasure hunts appeared to be on the rise, an idiosyncratic socio-economic indicator of the country's malaise. Cairo's *Daily News* (6 June 2008) reported that several Egyptians were buried alive while tunnelling for treasures whose locations were obtained from soothsayers. One died in Giza, 11 metres (36 ft) beneath his bedroom, where a 'magician' he paid E£5,000 (then £240) had advised him to dig. A young man in a village south of Cairo paid 'experts' E£2,000 to help find treasure under his house, which collapsed atop the tunnel, taking two lives with it. In Sohag (Middle Egypt) two friends sought the assistance of a 'Moroccan sheikh' to find treasure; both died beneath one of their fallen houses.[2] Commentators remarked that a deteriorating economic situation owed to the global downturn was as much at fault as gullibility, never mentioning the gloom surrounding an oppressed population. Treasure hunting is a crime punishable by up to ten years in prison, but like their distant ancestors, Egyptians risked arrest, injury and death because they had more faith in the ground than in government.

The contrast between rich and poor has always been stark in Egypt, but in 2008 most of its 80 million citizens belonged to the latter category and were obliged to compete for scarce resources. As the global financial crisis gathered momentum, Egypt's already dim fortunes plummeted amid reductions in tourism, Suez Canal revenues and foreign remittances. The country hovered in a befuddled stasis; Cairo seemed punch-drunk and about to go down for the count. The prevailing uncertainty mirrored that of the ancients' Intermediate Periods. Hosni Mubarak refused to appoint a vice-president; when he died, would his dynasty continue via his son Gamal (1963–), as he clearly intended? Or would the priests (Islamists) take over? Or the generals? Mubarak had outlasted the average 21-year rule of the great New Kingdom pharaohs. His only rival in recent history was Mohammed Ali who ruled for nearly half a century, and whose dynasty was overthrown by members of the Egyptian military establishment, to which Mubarak belonged. The Free Officers Revolution of 1952 was meant to afford citizens greater economic opportunities and civil rights, but Gamal Abdel Nasser proved unwilling to share power and responsibilities even when efforts to provide promised services like free education, jobs, healthcare and housing had long since failed to meet demand.

Mubarak was vice-president to Anwar Sadat (assassinated in 1981), whose 'open door policy', aimed at enabling private enterprise to pick up the slack, amounted to cronyism. The more vigorous neoliberal reforms championed by Gamal Mubarak did not produce jobs or benefits so much as sweetheart deals for cohorts who built fortunes on the backs of underpaid workers. Grandiose five-star hotels proliferated in the capital and billboards advertised lushly landscaped residential compounds with names like Dreamland, Beverly Hills and Gardenia Park, as an increasingly impoverished, demographically young and Internet-savvy population looked on. Heidegger defined longing as the 'agony of the nearness of the distant'. At the dawn of the new millennium, a decent life had never seemed so close to so many, yet so utterly out of reach. Uneasiness grew against a backdrop of rising poverty and overcrowded, sub-standard living conditions. Workers' strikes, though outlawed, became larger and more insistent.

Egypt was no longer a country of farmers; as people left their villages in search of work, Cairo absorbed a quarter of the country's total population.[3] Much of the city's growth was 'informal housing', built without licence and with minimal expertise, that has filled the cracks in the 'formal' city and spilled from its perimeter. Driving along the ten-lane ring road encircling the capital, the pyramids now appear on a foreshortened horizon like a slightly taller and more orderly pile of bricks. Dense conglomerations of red-brick boxes, from three to ten precarious storeys high, occupy what was once cultivated land, a precious resource in a desert country. The buildings have few windows, and in the long summers are oven-hot. Wide streets are rare; narrow dirt paths run around the buildings so that moving from place to place requires the endless zigzagging of a rat in a maze.

Hardly a month goes by without some archaeological discovery making headlines in Egypt; although each fresh find means there's one fewer left, it spurs the counter-intuitive impulse to dig for more. Most of the country's inhabited areas have been settled for millennia, reinforcing the long-standing belief that the earth is sown with treasures. Some still hope for gold, although they understand that the stock has been depleted over time. They know that artefacts of other sorts gained currency only in the last two hundred years, meaning there are truckloads waiting to be uncovered. Stories circulate about successful home-based digs, and small finds fetching thousands of Egyptian pounds. Whenever someone in a poor neighbourhood makes good or appears prosperous, it is rumoured that he or she found 'a piece' (*hetta*), something valuable enough to change their lives, echoing Middle Kingdom author Ipuwer's remark that 'paupers have become men of affluence,' not as a result of honest efforts, but from tomb-raiding.[4]

Early in August 2008, in an informal area on Cairo's Giza Plateau, the houses of eleven families collapsed when a neighbour decided to tunnel for treasure. Miraculously, there were no casualties. The quarter is called Saft al-Laban ('milk pot'). 'Don't ask me why,' said Faris, a friend who grew up there but was too young to recall, as I did, when his neighbourhood consisted exclusively of fields, many planted with *berseem*, fodder for the water buffalo that provided milk and meat. Faris was studying philosophy at Cairo University, which was challenging, he said, since students were discouraged from questioning the existence of God. He taught himself English by reading translations of Plato and Kant, and he had a Greek girlfriend he met at a small anti-Mubarak protest that the police dispersed by roughing up the demonstrators. Her name was Athena, and he was struck that the justice embodied in her name should sound at just that moment.

Saft al-Laban's main, paved thoroughfare is dominated by the massive concrete pillars of a ring road access-ramp, squeezed so tightly between the facing houses as to practically roof the street. On a midsummer evening in 2009, Faris and I walked beneath the ramp, where battered vehicles, pedestrian and animal traffic mingled freely. Dust and exhaust fumes wafted, brownish-red, on a hot abrasive breeze. A woman and a boy led a weary and disorientated water buffalo home from one of the few remaining fields a few kilometres away. The road was lined with grocers and other shops, and patches of dirt sporting scraggly blades of grass ringed with protective barbed wire, as if they were the last specimens on Earth. We visited a house adjacent to those that collapsed the previous year, its open door facing an alley just wide enough to walk single-file. An elderly woman veiled in black showed us around her three ground-floor rooms. She indicated several walls with floor-to-ceiling lightning-bolt-shaped fissures she had scrupulously hidden from view, one behind a full-length mirror, another behind a curtain, yet another behind a large wooden wardrobe

The nearby home of Salah Awad, a member of Saft al-Laban's municipal council, was better equipped, with a kitchen and bathroom that boasted running water for sometimes ten full hours a day. The reception area was lined with hard, high couches covered in riotous floral prints. One of Salah's six sons, a cameraman for a satellite TV channel, was present along with several neighbourhood friends. Salah's wife and only daughter sat on the floor in the kitchen shelling peas and squeezing limes. Everyone knew I was interested in the ill-fated treasure hunt that took place a block away, but such discussions are best not approached head-on, so I told a suitable story in my broken Arabic, the 351st tale of *The Thousand and One Nights*. It's about a man from Baghdad who was wealthy but lost everything he had. Someone asked if this was because of the American invasion of Iraq. Salah said it didn't matter; the point is he was rich and now he's broke, and urged me to go on.[5]

This man had a dream, I continued, where a voice tells him that his fortune waits in Cairo. So he walks all the way here, arrives at night and takes refuge in a mosque. While he's sleeping, a band of thieves rob a nearby house and the police come to investigate. Failing to find the real culprits, they round up whoever is available, in this case the man from Baghdad, beat him half to death and throw him in a cell where he languishes for several days. Everyone laughed at the familiarity of this scenario. Someone mentioned a book, entitled *So You Don't Get Hit on the Back of Your Head* (2008), by a former policeman named Omar Afifi. A guide for surviving police abuse, it outlined the constitutional rights theoretically protecting citizens from illegal arrest, detention and torture. It sold thousands of copies before it was banned and its author sensibly left the country. It was no coincidence that Egypt's uprising began on 25 January, a joyless national holiday called Police Day. Thanks to citizen journalism, cases of police brutality had circulated beyond the reach of state censorship, contributing to the growing anger and contempt for government.

The *Thousand and One Nights* story, however true to life, had a happy ending. The Chief of Police interrogated the man from Baghdad who confessed that his dream of finding riches had ended with a sound thrashing. The chief chuckled and said he too had a similar dream, but of course he wasn't dumb enough to believe it. A voice told him to go to Baghdad, he said, and dig beneath a house that he recalled in great detail. The two men shared a hearty laugh, and the chief let his prisoner go. The latter hastened back to his own house in Baghdad, which happened to be precisely the one the police chief had described. He dug there and sure enough, Allahu Akhbar, he found a great treasure. My listeners smiled and shook their heads in wonderment. None had read *The Thousand and One Nights*, but narratives like this may be counted among Egypt's cultural memes, deeply embedded in popular history. Today's treasure-related stories echo medieval ones trope for trope: Moroccan magicians, ancient books, jinn-subduing spells and the need to act during a window of opportunity governed by certain astrological conditions.

Modern versions of medieval treasure-hunting manuals are still published. A cursory perusal of the booksellers near Al-Azhar mosque (who trade largely in religion-related books) yielded *A Guide to Some Places of Treasure in Egypt*, an undated reprint of a handwritten manuscript. The frontispiece featured a photo of the author, a bemused and bearded young man, wearing a turban and holding prayer beads. In his preface he explained the book's genesis: 'With the rising of the computer and the Internet arriving in our country . . . the fates drove me to the seminar of one who embraces comprehensive knowledge of astronomy and astrology, and there I found what I was looking for,' namely, privileged information about treasure hunting that he proceeds to share. Religious types debate whether treasure hunting is *haram* (forbidden), with many condemning it and others providing ground cover for those who undertake it. A Salafi (ultra-conservative) sheikh raised an outcry when he weighed in on a Salafi-affiliated TV channel with a religious decree (*fatwa*) that contradicted antiquities laws, saying it's finders keepers if treasures turn up on your own property but things found on public land can't be sold, and should be reburied.[6] The author of the *Guide to Some Places of Treasure* was unequivocal. 'Treasures are contentment, so cleave unto them and you will live like a king,' he wrote, 'look to him who is a master of the world in its entirety [rich]. Did he die unknown without a shroud?'[7]

The author of a similar book, *Removing the Veil from Treasure and Antiquities Hunting*, was more circumspect, warning readers against scammers and relating anecdotes entitled 'The Price of Greed' and 'He Pays for Forgery with His Life'. He offered a chapter devoted to jinn and their powers, including possession of a human body; another on magic and Islam's prohibitions of it, but also what magicians can do, how to become one, and incantations designed to reveal hidden treasures. After 120 pages effectively encouraging treasure hunting, the book ends with an admonition:

> Wake up Muslims! Be aware that all these ideas are being promoted in our country. It's just the enemies of our religion, trying to distract us from our truths because they know of our weakened financial condition. They want us to live in dreams and fictions and forget the original reasons for awakening.[8]

In closing, the author remarked that he still gets calls from people asking him to help them hunt treasures, which was unsurprising since his mobile phone number was on the back cover.

The son of Salah, who works for a TV station, opened his computer and showed us his coverage of the houses that collapsed in his neighbourhood the previous year. The tunnel that caused it was almost as big as the room where it was dug. The nearly 2-metre-square (22 sq. ft) shaft, reinforced with wooden planks, reached an impressive depth of over 15 metres (49 ft) before the houses above it began tumbling like dominoes. 'A single dream', intoned the reporter, 'seduces the poor, because they know that Egypt is a house of many stories,' a poetic reference to the country's archaeological strata.[9] I asked if anyone did anything about the situation after the clip aired. This got another big laugh. What could be done? When asked why people risked their own and others' lives, one local man said, '[they] know that the area is an archaeological one, and it causes a mania among them.'

Salah noted how the 'the poor and naive' were easily hoodwinked by individuals claiming they can locate treasures and neutralize jinn, usually by reading a passage from the Qur'an. These self-styled sheikhs are called 'Moroccan' owing to their special skills, and are always strangers from another neighbourhood, not foreigners. Their talent lies in gauging people's weaknesses, their neediness and the real killer: hope. 'You wouldn't believe it,' Salah said 'but people with a little money will invest it in a treasure hunt, not a business. They don't expect great riches, only to find something, anything, worth even a few thousand pounds.' This would hardly cover the cost of repairing the floor tiles, providing the house was still standing. Despite the expense, and literally piles of proof that more often than not the jinn win, professional charlatans found clients.

Once committed to the hunt, people reportedly paid substantial sums for special jinn-busting incense, and still more for 'red mercury' (*al zaybaq ahmar*), a substance mentioned in Salah's son's reportage, whose value and properties depend on who you talk to. Some said it costs thousands, others millions of dollars, and that it was found only at the core of certain pharaonic statues; others thought it came from Russia. Red mercury not only disarms jinn, according to some, but can inspire knowledge of treasure locations and even grant eternal youth. One of my interlocutors was convinced that Hosni Mubarak possessed red mercury and would therefore live forever. No one I spoke to had actually ever seen it. Like their medieval counterparts, modern Egyptian con artists have masterfully exploited the appetite for buried treasure, inventing occult accessories like red mercury and spin-off *mises en scène*. One band of scammers promised victims they could change Egyptian pounds into u.s. dollars with the help of jinn. Some used impressive sleight-of-hand tricks, like making a plate of sand burst into flames, producing fire from within their clenched fist or making rocks rattle as it if they had something inside.[10]

Treasure-related cons constitute a cottage industry, with scammers cold-calling phone and Internet listings of wealthy professionals (often doctors). A brief and flattering preamble usually delivered by a girl ('I heard you were a wise and successful man') is followed by a plea for advice; the caller says one of her relatives has found antiquities while working on a construction site and is not sure what to do. Sell them? Look for more? Can the great man help? While most respondents told the caller to report the matter to the police, some took the bait in the hopes of either acquiring artefacts cheaply or else meeting the girl. Sometimes smartphone photos of artefacts were sent to elicit sales or involvement in promising digs. In one instance, an antiques dealer received a video clip shot in the desert where what he recognized as cheap replicas of Tutankhamun's funerary equipment were laid out in the sand, as if they'd just been found.[11]

Belief in the spell-like power of religious texts and invocations to protect treasure hunts is a long-standing tradition. But Egyptian magic also has a pragmatic side, providing in other circumstances a socially acceptable refutation of unpleasantness. Hence a man without a job or couples without children engage practitioners to remove the curses that have fallen upon them. The belief in possession (by jinn) is often related to marital problems, for example, where one partner wants out; stress, anger or the unwillingness or inability to have sex will be blamed on the invading jinn, as opposed to a partner. Exorcisms, usually involving religious texts, are not uncommon (Coptic priests are considered experts), though people are generally expected to deal with jinn's mischief themselves, that is, to refuse to allow them to cause discord. The *zar* ritual, exclusively for women, uses music and dancing as a therapeutic means of exorcising demons, aka the frustration and fatigue of caring for a family under difficult living conditions. The painful downside of scapegoating jinn for ordinary problems is that debilitating mental and physical conditions may be dismissed and left untreated. Religious scholars under whose mandate the jinn fall, do little to counter misconceptions.

The belief in nefarious jinn and in practices like dream interpretation and divination has never been confined to the poor and undereducated; Egypt's former monarchy regularly consulted astrologers. Gamal Abdel Nasser is said to have enlisted a well-known healer from Upper Egypt to identify the source of a nagging ailment, which was identified as a spell that had been cast against him.[12] These activities belong not to a class, but a culture that however grounded in the present is infused with remnants of its past. Representations of the hand, a pre-Islamic talisman, decorate shops and houses of every stripe, as does the protective eye of Horus. Egyptians still celebrate the pharaonic holiday of *Sham al-Nessim* ('sniffing the breeze') corresponding with the vernal equinox and later associated with Coptic Easter. On the Monday after Easter Sunday, Muslims and Christians picnic on whatever scrap of green they can find, including the landscaped islands separating street traffic. The traditional menu includes salted fish, lettuce (an aphrodisiac) and spring onion, a perennial staple whose salutary effects are associated with a story about a pharaoh's only son, who was dying until a priest broke one under his nose, like a popper, and cured him.

On the seventh day after a child's birth, families gather for a *sebua* ('the week'), a party that involves banging pots and pans to scare off whatever malevolent spirit might lurk in the newborn's vicinity. Since an Egyptian is born approximately every twenty seconds, this may help account for Cairo's background din.[13] The original version of the ritual is depicted on the walls of the funerary temple of Hatshepsut, where Anubis rolls a kitchen sieve, and the distance it travels before toppling foretells the length of a child's life. When someone dies in rural Egypt crowds of extended family and friends gather to wail for hours at a time, with women shrieking at the top of their lungs, 'oh my soul' (*ya ba-i*), harking back to the pharaonic concept of *ba*, an aspect of the deceased's spirit, one of many etymological links to ancient speech that survive in Egyptian Arabic via the Coptic language.[14]

It's not that Egyptians are more susceptible to superstition, or more attached to traditions, than other people; the dots between past and present behaviours are just easier to connect. With this in mind, death by treasure hunt seems bizarre only if taken out of context, the same way people boarding flimsy, overcrowded ships for Mediterranean crossings would sound crazy, if you didn't know they were refugees, and why.

In 2010, about six months before Egypt's uprising, Cairo-based bloggers and Egypt-watching social media users worldwide shared the trailer for *Chasing Mummies*, a History Channel programme starring Zahi Hawass, then secretary general of Egypt's Supreme Council for Antiquities (SCA), referred to in the voiceover as 'the daddy of all mummies'. This priceless cultural artefact opens with wind whistling over the desert as the sun sets behind the Step Pyramid of Saqqara. A man on horseback gallops toward the camera until his stocky silhouette is unmistakable: Hawass, wearing his Indiana Jones-style hat. '100,000 years of history', growls the narrator, 'belong to one man.' Cut to Hawass posing jauntily in front of the Great Pyramid, as if he just finished building it. The teaser shows the 64-year-old Egyptologist grunting gamely through tight tunnels, being lowered by rope into a pit, and shouting at the film crew, utterly unhinged. 'I don't want anyone to talk! Or I will leave! You do not understand archaeology! You understand! Nothing!' Zahi and the bedevilled crew set off into the desert and find an ancient burial, but one that tomb raiders despoiled long ago. 'They opened the sarcophagus,' Hawass yells, 'and they robbed! Everything!' A mummy is nonetheless produced and he gloats over his prize. 'Thisss,' Hawass says, with his peculiar finial hiss, 'is one of the beautiful mummiesss that I found in my career.'[15]

While damning the thieves who beat him to the punch, Hawass typically glossed over the motivations behind ancient raiding, perhaps because the parallels with the present day were uncomfortably close. He maintained amicable ties with the Mubarak regime that relied on his services as patriot, tourism generator and grand distraction; however outrageously self-promoting, his clowning for the media left the international public little surplus attention to pay to less amusing Egyptian foibles, like martial law. In his role as guardian of Egyptian antiquities, Hawass went so far as to try copyrighting the pyramids, miffed at the success of knock-offs like the Luxor Casino in Las Vegas, and desirous of royalties. He took credit for ending the practice of allotting a portion of archaeological finds to the foreign missions that unearthed them, although this was stipulated in legislation dating to 1922. 'I feel it is an honour for any expert just to work in Egypt,' he said, and he wasn't wrong.[16] But Hawass was also of the opinion that it was an honour for Egyptians to visit their own monuments. 'The pyramids should be for the people – but they're like a dish of gold,' he said, complaining that his compatriots lacked the proper table manners, especially those who earned their daily onion by peddling sodas, souvenirs, crafts or camel-rides on site. 'You cannot experience the magic of the pyramids when someone is bothering you to buy a scarf,' Hawass remarked.[17]

In 2001, construction began on a wall around the three Old Kingdom pyramids of Giza to prevent encroachment and curb the animal and human traffic that once moved there freely. Completed in 2008, the 4-metre-high (13 ft) concrete barrier topped with 3 metres (10 ft) of fencing had a double-based 1.5-metre-deep (5 ft) foundation to discourage tunnellers, and was equipped with CCTV cameras and twenty electronically controlled gates. The 22-kilometre-long (72 ft) wall enclosed Khufu, Khafre, Menkaure and a large swath of the plateau, while cutting Khufu ('the great pyramid') off from the adjacent (eastern) village of Nazlet al-Samman (Quail Landing), formerly a rural settlement by then thoroughly enmeshed in Cairo's urban fabric. Residents whose livelihood depended on tourism had to secure entry via metal detectors to what was once their backyard. The wall was essential, Hawass maintained, because otherwise the site was 'a zoo', but people living beside it said their neighbourhoods felt like a jail.[18]

In 2010, with a population of about a quarter-million, Nazlet al-Samman was a cluster of ragtag mud-brick homesteads and towering new brick buildings, bordered on one side by a four-lane street and on the other by the wall. Some residents claimed the village was founded by the pyramid builders, but it more likely arose to serve tourists who came in greater numbers after the 1869 opening of the Suez Canal. Known for its stables, Nazlet al-Samman was the departure point for many an exhilarating gallop around the pyramids, the same stretch of desert where pharaohs hunted or practised chariot warfare and Mamluks played polo. Pedestrians shared the town's rutted main boulevard with camels, horses, donkey-drawn carts, buses, cars and tuk-tuks. The main entrance to the pyramids swirled with traffic, the air redolent of incense, frying falafel, manure and exhaust fumes. The streets, lined with the usual greengrocers, bakers, opticians, pharmacies and photomats, were interspersed with perfume and souvenir shops, everything from small stalls festooned with talismans, to grand showrooms with chamfered, marble-clad facades aping those of ancient temples. The souvenir trade has changed since the days when they were expected to look like real artefacts, 'executed with a skill that almost defied detection'.[19] Today's versions rarely make such pretence, with some locally crafted statues so crude you can hardly tell a jackal-headed Anubis from a cat-headed Bastet. The Chinese have meanwhile cornered the machine-made pharaonic memorabilia market. The ancient gods would presumably be pleased that an industry remains devoted to replicating their image, but one wonders what they'd make of Nazlet al-Samman's Pizza Hut, built within whispering distance of the Sphinx.

Local news outlets reported a catastrophic treasure-hunting accident in Nazlet al-Samman in September 2009, where six men were buried alive while tunnelling.[20] The survivors of the eighteen-man crew were arrested and imprisoned; when I went looking for the house in November 2010, they had just got out of jail. I asked men seated in front of a small mosque about the collapsed house. They said it belonged to someone named Ragab, and indicated a dirt path running along the wall. On the way, I met a man in his mid-twenties named Amir who knew Ragab and took me to the ruins of his home on a plot of about 5 metres square (54 sq. ft), separated from the wall by a narrow path. The front of the two-storey mud-brick dwelling was shorn away, revealing a cross-section of tiny rooms, one on ground level filled with sand emptied from the tunnel, and another, covered in debris, where planks of reused wood poked haphazardly from the narrow, poorly reinforced shaft that collapsed at a depth of around 7 or 8 metres (23–26 ft). The antiquities authorities installed a low iron gate around the wrecked house and left it as a caution to those who would search for treasure. The neighbours, who said they were threatened with eviction if the illegal digging didn't stop, used the site as a rubbish dump. The CCTV cameras topping the wall looked like they'd long since been target practice for slingshots.

Amir said his family had lived in Nazlet al-Samman for 140 years. His sinewy arms were covered in cutting scars, dozens of short horizontal slashes and several thicker lengthwise ones intermingled with homemade tattoos in faded blue, the initials of his parents, his girlfriend's name in a lopsided heart. He said he was planning to make the engagement formal as soon as he could afford the requisite gifts of gold jewellery. Paying for his side of the marriage contract (including providing a home) would take a few more years and Amir wondered aloud if the girl would wait for him. A high-school graduate, he worked as an informal guide and knew a handful of strategic words in seven languages, including Russian and Japanese. To find work, he stood near the main entry to the pyramids and asked tourists if he could see their tickets, pretending that was his job. Having got their attention he offered to show them around, arrange for a horse or camel ride, and maybe sell them something. He said he could tell how much they would tip by how they were dressed, noting that nice clothes are often 'decoration' and people who wear them were usually cheap. Really rich people, the big tippers, he said, don't care how they look. Unfortunately for Amir and others like him, people travelling alone, rich or otherwise, were few. Tourists moved in groups monopolized by trained guides who steered them to the shops and stables where they received commissions. Business, judging by Amir's worn-out T-shirt, shorts and sandals, was not so good. Either that or he was trying to look rich.[21]

Amir demonstrated the artful technique he'd developed for piquing tourists' interest in acquiring an *orijinal*, slang for genuine artefact, but in his case signifying modest forgeries of shabti statuettes and scarabs. He turned a sale into an expedition, never showing the things right away, only saying he could get them, and would the visitors like to see. They usually did, and this required a walk to a particular boulder from whose base a wooden box was produced and furtively stuck in the back waistband of his jeans, like a plain-clothed TV cop might do with his weapon. Then he took them to Bondok's café out by the pyramid of Menkaure, a bench and a propane gas heater sheltered from the wind by fallen blocks of noble masonry. While Bondok rinsed the glasses in a bucket of tea-stained water and set his tarnished old copper kettle on the flame, Amir allowed the desert to impose its silence. At last, he opened the box, and from a welter of filthy rags (ersatz mummy wrappings) produced the objects to be examined. The tourists handled them with reverence, politely oo-ing and ah-ing and inevitably buying one or two. A few dollars or euros were a small price to pay for a magical workman in the shadow of the pyramid; even if it wasn't old, it was at least an authentic fake.

Amir shared his insider knowledge of Ragab's misadventure, both as a neighbour and because he happened to be in jail when Ragab and his crew arrived. Amir was arrested several weeks earlier for throwing stones at policemen when they stormed the house of a neighbourhood drug dealer and manhandled his sisters and mother. Amir said he was beaten and imprisoned for nine months. He recalled his release with satisfaction, returning home a hero, being well fed and given money and drugs. He said that Ragab arrived in jail with several broken teeth he'd acquired during interrogations to reveal the names of his accomplices and the location of any artefacts they might have found.[22] According to Amir, Ragab's father had told him never to dig for treasure and he didn't really want to. But a month after his father died, his mother said something along the lines of 'I'm old, we're broke, start digging,' so Ragab dug.

Speaking in a low conspiratorial tone, Amir said Ragab's men unearthed an *orijinal* and convinced a wealthy local, a member of parliament, to buy it for E£2.5 million. But why would they have kept digging until the tunnel collapsed, if they found something worth so much money, I asked. Amir looked at me like I was stupid. The crew was big and had many needs, he said, and besides, what if there were more statues? Not only was the mentioned sum fantastic, Amir described a *gahaz* (gadget) the size of a cigarette lighter that when placed beside an artefact can detect its age. This too was pure fiction, the kind that treasure hunting ceaselessly inspires. Stories became legends in the telling; a find worth E£5,000 in the morning was valued at E£500,000 by night. Even the reports of eyewitnesses varied, embellished according to the propensities of the teller and perceived expectations of the listener. Amir's fabrication betrayed the urge to keep the dream of treasure alive while incriminating a despised government official.

Through Amir I met Mahmoud, one of the men directly involved in Ragab's dig, who assured me they'd found nothing before the tunnel caved in. We talked at a café in the shade of the wall where someone had drawn a pharaonic-style solar boat with Allah's names written in the masts, all painted in talismanic turquoise. The 26-year-old Mahmoud was a bit chubby, soft-spoken and kind. He found a plastic stool for me to sit on and a piece of cardboard he placed on the ground for himself. Originally from a village near the Old Kingdom Step Pyramid of Saqqara, his mother and three siblings had lived in Nazlet al-Samman since he was a boy. Mahmoud, who had completed primary school and was now an electrician, pulled a wire cutter from his back pocket by way of credentials. He knew Ragab as he'd worked in his house, shared 'bread and salt' with his family, and everyone in the area anyway knew one another. Indeed, Mahmoud heard about the digging at Ragab's before he was asked to join the crew. It seems Ragab was very generous with his invitations to friends and relatives, and everyone (except the local police) knew what was going down.[23]

The digging began in September, which corresponded that year with the lunar Islamic month of Ramadan, when devout Muslims forgo water, food, smoke and sex from dawn to sunset and all activity, including police supervision, slows to a near halt. Ragab's crew may have also chosen Ramadan to start their dig since jinn are said to be less active in the Holy Month; all that praying and personal sacrifice puts them off. September is still summertime in Egypt, so it was hot work. The sand removed from the hole was placed in an adjacent room so as not to attract attention on the street. Near the month's end, the men hit a stone slab they believed was the ceiling of a tomb. At this point someone brought in a sheikh, a man in his late forties, to protect the men by reading the Qur'an. As Mahmoud pointed out, 'there is Qur'an – and there is "not Qur'an",' meaning the sheikh's invocations were not strictly by the book. Mahmoud said they failed to break through the stone slab, so they tunnelled laterally above it and found an opening at one end. Concerned about 'bacteria' (bad air) they lowered a lamp, peered inside and saw what they thought was a mummy or a statue. Nearing the prize they grew reckless; the ground was sandier and they failed to shore up the tunnel sides properly. The more sand they removed, the more took its place, and the tunnel, along with the house's meagre foundations, began to give.

On 24 September 2009 Mahmoud had done a bit of tunnelling but said 'my god told me not to go back down.' Six members of the group were working in the tunnel, several were away until their next shift and several more were in the house, including Mahmoud who was napping. His colleagues' screams awoke him; the house was filled with dust rising from the tunnel that had caved in on the workers below. Mahmoud and the others dug with their hands until they bled. Neighbours came to help; someone called the police because they had access to bulldozers but according to Mahmoud they refused to take action until the antiquities authorities could examine the site. According to one news report, heavy machinery was in fact brought in, then replaced by fifteen manual workers.[24] Ragab's house did not actually fall, but along with his neighbour's was partially demolished by bulldozers in the course of the rescue effort. Four days passed before distraught family members recovered their dead. Five of the men were in their twenties, one recently engaged, another just married, another who had just seen the birth of his first son. The sixth and eldest man was the sheikh hired to protect the dig. 'Sheikhs [like this one] are liars,' Mahmoud said, 'god have pity on his soul.'

Mahmoud was arrested and taken from the police station directly to prison. He hired a lawyer who proved more useful in getting food into the jail than in getting him out. Mahmoud said eating was expensive, because there were so many middlemen, and that his 5-metre-square (54 sq. ft) cell was packed. He considered himself lucky to have served only a year when he might have been jailed for much longer. Asked if having gone through all that for naught – the brush with death, the loss of friends, a year

Pyramid wall, Nazlat al-Samman, 2010.

in prison – would he dig again, Mahmoud said 'yes, but I would do it my way.' He believed his neighbourhood was full of possibilities; 'there's work down there,' he said. A friend of Mahmoud's joined us, Sami, who was part of the crew and present when the tunnel collapsed. Dressed in a galabiyya, Sami was in his late twenties and fresh out of jail but unlike Mahmoud, he'd had his fill of treasure hunting. 'I have children,' he told me. 'So much was lost, and all for what? For a dream, nothing more, just a dream.'

In December 2010, I met a man from Abu Sir (15 kilometres/9 mi. south of Nazlet al-Samman), a former farming village adjacent to an Old Kingdom necropolis. Taha was around 35, married with children and one of seven siblings. He worked in a perfume shop on the Pyramids Road, where we sat in a spacious basement filled with semicircular couches and glass shelves holding flasks and fluted hand-blown bottles, an empty room designed to accommodate busloads of tourists. Over coffee, I asked about the framed photo of a man who looked as if he'd leapt from a temple frieze, as did Taha, who said it was his grandfather, recently deceased at age ninety, co-author of books about the pyramids in a New Age vein. Taha, who spoke English well, said he learned a lot from his grandfather, who was interested in meditation and chakras. We discussed how the theory that aliens helped build the pyramids was held almost exclusively by foreigners, and eventually arrived at the topic of treasure hunting.

Taha said a man died beneath his house in Abu Sir earlier that year, but that was unusual, because people mostly dug in the antiquities-rich desert. Sheikhs were not needed to determine treasure locations, he said, but if a dig encountered trouble, like rising water, or snakes in the pit, or if someone felt they'd been kicked from behind when no one was there, they called in a sheikh. I mentioned a recent article in *Al-Masry Al-Youm*, an independent Arabic daily, reporting that archaeological sites were being plundered in the Fayoum, in Sohag (Middle Egypt) and Qena (Upper

Egypt).²⁵ Taha agreed that treasure hunts were on the rise, adding that the forgery business was also thriving and that Abu Sir was home to an expert, a former farmer who worked with several archaeological missions to educate himself. 'Ordinary people will do anything for money nowadays,' he said, because people needed it to marry and needed to marry to have proper sex. Forced to wait until they could earn enough, often until their mid-thirties, they will go to any extreme. 'This is important,' he said, meaning sex was a strong motivation for treasure hunting.²⁶

Taha invited me to his home and on 7 January 2011 we drove through a bleak labyrinth of informal buildings to a half-built house belonging to his brother Omar. The ground floor was enclosed by three walls, the unfinished fourth looking out on the desert. With Omar and a male cousin we sat on the frigid, thinly carpeted floor. Omar smoked a hookah, tended by his ten-year-old son. His barefooted four-year-old daughter cajoled a half-pound note from him and went out to buy a date bar at a nearby kiosk. The TV was on, an episode from a camp Iranian serial about Yussef of Qur'anic fame (the biblical Joseph) that transfixed them until the cousin brought a large round trayful of food: bowls of okra in minty tomato sauce, chunks of stewed water buffalo and large discs of freshly baked bread. While we ate, another brother called from Kuwait where he'd worked since after the Gulf War, and the phone was passed around so everyone could greet him. Like countless Egyptian families, Taha's relied in part on financial assistance from a relative who managed to find work abroad. After lunch, the men started talking, with Omar quoting passages from the Qur'an that he interpreted as warnings against treasure hunting, since whatever God put in the ground was meant to stay there. He was basically saying that while he and his brother knew a lot about the subject, I shouldn't assume they'd ever tried it.

Located at the edge of the desert on cultivatable land, Abu Sir is no longer a farming village but neither is it a town, only a mass of slapdash buildings flanking a canal. The area takes its name from the Coptic *busiri*, 'house of Osiris', god of the afterlife. The adjacent necropolis once served the ancient capital of Memphis and is known for the ruins of fourteen step pyramids, in varying states of decay. Used for burials throughout antiquity, the partially excavated site is a rich hunting ground. Like Gurna on Luxor's west bank, most of Abu Sir's residents belonged to one of several clans, each holding 'title' to certain areas where they dug. Taha said they sounded the ground with an iron rod that penetrates sand but stops at stone. Also like Gurna, family members hauled sand for archaeological digs in the winter, and kept their relatives informed as to what was found and where. They had more information about antiquities than the archaeologists, according to Taha, and had found many things they could never report. He claimed he once saw a 10-metre-long (33 ft) fossilized skeleton of a gigantic centipede, with sets of legs projecting from its spine. He'd seen burial chambers full of funerary equipment in Saqqara (3.5 kilometres/2 mi. south), site of another ancient necropolis and of the Step Pyramid of Djoser, and reckoned that in Saqqara alone there were more treasures than in Cairo's Egyptian Museum, enough 'to give everyone in the world a piece'.[27]

In Abu Sir's archaeological zone, territorial disputes sometimes resulted in death by gunshot, the brothers said, as people went to the desert armed with rifles. Omar remarked that while shots were once fired in warning when someone was seen poking around someone else's territory, people had grown less averse to shooting to wound or kill. The guns in question were almost invariably old, family heirlooms once used for hunting wild fowl, and not the most accurate of weapons. Gunshot deaths were certified as due to natural causes by a village official, perhaps a member of the family, the brothers said. They knew of four people who died in the last year in treasure-related incidents: the man buried beneath his home, one in a desert tomb shaft, and two by gunshot, one of them a young man shot accidentally by his father, tragic proof, Omar said, that seeking one's fortune from ill-gotten gains is bound to backfire. The fourth person was an antiquities guardian in Saqqara but no one knew who shot him or why, or whether or not it was an accident. Taha noted that antiquities guardians were sometimes in league with thieves, and who could blame them? 'They make only a few hundred pounds [under U.S.$50] per month,' he said; 'if they could steal the pyramids, they would.'[28]

Taha voiced a bitter complaint shared by the area's residents about a state-built wall that prevented them from expanding their cemetery into the desert, presumably because it would infringe on archaeological sites. He said they'd applied for permits to make more room but hadn't received an answer. Meanwhile, available crypts were packing them in, 'even the dead are overcrowded,' he said. Like many Egyptians, Taha was convinced that government officials trafficked in artefacts, and were uniformly corrupt. No one had any proof beyond the anecdotal, only a timeless rancour in the face of injustice, and a desire to balance the scales. 'If the government is stealing, why not us?' Taha said. 'We follow their example. If you give me no chance for a legitimate job, then I guess you want me to be a criminal.'[29]

The disparity of opportunities and freedoms afforded elite versus average citizens is old news, as is the former's ability to escape punishment for their misdeeds. As the Middle Kingdom author of the *Tale of the Eloquent Peasant* remarked, 'theft is natural to him who has nothing', but a rich thief, 'is he not to be rebuked?'[30] The peasant's story, meant to illustrate the concept of *maat*, cosmic order, upheld by even-handed application of the law, suggests instead that Egyptians have never stopped regretting *maat*'s absence. The peasant was robbed en route to market by a wealthy landowner who assumed he could get away with it. When the poor man threatened to take the matter to the authorities, the rich one beat him until he wept. For days he begged for the return of his goods but the villain ignored him, so he approached a magistrate who passed him off to a colleague, who turned him over to another, then another, each duly recording his pleas but doing nothing about them. All of the peasant's speeches were prefaced with wheedling adulation:

> My lord, you are the greatest of the great, the guide of all that is not and that is. When you embark on the sea of truth ... the waves shall not break upon you ... the shy fish shall

come to you . . . for you are the father of the orphan, the husband of the widow, the brother of the desolate . . . you great one, free from greed, free from arrogance, destroyer of falsehood, creator of truth.[31]

Pharaoh caught wind of the case and, impressed with the peasant's turn of phrase, ordered the magistrates to feed his family but not to render justice, because the peasant's descriptions of his plight and his sometimes barbed appeals to the authorities' higher values made such good reading. At last, after nine exhausting entreaties, the peasant got his goods back and was awarded the land of the man who robbed him, showing the pharaoh's generosity in the service of *maat*, albeit fictional. Never mind that justice was withheld at pharaoh's whim and the peasant only won because he managed to stay alive, or that the 'eloquence' that saved him consisted largely of high-blown flattery aimed at softening up his oppressors.

The ancients raised sycophancy to a high art, with their litanies of honorifics and lists of pharaohs' attributes, but Mubarak-era toadies gave them a run for their money. Presidential birthdays occasioned outpourings of praise in editorials and paid-for ads in the state-owned press and elsewhere. Buckets of honeyed ink were spilled for the anniversary of Mubarak's twentieth year in office (14 October 2001); the words 'love' and 'sacrifice' peppered paragraphs of loyalist froth describing Mubarak as 'a prophet of peace, an angel in the form of a president', lauding his determination, industriousness and his 'captivating simplicity'.[32] Mubarak's paternal rapport with his people was highlighted alongside his peerless leadership: 'we love to call him Papa Mubarak, because he is the father of us all,' one who treats his children with 'humanity and sensitivity . . . there is not a single [one of his actions] from which the fragrance of fatherliness does not waft.' Ranked alongside the Nile and the pyramids, Mubarak was part of an 'exquisite national melody . . . when the poets express Mubarak-love, the hearts tremble.' He was 'solid as a mountain, because he supports Truth and Justice', his 'eye always as clear as the eye of Horus'.[33] All the pharaohs put together couldn't boast as many monuments: libraries, airports, town squares, streets, a metro station and more than five hundred schools, all named after Hosni Mubarak.

Some of the tributes of 2001 referenced the recent attacks on New York's World Trade Center, stressing the wisdom Mubarak bestowed upon foreign leaders, without of course mentioning he'd acquired it in response to domestic terrorists who were typically sentenced in military courts and summarily hanged. Nobel Laureate Naguib Mahfouz was alone in politely requesting that the president put an end to laws restricting civil rights and allow for multi-party presidential elections to replace the yes/no vote by which Mubarak's six-year terms were repeatedly renewed.[34] The constitution was finally amended along those lines by referendum in May 2005, an election year, just in time for Mubarak's campaign to boast his commitment to democracy. Since the referendum was held shortly after the presidential birthday, the streets were already plastered with supportive messages. 'Even unborn children in their mother's wombs say "yes" to Mubarak,' read a billboard in Sayyeda Zeinab, a run-down quarter of old Cairo. But while multiple candidates could now stand against him, Mubarak had virtually no opponents. The only remotely viable one, a businessman named Ayman Nour, was arrested both before and after the election, which everyone believed was rigged.

Cairo was meanwhile choked with campaign propaganda, posters, banners and billboards bearing the image of an aged, somewhat rueful-looking Mubarak, his hair dyed dark and dressed in an open-collared shirt, captioned 'a crossing to the future'. 'What future?' a cab driver asked me. 'It should have said "*malesh*,"' a frequently used word whose meaning oscillates between 'too bad' and 'never mind'.[35] This would have been a more honest, and therefore highly original, campaign slogan, said the cabbie, who like millions of his countrymen saw no point in voting. Egyptians hunkered down for another six years of Hosni, vowing to form parties to challenge him in 2011, which was legally near impossible and guaranteed to attract the dreaded midnight door-knock from state security. Mubarak's younger son Gamal was positioned as his successor. The only political power people had left was the danger they might represent if they took to the streets, and on 25 January 2011 they started using it.

Downtown Cairo's Egyptian Museum is a stately neoclassical building, occupying the northern end of Tahrir (Liberation) Square. Opened in 1902, when fashionably racist Lord Cromer (Evelyn Baring) was British Consul General, it stands as a monument to Egypt's colonialist past, its pink facade embedded with plaques commemorating foreign Egyptologists. Auguste Mariette, founding director of the first Egyptian Museum in Bulaq, is actually buried in the Cairo Museum garden, within tunnelling distance of the world's greatest array of Egyptian treasures. Inside the museum's lofty halls, antiquities were stockpiled rather than displayed, a staggering profusion of monoliths, statuary, artefacts of every sort, including the gold of Tutankhamun.[36] Beginning Tuesday 25 January 2011, and for over two weeks, the museum was immersed in crowds numbering in the hundreds of thousands, Egyptians of every age and background who agreed it was time for change. Not everyone, however, agreed on the fate of the nation's cultural property, and on 28 January, while some protected the museum's contents, others helped themselves.

They called it 'the day of rage', as demonstrators held their ground against armed security forces after 72 hours of protests demanding President Mubarak's resignation. The state had shut down the Internet and mobile-phone services were interrupted, but people gathered in ever greater numbers. Met with tear gas, water cannons and large deployments of riot police, protestors retaliated by throwing whatever rubble was at hand, and it was a testimony to the condition of downtown Cairo's streets that for eighteen days they never ran out of ammunition. Molotov cocktails were used infrequently (owing to the cost of petrol) but strategically, and in the midst of the melee the high-rise headquarters of the hated ruling National Democratic Party, located just beside the museum, was set aflame. Night fell and the police retreated as smoke billowed and sparks flew. Who would protect the museum, not just from fire, but looters? A group of citizens took action, forming a human chain around the building while young men nimbly scaled the facade to stamp out flying bits of burning debris. Average Egyptians helped safeguard the Egyptian Museum that night, perceiving it as both symbol of a proud heritage and warehouse of national wealth.

At some point that same day, the museum was looted. Reports varied wildly as to the number of looters (from ten to a thousand) during an apparently brief and frantic foray; several stolen objects were found on the museum grounds, dropped by the thieves in their haste.[37] Some 54 items were later officially reported missing, including a gilded wood statue of Tutankhamun snapped off its base at the ankles, one of many treasures recovered in subsequent months.[38] Like the Cairo Museum, the Library of Alexandria had its protectors, and some brave antiquities guardians, tourist police and archaeologists warded off thieves at a smattering of sites, including Aswan, where the removal of a statue of Ramses II was prevented. But by and large, the heritage lovers were outnumbered by less altruistic citizens who launched a free-for-all raid nationwide. According to the state-sponsored *Al-Ahram Weekly*, warehouses of archaeological missions, usually reserved for statue fragments, pottery shards and archaeological evidence of no commercial value, were stormed in Abu Sir, in nearby Dashur and Giza, in Tel al-Basta in the Delta, Wadi al-Feiran (Sinai) and on Luxor's west bank. Inscribed blocks were removed from tombs in several locations, and two were described as 'entirely destroyed', one in Ismalia, and the Tomb of Impy, near the Sphinx. A Sinai storage facility housing artefacts slated for regional museums was sacked, and the contents left behind, thirty truckloads' worth, were subsequently sent to the Cairo Museum where they were stashed in its already cluttered basement under army guard.[39]

Reports indicated that crowds swarmed archaeological sites, digging randomly with whatever tools they could find. While the battle raged in Tahrir Square, children and teens thronged Saqqara's archaeological zone, scattering when shots were fired in the air,

Tomb B1, Gabbari (Alexandria), containing hundreds of loculi (burial niches), 1997. This necropolis (dating from the 3rd century BC to the 4th century AD) was unearthed and partially destroyed during road construction, and as of 2008 was buried again beneath the new road.

then gathering again, 'digging fruitlessly in the sand'.[40] A member of the military detail sent to Saqqara on 30 January expressed a widely held concern for the country's image. 'We don't want people around the world to hear rumors about us,' he said, referring to media accounts of rampant raiding, 'we can protect our history.'[41] Military guards were eventually posted in other high-profile areas, often after damage had already been done. There was no stopping it, according to Taha, one of many Egyptians who objected to the destruction. 'It's too much,' he said, when we spoke by phone in mid-March. 'If everything is broken what will [tourists] come to see?' While opportunistic diggers probably unearthed some finds, the finer things stolen from museums and warehouses were registered and hard to sell, especially for ordinary people unconnected to potential buyers. Considering the relatively few who might profit, the treasure-hunting frenzy unleashed during Egypt's popular uprising seems to have served largely to satisfy an irrepressible urge.

Hosni Mubarak resigned on 11 February 2011, amid cacophonous jubilation up and down the Nile. The official death toll of the nationwide protests was 846 (including 26 policemen) with an estimated 6,400 wounded civilians.[42] On 12 February the employees of the over-staffed Ministry of Antiquities picketed its Cairo headquarters, demanding higher pay and an end to layoffs that had left many of them idle for years. In March, just two months after his long-coveted appointment as antiquities minister, Zahi Hawass resigned, claiming distress at his inability to protect the monuments but also to mitigate liability arising from his ties to the fallen regime. In the ensuing months, while the authorities were busy elsewhere, people built houses in the buffer zones surrounding archaeological sites and on the sites themselves. In Cairo's medieval quarter, old, unregistered buildings were stealthily demolished to make room for high-rise informal housing. Perhaps the most tangible, near immediate outcome of the uprising in 2011 was the greatly improved availability of affordable housing, albeit unlicensed and typically occupying cultivatable or archaeological land.

Under the administration of the Supreme Council of Armed Forces (SCAF), Egypt held its first open presidential elections in

June 2012, where both religious and secular factions presented candidates. Campaigning against the corruption associated with secular government, the comparatively well-organized Muslim Brothers won, and, on 24 June 2012, Egypt had its first religious leadership since the priests of Amun. When the election results were announced in favour of a nondescript functionary named Mohammed Mursi, Tahrir Square, packed with supporters, erupted in deafening cheers, while the secular losers who hadn't bothered to vote wrung their hands. But 'it is a truism of history,' wrote Egyptologist Barry Kemp, 'that given the chance, the underdog imitates his master.'[43] And so it was with the Muslim Brothers, whose arrogance brought them in one short year to the same precipice it took Mubarak three decades to reach.

On 30 June 2013, in response to a call for protest on behalf of Tamarrod ('rebellion'), a secular youth group rumoured to have army backing, Tahrir Square seethed with citizens arriving in banner-bearing hordes from downtown's main arteries, as similar scenes unfolded in other cities.[44] The generals promptly stepped in to remove and, for good measure, imprison the ill-fated President Mursi, to the prolonged, high-decibel euphoria of the Egyptian majority. Demanding his restoration to power, thousands of Mursi's supporters staged a sit-in near a mosque that lasted until August, when they were violently dispersed, resulting in 817 deaths, a show of force that sent a clear message to all Egyptians, no matter which god they worshipped. 'In order for things to remain the same, everything must change,' runs the classic line from Lampedusa's *The Leopard*. Egypt had its revolution, circling 360 degrees back to where it started.

In May 2014, the people chose former director of military intelligence, and commander-in-chief of the armed forces, Abdel Fattah el-Sisi (1954–) as their elected president over a little-known Nasserist opponent. Whereas the Intermediate Periods of antiquity lasted at least a century, this one took a few short years, time enough for the nominally civilian government to establish a soldierly grip on most aspects of Egyptian life and material heritage. In the interim, archaeological sites were looted, unlicensed housing was built and the residents of Abu Sir and of Dashur successfully expanded their cemeteries, keeping a weather eye out for antiquities as they dug their new crypts. The unrest froze tourism, depleting both the crowds that normally filled the sites and the funds available to the Ministry of Antiquities to secure them. Photographs of plundered archaeological zones recalled the Middle Kingdom *Admonitions of an Egyptian Sage*, depicting wanton raiding. 'Verily bodies which were in the tombs are cast out into the desert/And the skills of the embalmers are undone.'[45] Abu Sir al-Malek (125 km/78 mi. south of Cairo), a burial ground used for several millennia that covers over 200 hectares (500 ac), resembled the scene of a zombie massacre, a bone-strewn expanse of desert, skulls spilling sand from the eye sockets, mummy bandages fluttering in the wind.[46] Satellite imagery of illegally excavated sites showed them as pitted and cratered as the dark side of the moon.[47]

According to Egyptian Egyptologist Monica Hanna, who risked her life documenting looting in the wake of the uprising, treasure hunters fell into the same two categories they always have, rich and poor. The latter used shovels and picks, digging wherever possible, whereas the former were armed with automatic weapons smuggled from Libya, heavy excavation machinery and connections to international traffickers.[48] Brigadier General Ahmed Abdel Zaher, then chief of operations for the Egyptian antiquities police, described the rich raiders' business model as 'a pyramid, of course', with otherwise jobless locals at the base, a middle tier organizing crews and gathering finds, and top guns smuggling them out of the county.[49] Hanna, a mother and the dean of the Cultural Heritage and Archaeology Unit at Cairo's Arab Academy for Science, Technology and Maritime Transport, focused on solutions, using social media to alert the public to thefts and lobby for a grassroots education campaign connecting people with their heritage. Unless they live near monuments, Egyptians rarely visit them, and limited school curricula unsupported by field trips offer little incentive to explore history or careers in heritage preservation. Until recently, scholarly research about Egyptian heritage, published mainly in the West, was not always easy for Egyptians to access, and Hanna is an outspoken proponent of online tools such as Google Scholar and Google Maps.[50]

Whereas looters once operated relatively freely in secluded areas, now they must look both over their shoulders and above their heads, as their activities are visible from space. Egyptian geologist Farouk el-Baz (1938–) pioneered the use of satellite imagery for detecting surface signs of underground water in Egypt's desert, a spin-off of his work with NASA mapping locations for the first lunar landing. Like aerial photography, he pointed out in the 1980s, remote sensing could be used for finding ancient settlements.[51] Archaeologists have since added it to their kit, for identifying both ancient sites and illegal excavations. Sarah Parcak, founding director of the Laboratory for Global Observation at the University of Alabama at Birmingham, has reportedly found the 'potential' locations of seventeen pyramids, 3,100 settlements and 1,000 tombs.[52] Keeping track of Egypt's multitudinous archaeological sites, both known and as yet unexplored, has proved a daunting task for the antiquities authorities, whose ongoing effort to digitally map sites (using a Geographic Information System database) began in 2000.[53]

Parcak's satellite imagery analysis showed a clear spike in looting in the aftermath of Egypt's uprising in 2011, but also in the years preceding it, corresponding with the 2008 global financial crises, more proof that tomb-raiding is a barometer of hard and/or uncertain times.[54] Winner of the million-dollar TED Award (2016), Parcak created an online platform (GlobalXplorer) enlisting public participation to police archaeological sites, a cyber-Medjay that would share information with governments and archaeologists. Users were provided with tiles (satellite images of specific areas) and offered a tutorial on how to spot covert digs, though it was unclear from the website how the process of information-sharing actually worked. For monitoring ongoing theft, Parcak envisaged a 'global alarm system where areas would glow red when they are being looted', a bit like an angry jinn. She described her aim to stop looting by involving and educating the public as 'the democratization of discovery', but the online tools that might protect cultural property have turned out to be a double-edged sword.[55]

Surveying the decimation of heritage sites worldwide, many of them suffering the effects of climate change, one easily shares the grief and urgency of archaeologists. In their mission to decipher the past, they find themselves in a paradoxical fight against time, searching for answers to questions that only multiply as glimpses of ancient life are revealed, scrambling to learn what they can before the slate is wiped clean. In Egypt as elsewhere, urban and rural development cause irreparable loss, as the needs of the present increasingly trump the past's preservation.[56] War is another problem. Planting the military base known as Camp Alpha squarely on the ruins of ancient Babylon during the 2003 U.S. invasion of Iraq was no less reprehensible than the destruction of archaeological sites in conflict zones by fanatics, whose abhorrence of ancient art did not prevent them from selling it for profit, aided and abetted by Facebook and WhatsApp.[57] In the wake of the Arab Spring, when the Islamic State turned the cultural heritage of Syria and Iraq into a revenue stream, antiquities trafficking across the Middle East captured the world's attention. While it was clear that online networking among the largely young populations of Middle Eastern countries helped ignite the region's uprisings, only lately has social media's use by latter-day tomb raiders been addressed.

Between 2014 and 2019 the number of Facebook users in the Middle East rose from 56 million to nearly 190 million; one in ten young Arabs logs on daily and Egypt ranks among the top ten users worldwide.[58] While 'community standards' on Facebook and WhatsApp disallowed the movement of drugs and arms through their platforms, prospective treasure hunters could nonetheless find the online equivalent of *The Book of Hidden Pearls*, instructions on what to look for, maps and diagrams and instead of spells, helpful hints about how to rig pumps to drain groundwater. One of many Facebook groups had over 50,000 members, 5,000 of them active posters, and others requesting private communication via WhatsApp. Images of fresh finds in different countries, some still in the ground, were posted for sale and authenticated by crowd-sourced experts; in some cases forms were available for the looting-to-order of particular kinds of items. One group member focused on assisting others in finding Roman-era tombs, and Roman artefacts began appearing in postings soon after. Another member posted a detailed, illustrated log of his ongoing dig, entitled 'memoirs of a professional raider', complete with warnings about asphyxiation and tunnel collapse. For less tech-savvy users, instead of GPS coordinates and Google Earth screen shots, simplified infographics illustrated the location and layouts of underground tomb chambers, replete with cartoonish pots of gold.[59]

Predictably, Covid-19 lent global impetus to the online trade in antiquities, with theft facilitated by the dearth of tourists animating heritage sites, and the loss of tourism-related and many other kinds of jobs. One research project monitored 120 Facebook groups dedicated to trafficking during the pandemic, each with anywhere between a few hundred and 300,000 followers.[60] In July 2020, Facebook updated its community standards to include a ban on 'content that attempts to buy, sell, trade, donate, gift or solicit historical artifacts', a feeble measure unlikely to put more than a dent in these activities. Citing data privacy concerns, Facebook declined to preserve evidentiary posts that might serve to identify the provenance of artefacts photographed in situ that may appear on the market and to catch the people who put them there.[61] Whereas looters once operated based on local, person-to-person information and expert knowledge possessed by the few, social media has effectively democratized tomb-raiding.

In 2018, the British Museum launched an ambitious programme aimed at discouraging looting by strangling the black market for antiquities. Uniting government agencies and law enforcement with dealers, collectors, auction houses, museums and concerned members of the public, the Circulating Artefacts (CircArt) project is creating an accessible database focused on items illegally removed from Egypt and Sudan, pooling information to track their whereabouts, detail their provenance and render them impossible to sell by reputable dealers and traceable if sold by anyone else.[62] The market for antiquities is often blamed for fostering looting, with reason. But if global demand somehow ground to a halt, the underlying causes would remain: the hardship of the needy at the bulging base of a pyramid that's looking more like a pear; mistrust of government; and entrenched beliefs regarding the availability and life-changing potential of buried treasure. Even supposing it was all definitively unearthed, down to the last scarab, people would still hunt treasure in Egypt, such is the power of the country's reputation for possessing it.

Egypt's historic wealth has left an indelible mark on the collective imagination, stories we can't stop telling or enjoy being told, of kings who live large, die young and are buried in a mountain of gold. Putting an end to looting would require the dismantling of an arsenal of narratives, presumably by educating people about the comparative value of preserving a shared human history. But in places like Egypt, where the bulk of the population is underprivileged, an appreciation for history will never be as valuable as survival, which is what makes history in the first place. The penalties for tomb-raiding and antiquities trafficking are severe, ten years in prison for stealing and fifteen years and a million-pound fine for smuggling. Yet the threat of arrest, injury or death has never outweighed the urge to hunt treasure. It is stylish nowadays to speak of 'controlling the narrative', storytelling as a sociopolitical tool, but when it comes to treasure hunting in Egypt, the narrative's in control.

However opposed to the looting of cultural property, most experts would agree that while the actions of needy and hopeful amateurs are understandable, if not forgivable, the organized gangs that exploit poor labourers are criminal. Yet buried treasure has sustained individuals from all walks of life throughout Egypt's history, to such an extent that it is impossible to imagine the country having made it this far without it. The ancients' legacy served to prop up failing economies, build public works and propel multiple spin-off industries, not to mention inspire reams of scholarship and drive myriad, entertaining plot-lines in every medium. All in all, these wonderful things crafted with eternity in mind have rendered such incalculable dividends, tangible and otherwise, one might almost call it magic.

Shards, Medinat Habu Temple precincts, west bank of the Luxor, 2010.

EPILOGUE

WONDERING

The bicentennial of Champollion's decoding of the Rosetta Stone and the hundredth anniversary of the unearthing of Tutankhamun's tomb make 2022 a big year for Egyptology. Museum exhibitions, Egypt-themed books and media mark these and other discoveries while airing issues surrounding the conservation, acquisition and sharing of cultural treasures. As we look back on a pair of centuries that have proved more transformative for life on this planet than the previous several millennia, it's worth recalling that Egyptology, like archaeology and other disciplines contributing to the present body of scientific knowledge, is very young, at tops two hundred years, the blink of a kohl-lined eye. A world of information has nonetheless been laid before us, solving conundrums and suggesting others, while feeding the public appetite for all things pharaonic. Ancient Egypt is surely unique in having inspired as much scholarly scrutiny as popcorn-crunching entertainment. So variously has it been re-envisaged, whether by academics, scientists, authors, artists or interested individuals, as to beg the question whether its paradoxically absent yet materially present reality, hard archaeological data notwithstanding, can ever be grasped with something resembling objective clarity. Egyptology, as a discipline, must defy the very subjectivity on which in many ways it thrives.

Egyptians themselves are generally unconcerned with their deep history beyond the basic pride of ownership. It's the rest of the world that's bedazzled because Egypt has always had something for everyone, with each generation seeing it through the filter of its times. The works of early Egyptologists convey a Victorian deference, an almost devotional appreciation for ancient achievements, the mannerly gods, elegant religious ritual, the simple yet refined pastoral lifestyle. Sir J. Gardner Wilkinson's encyclopedic *The Ancient Egyptians, Their Life and Customs* (1854) revelled in the detailed documentation the ancients bequeathed, thanks to their dedication to bureaucratic order, reflecting his own era's passion for naming and cataloguing everything on earth. In his *Life in Ancient Egypt* (1894), Adolf Erman was suitably impressed with the art and monuments, but felt that the rest of the civilization looked wanting in 'the pitiless sun of science' that shone so brightly in his day.[1] Modern preoccupations are reflected in more recent interpretations of archaeological evidence revealing the ancients' shortcomings, notably, the corruption and costly obsession with (tomb) security that contributed to New Kingdom Egypt's downfall. Likewise, cutting-edge technologies are increasingly applied to more accurately reconstitute the past.

In 2020 the mummy of Nesyamun, a priest who lived in the eleventh century BC, was CT-scanned to digitally map his vocal tract and replicate it with 3-D printing. The idea was to reproduce Nesyamun's voice, or at least the sound he might have made before he died, of an allergic reaction to an insect bite on his tongue. A member of the research team remarked how the ancients called the deceased who successfully passed into the afterlife the 'true of voice'. When Nesyamun's ersatz vocal cords were activated, 'the vocalization produced sounded rather like *eeuughhh.*' The team was developing a computer model that would enable them to produce words, citing 'the sheer excitement and the extra dimension this could bring to museum visits'.[2] This ingenious quest to awaken awe overlooks a path requiring no special equipment, other than a willingness to be awed. Or perhaps awe is a capacity, a state of being, like youth, that gets buried and needs to be dug back up.

I began excavating mine in 2010 on Luxor's west bank, where I spent time at the Ramesseum Cafeteria, acquired by Hussein

Abdel Rasul from the Ministry of Tourism in the 1960s. A family-owned operation, it is beautifully situated beside the funerary temple of Ramses II with a view of the cultivated plain to the east and the desert mountains to the west. Of an evening, the terrace filled with burly, jovial Gurnawi wearing galabiyyas and drinking Stella beer. A cousin of the Abdel Rasuls told me they were all either treasure hunters, con artists, forgers or smugglers, some Muslim, some Copt. They told stories and asked me to imagine the largest room in the world, then fill it with antiquities. 'More than that', they said, 'still comes from here.' Their enthusiasm was perhaps buoyed by the massive USAID-funded drainage project then underway to prevent the Temple of Medinat Habu (Ramses III) from succumbing to dampness, as it sank nearer the rising water table. A trench was dug around the complex, and all the way to the Ramesseum, under the locals' close watch. At night, the heaps of soil removed in the daytime were discreetly examined by mobile-phone torchlight in case anything interesting had turned up. Peering into temple-adjacent parts of the trench's 3-metre (10 ft) depth, archaeological strata were readily visible, levels of settlement, sections of rooms and walls that were hastily noted by antiquities inspectors before pipes were laid and the earth filled back in.

Scores of experts could spend their lives recording remains such as these, and never catch up with the past. There's too much of it. The more than 3,000-year-old Habu Temple has been studied and documented for nearly a century by the University of Chicago Oriental Institute's archaeological mission, and they haven't finished yet. The temple precincts are carpeted with clay shards that clank and crunch beneath your feet, remnants of ancient pitchers and plates in shades of ochre and sienna, some bearing traces of decoration; it's difficult to tear one's eyes from the ground. Clay jar handles have proved particularly resilient; there are loads of them. I found it far easier to imagine the people who had lifted those jars a couple of thousand years ago than to picture our descendants two hundred, much less 2,000, years hence.

Egyptologists must be thanked for bringing us closer to the ancients and their understanding of the quandary of life and death, reminding us that no greater, more compelling mystery stands before us, much as it stood before them. They negotiated the enigma by casting in stone, building to concretize thought, specifically the soothing concept of eternity. But if Egyptology has taught us anything, it's that the ancients were as baffled as we are, and that the coming centuries are unlikely to deliver us from bewilderment. Perhaps the future study of Egypt will transcend archaeological investigation to join a broader enquiry, focused on the effects of ideological conceits on human survival, with a specialized branch devoted to Egyptologists as artefacts of the history of science. Or who knows? We may all be the subject of some interplanetary study by then, we and our broken treasures. Even so, I'd bet that Egypt, the whole unfurled fabric of it, would still have something for everyone: proof, if only in hindsight, that we belong not to a civilization, nation, race or even species, but to a wondrous process whose outcome is unknowable and doesn't really matter, so long as it continues.

CHRONOLOGY

Egyptologists determined the nomenclature of Egypt's historic periods; the ancients did not refer to their eras as 'old', 'middle' or 'new' kingdoms, counting their years instead by the rule of successive kings (for example, 'Year 1, in the rule of Ramses I'). The ancients did, however, list their kings, and the dynasties that fall within each period were characterized by the orderly succession of subsequent rulers, whether or not they belonged to the same bloodline. The Intermediate Periods refer to times of division and instability when central authority was absent. In the First Intermediate Period, regional governors (nomarchs) held sway. In the Second Intermediate the invading Hyksos ruled the north and Egyptians ruled the south from Thebes. In the Third Intermediate Period, the priesthood of Amun ruled Upper Egypt and relatives of the priests ruled as pharaohs from Tanis in the Delta. During the Third Intermediate Period, divisions arose from power struggles between the self-styled kings of urban centres (Herakleopolis, Tanis, Hermopolis, Thebes, Memphis and Sais), paving the way for foreign rule, invasion and occupation.

The following dates are based on Salima Ikram, *Death and Burial in Ancient Egypt* (London, 2003).

> **Predynastic Period:** 5000-3000 BC
>
> **Archaic Period:** 3000-2663 BC
> Dynasty 1-2
>
> **Old Kingdom:** 2663-2195 BC
> Dynasty 3-6
>
> **First Intermediate Period:** 2195-2066 BC
> Dynasty 7-10

Middle Kingdom: 2066–1650 BC
Dynasty 11–14

Second Intermediate Period: 1650–1549 BC
Dynasty 15–17

New Kingdom: 1549–1069 BC
Dynasty 18–20

Third Intermediate Period: 1064–656 BC
Dynasty 21–5

Late Period: 525–332 BC
Dynasty 26–31

Greek Period: 332–30 BC
Alexander the Great and Ptolemaic Dynasty

Roman Period: 30 BC–AD 324

Byzantine Period: 324–641

Medieval Islamic Period: 641–1517

Ottoman Turkish Period: 1517–1805

Mohammed Ali Dynasty: 1805–1953

British Occupation: 1882–1957

Republic: 1953–present

REFERENCES

Introduction

1 Patricia Crone quoted in Robert Irwin, *Ibn Khaldun: An Intellectual Biography* (Princeton, NJ, 2018), p. xiii.
2 Barry Kemp, *Ancient Egypt: Anatomy of a Civilization* (London, 1991), p. 3.
3 Ibid., p. 178.

ONE: Never Say Die

1 William Kelly Simpson, ed., *The Literature of Ancient Egypt* (Cairo, 2003), p. 242.
2 See a chronology of Egypt's kingdoms and dynasties, on p. 268.
3 E. A. Wallis Budge, *The Book of the Dead: The Chapters of Coming Forth by Day* (London, 1898), Spell 125, pp. 191-2, available at https://archive.org.
4 The Book of the Dead, 'Of Bringing the Mahkent Boat', from the papyrus of Book of the Dead of Nu (British Museum; EA10477). Available online at https://archive.org.
5 Inscription in the New Kingdom tomb of Amen-User, who served as vizier during the reigns of Thutmose II, Hatshepsut and Thutmose III; quoted in Pascal Vernus, *Affairs and Scandals in Ancient Egypt*, trans. David Lorton (Ithaca, NY, 2003), p. 3.
6 A. J. Spencer, *Death in Ancient Egypt* (Harmondsworth, 1986), pp. 46-7.
7 Reg Clark, *Securing Eternity* (Cairo, 2019), pp. 53-65. See also Spencer, *Death in Ancient Egypt*, pp. 46-7.
8 A mineral occurring naturally and found in Wadi Natrun (Lower Egypt), natron is a mix of sodium bicarbonate, sodium carbonate, sodium sulphate and sodium chloride. Later Christian burials used common salt as a desiccant. For a full description of mummification, see Salima Ikram, *Death and Burial in Ancient Egypt* (London, 2003).

9 Ibid., p. 66.
10 Ibid., p. 54.
11 H. E. Winlock, *Excavations at Deir El Bahri, 1911-1931* (New York, 1942), p. 225.
12 Ikram, *Death and Burial in Ancient Egypt*, p. 60.
13 Christina Riggs, *Unwrapping Ancient Egypt* (London, 2014), pp. 94-5.
14 Ikram, *Death and Burial in Ancient Egypt*, p. 68.
15 For *mummia*/bitumen see Chapter Three, pp. 130-31.
16 Spencer, *Death in Ancient Egypt*, p. 128.
17 Lise Manniche, *Egyptian Luxuries: Fragrance Aromatherapy and Cosmetics in Pharaonic Times* (Cairo, 1999), pp. 53, 129.
18 Spencer, *Death in Ancient Egypt*, p. 49.
19 For an experiment replicating ancient beer-brewing techniques, see Tasha Marks, 'A Sip of History' (25 May 2018), blog.britishmuseum.org.
20 Ikram, *Death and Burial in Ancient Egypt*, pp. 81-3.
21 Spencer, *Death in Ancient Egypt*, p. 72.
22 The Internet has provided a solution to the ongoing problem of family tomb upkeep. Several Chinese websites offer the possibility to build virtual memorials and make virtual offerings by clicking on 'candles', 'flowers' or 'incense'. Online rituals are also available.
23 Peter Green, 'Tut-Tut-Tut', *New York Review of Books* (11 October 1979).
24 Adolf Erman, *Life in Ancient Egypt*, trans. H. M. Tirard (New York, 1971), pp. 119-21.
25 Ibid., p. 121.
26 Ibid.
27 Ikram, *Death and Burial in Ancient Egypt*, p. 79.
28 Barry Kemp, *Ancient Egypt: Anatomy of a Civilization* (London, 1991), p. 129. The expedition of 1933 BC included thirty hunters, a contingent of soldiers, millers, brewers and bakers, and twenty mayors of towns who provided conscripts, the entire undertaking managed by eight scribes.
29 Sir J. Gardner Wilkinson, *The Ancient Egyptians: Their Life and Customs*, 2 vols (New York, 1989), pp. 143-4.
30 Ibid., p. 145.
31 Ikram, *Death and Burial in Ancient Egypt*, p. 97.
32 The weight of a *deben* varied over time and there is some disagreement as to its exact value. In the New Kingdom the *deben* probably weighed around 91 grams (3 oz), and was divided into ten *kite*, equivalent to 9 grams (2 tsp) each.
33 Kemp, *Ancient Egypt*, pp. 248-51.
34 Nigel Barley, *Dancing on the Grave: Encounters with Death* (London, 1997), p. 221.
35 Vernus, *Affairs and Scandals in Ancient Egypt*, p. 159.
36 Erman, *Life in Ancient Egypt*, p. 141.

References

37 Ibid.
38 John Romer, *Ancient Lives: The Story of the Pharaoh's Tombmakers* (London, 1984), p. 53.
39 Ibid. According to Romer, the song was already three hundred years old when sung at festivals during the nineteenth-dynasty rule of Merenptah (1212–1201 BC).
40 Nicholas Reeves, *Ancient Egypt: The Great Discoveries* (London, 2000), p. 43.
41 Julie Hankey, *A Passion for Egypt* (London, 2007), pp. 56–7.
42 Jacques de Morgan, *Fouille a Dachour, 1894–5* (Vienna, 1903), p. 97. Author's translation.
43 Kemp, *Ancient Egypt*, p. 53.
44 Architect of the first step pyramid at Saqqara for third-dynasty pharaoh Djoser, Imhotep was still remembered 1,500 years later in the New Kingdom, not as a genius builder but as the author of wisdom texts. Songs were written about him and in the 26th dynasty he became a minor god associated with healing powers, identified by the Greeks as Asklepios. See ibid., p. 106.
45 Aidan Dodson and Salima Ikram, *The Tomb in Ancient Egypt* (London, 2008), p. 204.
46 The mummy's jewels and amulets were preserved and are now in the Manchester Museum in England.
47 The entrance to Tutankhamun's tomb must have been entirely concealed by the time Ramses VI's tomb was built, directly above it, two hundred years later; the workmen were apparently unaware of its proximity and the rubble from their excavations lent additional, inadvertent protection to Tut's burial place.
48 Dodson and Ikram, *The Tomb in Ancient Egypt*, p. 197.
49 Spencer, *Death in Ancient Egypt*, pp. 88–9.
50 Ibid., pp. 106–8.
51 T. Eric Peet, *The Great Tomb-Robberies of the Twentieth Egyptian Dynasty* [Oxford, 1930] (Eastford, CT, 2005), pp. 9–10.
52 At the time of this writing (2021) the Tomb of Seti I may still be visited for a relatively high (£45) ticket price. The tomb is currently being digitally recorded by a team of local residents, trained by Factum Arte, experts in digital documentation and 3-D routing who produced a replica of Tutankhamun's burial chamber, installed underground beside the house of Howard Carter, at the entry to the Valley of the Kings.
53 William Kelly Simpson, ed., *The Literature of Ancient Egypt* (Cairo, 2003), p. 198.
54 Ibid., pp. 189–91.

TWO: Grave Matters

1 William Kelly Simpson, ed., *The Literature of Ancient Egypt: An Anthology of Stories, Instructions, Stelae, Autobiographies, and Poetry* (Cairo, 2003), p. 230.
2 The Greeks called it *Thebai* (from the Coptic *Ta-opet*) and referred to it as *Diospolis Magna*, the 'great city of the gods'.
3 The first eighteenth-dynasty pharaohs were from Thebes and lived there. Mid-eighteenth-dynasty pharaohs spent a portion of their year in Thebes but were based in Memphis. Amenhotep IV, who restyled himself as Akhenaton, built a new capital, Amarna (400 kilometres/250 mi. north of Thebes). Tutankhamun, son of Akhenaton and Nefertiti, restored Thebes as the religious capital. Army General Horemheb was the last pharaoh to use Thebes as an administrative capital. His successor, Ramses I, ruled from Tanis (in the Nile Delta). Ramses II made Per-Ramesses (in the eastern Nile Delta) his principal residence (r. 1279–1213 BC).
4 John Romer, *Ancient Lives: The Story of the Pharaohs' Tombmakers* (London, 1984), p. 4.
5 Book of Nahum, 3:8. The earliest traces of human presence, found in mountains of west bank Thebes, date to the Stone Age.
6 See www.altair4.com for a 3-D model (with video) of Karnak reconstructed.
7 Archaeologists still debate as to whether the architraves were levered into place or rolled up ramps into position.
8 Benedict G. Davies, *Egyptian Historical Records of the Later Eighteenth Dynasty* (Warminster, 1992), pp. 11–12.
9 Barry Kemp, *Ancient Egypt: Anatomy of a Civilization* (London, 1991), p. 201, quoting from Papyrus Leiden i350 (c. 1215 BC, end of Ramses II reign).
10 Ibid., pp. 191–2. Portions of the Ramesseum granaries still stand.
11 Ibid., p. 190.
12 Ibid., p. 193.
13 Adolf Erman, *Life in Ancient Egypt* [London, 1894] (New York, 1971), p. 96.
14 Kemp, *Ancient Egypt*, p. 111.
15 Ibid., p. 223.
16 Erman, *Life in Ancient Egypt*, p. 115. The Hyksos who had occupied portions of Egypt during the Second Intermediate Period introduced horses and chariot warfare to Egypt.
17 Ibid., p. 57.
18 Lise Manniche, *Sexual Life in Ancient Egypt* (London, 1987), p. 30.
19 Erman, *Life in Ancient Egypt*, p. 76.
20 Romer, *Ancient Lives*, pp. 53–4.
21 Deir al-Medina ('the monastery of the town') was named after a monastery built nearby and abandoned in the eight or ninth

century AD. A 3-D video reconstruction of Deir al-Medina is available online: www.altair4.com.
22 For a moving account of the research surrounding Deir al-Medina, including the roles of Černý, Alan Gardiner and T. Eric Peet, see John Romer, *Ancient Lives*, pp. 202–9.
23 Morris Bierbrier, *The Tomb-Builders of the Pharaohs* (London, 1982), p. 52.
24 Ibid., p. 16.
25 Romer, *Ancient Lives*, pp. 44–6.
26 Bierbrier, *The Tomb-Builders*, p. 54.
27 Pascal Vernus, *Affairs and Scandals in Ancient Egypt*, trans. David Lorton (Ithaca, NY, 2000), p. 83.
28 *The Satire on the Trades: The Instruction of Dua-Khety*, in Simpson, *The Literature of Ancient Egypt*, p. 432.
29 Vernus, *Affairs and Scandals in Ancient Egypt*, p. 130, quoting from the Papyrus Chester Beatty IV, available online at http://archive.org.
30 Romer, *Ancient Lives*, pp. 32–3. Qen's dates based on Romer's estimation that he was around 50 when he started work on the tomb of Merenptah and around 85 when he died.
31 O. (ostracon) Deir al-Medina 303, quoted in Koenraad Donker van Heel, *Mrs Naunakhte and Family* (Cairo, 2016), p. 45.
32 'Instruction of Amenemope', in Simpson, *The Literature of Ancient Egypt*, pp. 234–5.
33 Vernus, *Affairs and Scandals*, pp. 151–3.
34 Ibid., p. 134.
35 Kasia Szpakowska, 'Demons in Ancient Egypt', *Religion Compass*, III/5 (2009), p. 800. Available online at www.researchgate.net.
36 Victor Grace, *Godhood in Ancient Egypt* (Cairo, 2003), pp. 13, 57.
37 'Tale of the Eloquent Peasant', in Simpson, *The Literature of Ancient Egypt*, p. 33.
38 Vernus, *Affairs and Scandals*, pp. 138–9.
39 The document found in Qen's library is known as the Papyrus Chester Beatty III (British Museum; EA10683). See A. H. Gardiner, *Hieratic Papyri in the British Museum*, Third Series, Chester Beatty Gift (London, 1935), with translation in vol. I, p. 20, available at www.academia.edu.
40 H. te Velde, 'The Egyptian God Seth as a Trickster', *Journal of the American Research Center in Egypt*, VII (1968), p. 37.
41 Károly Kerényi quoted ibid., p. 37. In retaliation for his lost eye, Horus stole Ma's testicles during the 'battle of Horus and Seth'.
42 H. te Velde, 'Seth, God of Confusion: A Study of His Role in Egyptian Mythology and Religion', *Probleme der Ägyptologie*, VI (Leiden, 1977), p. 68.
43 Ibid., pp. 23–4.
44 Papyrus Chester Beatty III, in Gardiner, *Hieratic Papyri in the British Museum*, p. 20.

45 Paneb's misdeeds as outlined by Amenakht are preserved in the Papyrus Salt 124 (late nineteenth to early twentieth dynasty) held in the British Museum, published by Jaroslav Černý, *Journal of Egyptian Archaeology*, xv/3–4 (November 1929), pp. 244–6, www.jstor.org.
46 Ibid., p. 245.
47 Ibid., p. 246.
48 Siptah's stepmother, Tawosret, ruled as pharaoh for two years (1189–1187 BC), the first woman to do so since Hatshepsut several centuries earlier.
49 Romer, *Ancient Lives*, p. 82.
50 Al Berens, 'Sex, Lies and Ostraca: A New Look at the Foreman Paneb', lecture delivered at the American Research Center in Egypt, Northern California chapter (25 January 2009).
51 Černý, Papyrus Salt 124, p. 246.
52 H. te Velde, 'The Egyptian God Seth as a Trickster', p. 54.
53 Papyrus Chester Beatty III, in Gardiner, *Hieratic Papyri in the British Museum*, pp. 11–18. The bulk of the dreams and portents legible on the papyrus were specified as those of followers of Horus. Only a few of Seth's followers' dreams survived, all good omens, including standing on a hill with a sceptre in one's hand, p. 21.
54 Manniche, *Sexual Life in Ancient Egypt*, p. 8.
55 Translation of Papyrus Deir al-Medina 27 by Pascal Vernus, *Chants d'amour de L'Égypte antique* (Paris, 1992), p. 165.
56 For more on the women of Deir al-Medina, circa twentieth dynasty, see van Heel, *Mrs Naunakhte and Family*.
57 Černý, Papyrus Salt 124, p. 245.
58 Papyrus Chester Beatty III in Gardiner, *Hieratic Papyri in the British Museum*, pp. 12–18.
59 'Love Songs of Papyrus Harris 500' and 'Love Songs of Papyrus Chester Beatty I', in Simpson, *The Literature of Ancient Egypt*, pp. 310, 323.
60 Manniche, *Sexual Life in Ancient Egypt*, p. 109, with reproductions from the Turin Erotic Papyrus, pp. 108–11.
61 Ibid., acrobatic girl ostracon from Deir al-Medina (Turin 7052), p. 85; woman's torso ostracon (Turin 5639), p. 90, both *circa* nineteenth dynasty.
62 Paneb's tomb, designated Theban Tomb (TT) 211, in Deir al-Medina is currently closed to visitors.
63 Several New Kingdom love songs use geese in an erotic context, for example, 'the goose soars up and alights/ It has plunged into the snare.' Simpson, *The Literature of Ancient Egypt*, p. 313.
64 Romer, *Ancient Lives*, p. 69.
65 'Instruction of Amenemope' (late 20th to early 21st dynasty), in Simpson, *The Literature of Ancient Egypt*, p. 232.
66 Ibid., pp. 133–4.

67 Romer, *Ancient Lives*, p. 58, Papyrus Harris I (British Museum; EA9999).
68 Ibid., pp. 150–51.
69 The donkey magistrate and victorious mice appear on a portion of the Turin Papyrus 2031, Turin Museum RCGE46617, which also shows the aforementioned erotic drawings. The fox piper is depicted on papyrus EA10016 at the British Museum; and the noblewoman mouse on an ostracon in the Brooklyn Museum. All are reproduced in varying degrees of clarity in Vibeke C. Berens, 'The Ramesside Satirical Papyri' (Leiden, 2014), available at www.academia.edu; and Keely A. Wardyn, 'Satirical Imagery of the Ramesside Period: A Socio-Historical Narrative', *Journal of Undergraduate Research at Minnesota State University*, vol. XVII, article 8 (Mankato, 2017), available at http://cornerstone.lib.mnsu.edu.
70 Turin Strike Papyrus, in William F. Edgerton, trans., 'The Strikes in Ramses III's Twenty-Ninth Year', *Journal of Near Eastern Studies*, X/3 (July 1951), pp. 137–45. Available online at www.jstor.org.
71 Jack Shenker, *The Egyptians: A Radical Story* (London, 2016), p. 311.
72 Turin Strike Papyrus, in Edgerton, 'The Strikes in Ramses III's Twenty-Ninth Year', pp. 139–41.
73 Zahi Hawass and Sahar N. Saleem, *Scanning the Pharaohs: CT Imaging of the New Kingdom Royal Mummies* (Cairo, 2018), pp. 187, 190.
74 Romer, *Ancient Lives*, p. 127.
75 For a full account of the so-called harem conspiracy, recorded in the Judicial Papyrus of Turin, see Vernus, *Affairs and Scandals in Ancient Egypt*, pp. 108–20.
76 Thomas Hikade, 'Expeditions to the Wadi Hammamat during the New Kingdom', *Journal of Egyptian Archaeology*, XCII (2006), pp. 153–68, available at www.jstor.org.
77 Donald R. Hopkins, 'Ramses V: Earliest Known Victim?', *World Health* (May 1980), pp. 22–6.
78 Kemp, *Anatomy of a Civilization*, pp. 204–5.
79 Ibid.; Teresa Moore, 'Oracles, Pharaonic Egyptian', in *The Encyclopedia of Ancient History*, ed. Roger S. Bagnall et al. (Hoboken, NJ, 2012), pp. 4917–19.
80 Linda Rodriguez McRobbie, 'The Strange and Mysterious History of the Ouija Board', *Smithsonian Magazine* (27 October 2013), available at www.smithsonianmag.com.
81 Neil Tweedie, 'Sales of Ouija Boards Up 300% and Threatening to Become a Christmas "Must Buy" Despite Warning from Churchmen', *Daily Mail* (1 December 2014).
82 Moore, 'Oracles, Pharaonic Egyptian', pp. 4917–19.
83 On the use of oracles and the New Kingdom 'crisis of values', see Vernus, *Affairs and Scandals in Ancient Egypt*, pp. 121–49.
84 Kemp, *Anatomy of a Civilization*, p. 244.

85 T. Eric Peet, *The Great Tomb-Robberies of the Twentieth Egyptian Dynasty: Being a Critical Study, with Translations and Commentaries, of the Papyri in which these are Recorded* [Oxford, 1930] (Eastford, CT, 2005), complete with Peet's renderings of the papyri and their hieroglyphic texts.
86 Papyrus EA10052 (British Museum), ibid., p. 152.
87 Ibid., p. 46. Peet was obliged to work from photo reproductions of the Amherst Papyrus that were published by Percy Newberry in 1899. It was named after Lord Amherst of Hackney who acquired it in Egypt in the 1880s and whose heirs sold it to J. P. Morgan around 1912.
88 Papyrus Ambras, ibid., p. 177.
89 Belgian Egyptologist Jean Capart (1877–1947) found the missing half of the Amherst Papyrus among Leopold II's souvenirs.
90 Papyrus EA10052 (British Museum) in Peet, *The Great Tomb-Robberies*, p. 156.
91 Abbott Papyrus (British Museum; EA10221, purchased in 1857 from Dr Henry Abbott with the aid of Sir J. Gardner Wilkinson), ibid., p. 37.
92 Amherst Papyrus, ibid., pp. 48–9.
93 Ibid., pp. 46, 49.
94 Ibid., p. 41.
95 Papyrus EA10068 (British Museum), ibid., pp. 80–81. Around 0.5 kg of gold and nearly 3 kg (6½ lb) of silver were recovered from traders, and another 70 grams (2½ oz) of gold and 400 grams (14 oz) of silver, in addition to bronze vessels from other individuals.
96 Papyrus EA10068 and papyrus EA10053 (both British Museum), ibid., pp. 90–93, 109.
97 Kemp, *Anatomy of a Civilization*, p. 246.
98 Papyrus EA10383 (British Museum), in Peet, *The Great Tomb-Robberies*, p. 124.
99 Vernus, *Affairs and Scandals*, p. 21.
100 Papyrus EA10052 (British Museum), in Peet, *The Great Tomb-Robberies*, p. 143.
101 Ibid., p. 149.
102 Ibid., p. 146.
103 Ibid., p. 151.
104 Ibid., p. 146.
105 Vernus, *Affairs and Scandals*, p. 39, quoting Papyrus Mayer B.
106 Papyrus EA10083 (British Museum), in Peet, *The Great Tomb-Robberies*, p. 125.
107 Vernus, *Affairs and Scandals*, p. 25.
108 Papyrus EA10053 (British Museum), in Peet, *The Great Tomb-Robberies*, p. 113.
109 Ibid., p. 118.
110 Ibid., p. 119.

References

111 Papyrus EA10403 (British Museum), in Peet, *The Great Tomb-Robberies*, p. 172.
112 Papyrus EA10052 (British Museum), ibid., p. 153.
113 Salima Ikram, 'Hunting Hyenas in the Middle-Kingdom: The Appropriation of a Royal Image?', *Bibliothèque d'Étude*, CXXXVIII (Cairo, 2003), pp. 141-8.
114 Romer, *Ancient Lives*, pp. 192-5; Nicholas Reeves, *Ancient Egypt: The Great Discoveries* (London, 2000), p. 66.
115 Edward F. Wente, 'Late Ramesside Letters', *Studies in Ancient Oriental Civilization*, 33 (Chicago, IL, 1967), pp. 61, 53.
116 Reeves, *Ancient Egypt*, p. 66.
117 Nicholas Reeves and Richard H. Wilkinson, *The Complete Valley of the Kings* (London, 1996), pp. 202-7.
118 There are 65 numbered royal and private tombs in the Valley of the Kings, ranging from small pit tombs to huge labyrinths with over 120 corridors and chambers. A few tombs have been found only in the past century (KV62: Tutankhamun; KV46: Yuya and Thuya; KV36: Maiherperi; KV5: Sons of Rameses II). For detailed information and images, see www.thebanmappingproject.com.
119 Henry Wadsworth Longfellow, 'A Psalm of Life' (1838): 'Lives of great men all remind us/ We can make our lives sublime/ And, departing, leave behind us/ Footprints on the sands of time.'

THREE: The Seekers

1 Petra M. Sijpesteijn, 'The Arab Conquest of Egypt and the Beginning of Muslim Rule', in *Egypt in the Byzantine World, 300-700*, ed. Roger S. Bagnall (Cambridge, 2007), pp. 437-59.
2 Okasha El Daly, *Egyptology: The Missing Millennium: Ancient Egypt in Medieval Arabic Writings* (London, 2005), p. 117. Medieval Arabs counted the Pharos of Alexandria, the world's tallest structure when erected, as one of the marvels of pre-Islamic science. Its condition at the time of the Arab conquest is uncertain, but it was severely damaged by the earthquake of AD 956, and subsequent earthquakes reduced it to ruin by the early 1300s.
3 Ian Blanchard, 'Gold Mining and Trade in the World of Islam: Dishoarding and the Intensification of Production in the Mines of Antiquity', in *Mining, Metallurgy and Minting in the Middle Ages: Asiatic Supremacy, 425-1125*, I (Stuttgart, 2001), p. 103.
4 Ibid.
5 For images of the Nabataean monuments of the northern Hejaz, lately opened for tourism, see Maria Golia, 'Saudi Arabia's Hidden Gem: Al-Ula', *Middle East Institute* (3 October 2018), available at www.mei.edu.
6 Gustave Flaubert, *Flaubert in Egypt*, ed. and trans. Francis Steegmuller (New York, 1972), pp. 50-51.

7 Ulrich Haarmann, 'Medieval Muslim Perceptions of Pharaonic Egypt', in *Ancient Egyptian Literature: History and Forms*, ed. Antonio Loprieno (Leiden, 1996), p. 611.
8 Emilie Savage-Smith, ed., *Magic and Divination in Early Islam: The Formation of the Classical Islamic World*, XLII (Aldershot, 2004), p. xix.
9 Haarmann, 'Medieval Muslim Perceptions', p. 617. Quote from al-Idrisi's (d. 1251) *Lights of the Translunar Bodies*.
10 Sura 28 ('The Stories'), verse 76.
11 El Daly, *Egyptology: The Missing Millennium*, p. 41, quoting al-Masudi's *Fields of Gold*.
12 On the possible origins of this story attributed to al-Masudi, related less to treasure hunting than attempts to destroy symbols of previous empires' greatness so as not to be overshadowed by them, see Martyn Smith, 'Pyramids in the Medieval Islamic Landscape: Perceptions and Narratives', *Journal of the American Research Center in Egypt*, XLIII (Cairo, 2007), pp. 4–8.
13 Christopher Braun, 'Treasure Hunting and Grave Robbery in Islamic Egypt: Textual Evidence and Social Context', doctoral dissertation, Warburg Institute, University of London, March 2017, p. 53. Quote from al-Masudi's *Fields of Gold*.
14 Ibid., p. 50, quoting Fatimid historian al-Qudai (d. 1062).
15 Ibid., quoting Ibn al-Wardi's *The Pearl of Wonders and Uniqueness of Strange Things*.
16 Ibid., p. 71. Ibn Tulun's biography was written by tenth-century Egyptian historian Mohammed al-Balawi.
17 Blanchard, 'Gold Mining and Trade in the World of Islam', pp. 106–8.
18 Ahmad Fu'ad Sayyid, ed., *Al-Maqrizi's Khitat*, II (London, 2013), p. 88.
19 Fatimid chronicler Ibn Hammad (1153–1230) quoted in Jonathan M. Bloom, 'The Origins of Fatimid Art', *Muqarnas*, III (1985), p. 28. The Fatimid palaces are gone but Al-Azhar mosque still stands.
20 This oft-repeated quote is attributed to the *Hadith*, the record of the Prophet Muhammad's words as related by his companions and subsequently compiled.
21 Zin Eddine Dadach, 'Muslim Chemists: From Alchemy to Chemistry', paper presented at the Higher Colleges of Technology, Abu Dhabi (4 March 2019), available at www.researchgate.net.
22 Paul Lunde, 'Science: The Islamic Legacy', *Saudi Aramco World*, XXXIII/3 (May/June 1982), available online at www.aramcoworld.com.
23 Richard Covington, 'Rediscovering Arabic Science', *Saudi Aramco World*, LVIII/3 (May/June 2007), pp. 2–5, available with illustrations at www.aramcoworld.com.
24 J. M. Bloom, 'Papermaking: The Historical Diffusion of an Ancient Technique', in *Mobilities of Knowledge*, ed. H. Jöns, P. Meusburger and M. Heffernan, X (Berlin, 2017), pp. 51–66, available at https://library.oapen.org.

25 Lunde, 'Science: The Islamic Legacy'.
26 Taner Edis, *An Illusion of Harmony: Science and Religion in Islam* (New York, 2007), pp. 41, 44.
27 Richard Covington, 'Rediscovering Arabic Science', *Saudi Aramco World*, LVIII/3 (May/June 2007), p. 13, available with great illustrations at https://archive.aramcoworld.com.
28 Braun, 'Treasure Hunting', p. 75, quoting thirteenth-century historian Ibn al-Dawadari.
29 Blanchard, 'Gold Mining and Trade in the World of Islam', p. 105, quoting Ibn Hammad.
30 Braun, 'Treasure Hunting', pp. 74-5.
31 A cubit, measured by the distance between the elbow and the fingertips, was around 457 millimetres (18 in.).
32 Yacov Lev, 'Famines in Medieval Egypt: Natural and Man-Made', *Leidschrift*, XXVIII/2 (September 2013), pp. 57-8. Lev's paper draws on the first-hand account (1023-5) of historian Mohammed al-Musabbihi.
33 Ibid., pp. 59-61.
34 Deborah Manley and Sagar Abdel-Hakim, eds., *Traveling through Egypt: From 450 BC to the Twentieth Century* (Cairo, 2004), p. 56.
35 Abdullah Mesut Ağir, 'Al-Maqrizi's Khitat and the Markets in Cairo during the Mamluks Era', *Belleten*, LXXXI/291 (Istanbul, 2017), p. 340. It is uncertain whether Khusraw referred to the people of Cairo (the walled Fatimid city) or the adjacent Fustat (whose markets he described) or both.
36 Ibid., p. 340.
37 Yedida K. Stillman, *Female Attire of Medieval Egypt: According to the Trousseau Lists and Cognate Material from the Cairo Geniza*, doctoral dissertation, University of Pennsylvania, Philadelphia, 1972, n.p.
38 Ağir, 'Al-Maqrizi's Khitat', p. 340.
39 Blanchard, 'Gold Mining and Trade in the World of Islam', p. 106, quoting Ibn Hammad (1153-1230).
40 André Raymond, *Cairo, City of History*, trans. Willard Wood (Cairo, 2001), p. 71. The woman's letter to her husband, Judah ibn Sighar, was found in the Geniza archive.
41 Ibid., p. 93.
42 Savage-Smith, *Magic and Divination*, p. xxvii. Savage-Smith notes an increased twelfth-century interest in magic, 'for whatever reason'. See also Matthew Melvin-Koushki, 'Magic in Islam between Religion and Science', *Magic, Ritual, and Witchcraft*, XIV/2 (Philadelphia, PA, 2019), pp. 255-87, available at https://muse.jhu.edu.
43 Haarmann, 'Medieval Muslim Perceptions', p. 616.
44 Ibid., p. 609.
45 Isaac Newton (1643-1727) shared the belief that the pyramids held mathematical and metaphysical secrets. Harriet Sherwood,

'Revealed: Isaac Newton's Attempts to Unlock Secret Code of Pyramids', *The Guardian* (6 December 2020).
46 Blanchard, 'Gold Mining and Trade in the World of Islam', p. 105, quoting al-Masudi's *Fields of Gold*.
47 Braun, 'Treasure Hunting', p. 100. Many copies of the *Sun of Gnosis* still exist, an indication of enduring popularity.
48 Haarmann, 'Medieval Muslim Perceptions', p. 621.
49 Manley and Abdel-Hakim, *Traveling through Egypt*, p. 75, quoting -'Abd al-Latif al-Baghdadi (c. 1200). The ancients painted male nudes in red, and lions in red or yellow. The Sphinx originally had green eyeliner, white corneas and black irises. See Silvio Curto, 'The History of the Great Sphinx', *Book of Proceedings of the First International Symposium on the Great Sphinx* (Cairo, 1992), p. 152.
50 Braun, 'Treasure Hunting', p. 84, quoting Ibn al-Dawadari, first half of the thirteenth century.
51 Haarmann, 'Medieval Muslim Perceptions', pp. 610–12.
52 Ibid., p. 607; Braun, 'Treasure Hunting', p. 191.
53 El Daly, *Egyptology: The Missing Millennium*, pp. 163–4, quoting *Book of Roads and Kingdoms* by Andalusian geographer Ibn al-Bakri (1040–94).
54 Braun, 'Treasure Hunting', p. 90, quoting from *History of Islam and the Obituaries of Outstanding and Famous Persons* by Ibn al-Dhahabi (d. c. 1350).
55 Braun, 'Treasure Hunting', p. 277.
56 El Daly, *Egyptology: The Missing Millennium*, p. 44. Al-Idrisi dates the story of the red-faced man to the time of Fatimid vizier al-Afdal (1074–1094).
57 Haarmann, 'Medieval Muslim Perceptions', pp. 615, 623–4. Al-Idrisi's contemporary -'Abd al-Latif al-Baghdadi (d. 1231) also described how ancient monuments were destroyed to salvage building materials.
58 Joseph Henninger, 'Beliefs in Spirits among the Pre-Islamic Arabs', in Savage-Smith, *Magic and Divination*, p. 44.
59 Qur'an, Sura 15 al-Hijr ('the valley of stone'), Verse 27.
60 Savage-Smith, *Magic and Divination*, p. xxix.
61 Braun, 'Treasure Hunting', p. 96.
62 Savage-Smith, *Magic and Divination*, p. xiii.
63 Ibid., pp. xviii, xxi.
64 Ibid., pp. xix–xx.
65 Ibid., p. xxv.
66 Ibid., p. xxxiv.
67 Ibid., pp. xxx–xxxiv. The still-current practice of reading the coffee-cup dregs by reversing the cup on a saucer and interpreting the rivulets formed inside the cup may be understood as a variant of hydromancy.
68 Ibid., p. xxxiv.

69 Ibid., pp. xxxv–xxxvi. *Za'irja* resembles a system or 'diagram of divine attributes' developed by Catalonian polymath Ramon Llull (1232–1316) that Borges referred to as 'a thinking machine'. See Jorge Luis Borges, *The Total Library, Non-Fiction, 1922–1986* (London, 1999), pp. 155–9.
70 Savage-Smith, *Magic and Divination*, p. xxiv, quoting seventeenth-century Ottoman historian Hajji Khalifa.
71 Noah Gardiner, 'Forbidden Knowledge? Notes on the Production, Transmission, and Reception of the Major Works of Ahmad al-Buni', *Journal of Arabic and Islamic Studies*, XII (Ann Arbor, MI, 2012), p. 94.
72 Savage-Smith, *Magic and Divination*, p. xxxiv.
73 Emilie Savage-Smith and Marion B. Smith, 'Islamic Geomancy and a Thirteenth-Century Divinatory Device: Another Look', in Savage-Smith, *Magic and Divination in Early Islam*, p. 236.
74 Braun, 'Treasure Hunting', p. 94.
75 Edmond Doutté, *Magie et Religion dans l'Afrique du Nord* [Algiers, 1909] (Paris, 1984), pp. 265–6.
76 Charles Burnett, Keiji Yamamoto and Michio Yano, 'Al-Kindi on Finding Buried Treasures', *Arabic Sciences and Philosophy*, VII (Cambridge, 1997), pp. 59–60.
77 Braun, *Treasure Hunting*, p. 101.
78 Doutté, *Magie et Religion*, pp. 266–8. Medieval 'dousing' (*ruyafa*) is mentioned by Braun, 'Treasure Hunting', p. 87.
79 Braun, 'Treasure Hunting', p. 183. Often attributed to al-Masudi, the *Book of Mirabilia* was likely authored by Ibn Wasif al-Sabi, see ibid., p. 24. Egyptologists I consulted were unaware of any textual proof or material remains of ancient automatons.
80 Homer's *Iliad* (book 18, verses 368–88), trans. Samuel Butler, available at classics.mit.edu.
81 Apollonius Rhodius, *Argonautica*, available online at gutenberg.org.
82 Robert W. Lebling, 'Robots of Ages Past', *Aramco World Magazine*, LXX/6 (November/December 2019), pp. 32–3; Philip Vance, 'Philo of Byzantium', in *The Encyclopedia of Ancient History*, ed. R. S. Bagnall et al. (Malden, MA, 2013), pp. 5266–8; 'Heron of Alexandria, Greek Mathematician', *Encyclopedia Britannica*, www.britannica.com. accessed 1 November 2021.
83 Gunalan Nadarajan, 'A Reading of al-Jazari's *The Book of Knowledge of Ingenious Devices* (1206)', Foundation for Science, Technology and Civilization (Manchester, 2007), p. 8.
84 See 'Animation of al-Jazari's Elephant Clock', at www.youtube.com.
85 Nadarajan, 'A Reading of al-Jazari's *The Book of Knowledge*', p. 12, quoting Donald H. Hill, translator and editor of al-Jazari's book (Dordrecht, 1974).
86 Ibid., pp. 9–10.
87 Ibid., p. 15.

88 Robert Irwin, 'Ancient Mechanical Horrors', *Critical Muslim*, XXXIV (May 2020), pp. 39-50.
89 Nadarajan, 'A Reading of al-Jazari's *The Book of Knowledge*', p. 9.
90 Arie Nissenbaum, 'Ancient and Modern Medicinal Applications of Dead Sea Asphalt (Bitumen)', *Israel Journal of Earth Sciences*, LXVIII (January 1999), pp. 301-8.
91 W. R. Dawson, 'Mummy as a Drug', *Journal of the Royal Society of Medicine*, XXI/1 (1927), pp. 34-6.
92 El Daly, *Egyptology: The Missing Millennium*, p. 103.
93 While recent studies have identified trace elements of bitumen in late New Kingdom and later mummies, according to Egyptologist and mummy expert Salima Ikram, 'The burden of the material remains resin, oil and beeswax. Some samples that had previously tested negatively for bitumen are coming up positive, though this might once again be reversed.' Correspondence with author, 22 May 2020. More recently, a mummy possibly dating to the Old Kingdom was identified as containing the higher-quality resins usually associated with later mummification techniques. See Dalia Alberge, 'Mummy's Older than We Thought: New Find Could Rewrite History', *The Guardian*, 24 October 2021.
94 Rosalie David and Rick Archbold, *Conversations with Mummies: New Light on the Lives of Ancient Egyptians* (London, 2000), p. 40.
95 Dawson, 'Mummy as a Drug', pp. 35-6.
96 El Daly, *Egyptology: The Missing Millennium*, p. 97.
97 Ibid., p. 104.
98 Raymond, *Cairo*, p. 93.
99 Ibid.
100 Portions of the first Latin edition of ʿAbd al-Latif al-Baghdadi's *Account of Egypt*, trans. Joseph White (Oxford, 1800), were translated into English in *Critical Review*, XXXV (July 1802), pp. 241-51; and XXXVI (November 1802), pp. 252-9, available at www.archaeologicalresource.com.
101 Raymond, *Cairo*, p. 93.
102 *Critical Review*, XXXVI, p. 256.
103 Lev, 'Famines in Medieval Egypt', p. 62.
104 *Critical Review*, XXXVI, p. 257.
105 Braun, 'Treasure Hunting', pp. 57, 59.
106 Raymond, *Cairo*, p. 100.
107 Gaston Wiet, *Cairo: City of Art and Commerce* (Westport, CT, 1983), p. 68.
108 Raymond, *Cairo*, pp. 136-7, 139-40.
109 Ibid., p. 139.
110 Michael W. Dols, 'The Second Plague Pandemic and Its Recurrences in the Middle East: 1347-1894', *Journal of the Economic and Social History of the Orient*, XXII/2 (May 1979), pp. 163-4, 168-9, available at www.jstor.org.

111 Robert Irwin, *Ibn Khaldun: An Intellectual Biography* (Princeton, NJ, 2018), p. 9, quoting Ibn Khaldun's major work, *Muqaddimah* (*An Introduction* or *Prolegomenon*) to his universal history, *Kitab al-'ibar* (*Book of Lessons to Be Drawn*).
112 Ibid., p. 87, quoting the *Book of Lessons*.
113 Ibid., p. 86. First quote from the *Muqaddimah*; second quote from Ibn Khaldun's biography, *Al-tàrif bi-Ibn Khaldun wa rihlatuhu gharban wa sharqan* (*Presenting Ibn Khaldun and His Journeys in the East and West*).
114 Robert Irwin, 'Al-Maqrizi and Ibn Khaldun: Historians of the Unseen', *Mamluk Studies Review*, VII/2 (Chicago, IL, 2003), pp. 224–5.
115 Ağir, 'Al-Maqrizi's Khitat', p. 341.
116 Irwin, *Ibn Khaldun*, p. 51, from Ibn Khaldun's autobiography. See Irwin's chapter three, 'The Nomads', for Ibn Khaldun's rapport with Berber and Arab tribesmen.
117 Ibn Khaldun, *The Muqaddimah: An Introduction to History*, ed. N. J. Dawood, trans. Franz Rosenthal (Princeton, NJ, 1981), p. 301.
118 Ibid., p. 302.
119 Braun, 'Treasure Hunting', p. 58.
120 El Daly, *Egyptology: The Missing Millennium*, p. 38, quoting al-Jawbari (d. 1264).
121 Ibid., p. 38.
122 Ibn Khaldun, *The Muqaddimah*, pp. 301–2.
123 Ibid., p. 304.
124 Irwin, *Ibn Khaldun*, p. 120, quoting the *Muqaddimah*.
125 Ibid., p. 17, quoting the *Muqaddimah*.
126 Ibid., p. 125, quoting the *Muqaddimah*.
127 Irwin, 'Al-Maqrizi and Ibn Khaldun', pp. 217–19.
128 Matthew Melvin-Koushki, 'Magic in Islam between Religion and Science', *Magic, Ritual, and Witchcraft*, XIV/2 (Philadelphia, PA, 2019), pp. 265–6, available at Project Muse, https://muse.jhu.edu. Market inspectors' manuals dating to the eleventh to fourteenth century from Egypt, Syria, Iberia and India address the regulation of occult practices.
129 Ibid. Melvin-Koushki notes the 'de-esotericization' of the occult sciences as beginning in the twelfth century, based on the market inspectors' manuals.
130 Ibid., p. 266.
131 Braun, 'Treasure Hunting', p. 64.
132 Robert Irwin, *The Arabian Nights: A Companion* (London, 1994), p. 141.
133 Braun, 'Treasure Hunting', p. 275, quoting alchemist Jabir Ibn Hayyan's *Kitab al-Naqd*; p. 277, in relation to al-Baghdadi.
134 Humphrey T. Davies, trans., *Al-Jawbari: The Book of Charlatans* (New York, 2020), p. 93.
135 Savage-Smith, *Magic and Divination*, p. xxviii.
136 Davies, *The Book of Charlatans*, p. 193.
137 Ibid., p. 195.

138 Ibid., pp. 195–7.
139 Ibid., p. 199.
140 Ibid., p. 201.
141 Irwin, *Ibn Khaldun*, p. 124.
142 Braun, 'Treasure Hunting', p. 61, quoting Ibn Ilyas.
143 Ibid., p. 61.
144 Wiet, *Cairo*, p. 67.
145 Ağir, 'Al-Maqrizi's Khitat', p. 349.
146 Wiet, *Cairo*, pp. 156–7.
147 While stick-fighting is no longer a martial art in Egypt, it survives in ritualized form as a dance performed by men (often at wedding parties in Upper Egypt) who gracefully feign combat.
148 Irwin, *Arabian Nights*, pp. 131–5.
149 Ibid., p. 208.
150 Ibid., p. 4.
151 Ibid., p. 113.
152 Ibid., pp. 50–51.
153 Malcolm and Ursula Lyons, trans., *Three Tales from the Arabian Nights* (London, 2008), p. 136. For more on treasure hunting in *The Thousand and One Nights*, see Irwin, *Arabian Nights*, pp. 185–90.
154 Malcolm Lyons, trans., *Tales of the Marvellous and News of the Strange* (London, 2014), p. 76.
155 Ibid., pp. 73–8.
156 Ibid., pp. 79–83.
157 Ibid., pp. 83–94.
158 Ibid., pp. 94–6.
159 'The Romance of Setna Khaemuas and the Mummies', in William Kelly Simpson, ed., *The Literature of Ancient Egypt* (Cairo, 2003), pp. 453–4, 456, 459. While the demotic script of the copy that was found was used in the early Ptolemaic Period, the story itself may be older. See also W. M. Flinders Petrie, *Egyptian Tales* [London, 1895] (New York, 1999), including translations of tales involving magicians (pp. 5–21) from a Middle Kingdom papyrus.
160 Simpson, *The Literature of Ancient Egypt*, pp. 456, 462.
161 Lyons and Lyons, *Three Tales*, pp. 66–7.
162 Robert Irwin's introduction to Lyons, *Tales of the Marvellous*, p. xxxi.
163 Franz Rosenthal, *Gambling in Islam* (Leiden, 1975), pp. 154, 23.
164 Irwin, *Arabian Nights*, pp. 155–6.
165 El Daly, *Egyptology: The Missing Millennium*, p. 35, quoting Ibn Qadi Shuhba's chronicle of the events of 1403.
166 Johan Huizinga, *Homo Ludens: A Study of the Play Element in Culture* [1938] (London, 1949), pp. 4, 10.
167 Chris Bumbaca, '16-Year-Old Kyle "Bugha" Giersdorf Takes Home $3 Million Prize for Fortnite World Cup Win', *USA Today* (28 July 2019). On computer games involving tomb-raiding, see Philip Boyes,

'Traps, Treasure and Ancient Tomb-Raiders' (13 October 2018), www.eurogamer.com.
168 Huizinga, *Homo Ludens*, p. 8.
169 Braun, 'Treasure Hunting', pp. 275-7, 280.
170 Ahmed Bey Kamal, trans., *Livre des Perles Enfouies et du Mystère Précieux, au sujet des indications des cachettes, des trouvailles et des tresors* (Cairo, 1907), pp. iii-iv.
171 Ibid. On pp. vi-vii Kamal describes the manuscripts then held in the library of the Cairo Museum from which the material was drawn. All excerpts appearing here are my translation from the French, except for those citing Braun, who worked from the original Arabic. I am grateful to the Institut français d'archéologie orientale (Cairo) for granting access to their copy.
172 Braun, 'Treasure Hunting', p. 294.
173 Haarmann, 'Medieval Muslim Perceptions', p. 607.
174 Ibn Khaldun, *The Muqaddimah*, p. 303.
175 Kamal, *Livre des Perles Enfouies*, p. vi, cites the work of Mohammed ibn Mohammed ibn al-Hagg al-Fasi al-Abdari al-Qairawani al-Tilmisani al-Maghrabi (born in Fez; d. 1336, Cairo).
176 Braun, 'Treasure Hunting', pp. 233, 214.
177 Kamal, *Livre des Perles Enfouies*, pp. 17, 97, 99.
178 Ibid., pp. 28, 5.
179 Irwin, *Ibn Khaldun*, p. 12.
180 'Dr. Johnson's etymology of "gibberish"', available at www.thefreelibrary.com; Braun, 'Treasure Hunting', p. 16. Braun calls the French translation 'cursory' but even allowing for that, many of the directions are still abstruse.
181 Braun, 'Treasure Hunting', p. 181. Whereas magical practices of late antiquity frequently involved animal sacrifice, these were rare in medieval Islamic traditions.
182 Kamal, *Livre des Perles Enfouies*, p. 33.
183 Ibid., p. 68.
184 Ibid., pp. 33, 9.
185 Ibid., p. 35.
186 Ibid., p. 9.
187 Ibid., pp. 28, 14.
188 Ibid., p. 6.
189 Ibid.
190 Ibid., p. 97
191 Ibid., p. 23.
192 Ibid., p. 7.
193 Braun, 'Treasure Hunting', pp. 201, 213.
194 Kamal, *Livre des Perles Enfouies*, pp. 68-9.
195 Ibid., p. 69.
196 Ibid., p. 61.
197 Braun, 'Treasure Hunting', p. 248.

198 Kamal, *Livre des Perles Enfouies*, p. 21.
199 Items culled from throughout the *Livre des Perles Enfouies* in addition to some noted in Braun, 'Treasure Hunting', pp. 214, 219.
200 Braun, 'Treasure Hunting', p. 241, notes that, in some cases, the animal carcass was thrown into a passageway, to ensure safe entry. During the Islamic feast involving animal sacrifice, people still mark the entries to their homes with bloody handprints to protect them, a practice that echoes the Jewish Passover.
201 Website for Goop, a 'modern lifestyle brand' owned and promoted by a Hollywood actress: www.goop.com.
202 Kamal, *Livre des Perles Enfouies*, p. viii.
203 Ibid., pp. iii, viii.
204 Ibid., p. viii.
205 Braun, 'Treasure Hunting', p. 20, quoting an unpublished manuscript by Gerald Avery Wainwright, 'The Search for Hidden Treasure'.

FOUR: Den of Thebes

1 H. G. Wells, *The Outline of History* (New York, 1956), vol. II, p. 783.
2 Deborah Manley and Sahar Abdel Hakim, eds, *Traveling through Egypt: From 450 BC to the Twentieth Century* (Cairo, 2004), pp. 141-2.
3 Ibid. After Egypt, Browne visited Turkey, the Levant and finally Tabriz (Iran), where he was murdered in 1813.
4 Ibid., p. 143.
5 Edward William Lane, *Description of Egypt*, ed. Jason Thomas (Cairo, 2000), p. 328.
6 Ibid.
7 Bayle St John, *Village Life in Ancient Egypt: With Sketches of the Saïd* (Boston, MA, 1853), vol. II, pp. 210-11, 218.
8 Mohammed Ali made his title of 'wali' hereditary, though his descendants were reduced to figureheads under the British occupation.
9 Laverne Kuhnke, *Lives at Risk: Public Health in Nineteenth-Century Egypt* (Cairo, 1990), p. 32.
10 Ibid., p. 20.
11 St John, *Village Life*, p. 218. St John seems to refer to the policy of taking a fifth of all finds as a tax for treasure hunting that Ibn Tulun instituted in the ninth century, though it is highly unlikely that it was consistently adhered to in the interim.
12 E. W. Lane, *Manners and Customs of the Modern Egyptians* [1836] (London, 1989), pp. 249, 251, 262-3.
13 Donald Malcolm Reid, *Whose Pharaohs?* (Cairo, 2002), p. 100.
14 Ibid., p. 82, quoting Egyptologist John Gardner Wilkinson (1797-1875), who authored the *Handbook*.
15 Nicholas Reeves, *Ancient Egypt: The Great Discoveries* (London, 2000), p. 42.

16 King James Version, Ezekiel 29:12–14.
17 David Gange, *Dialogues with the Dead* (Oxford, 2013), p. 59. Gange masterfully captures the significance of ancient Egypt to the articulation of nineteenth- and early twentieth-century British culture, alongside the Bible's influence on Egyptology's development.
18 Ibid., pp. 65–6.
19 Deirdre E. Lawrence, 'Walt Whitman and the Arts in Brooklyn', available at www.brooklynmuseum.org.
20 Henry Abbot's collection is now in the Brooklyn Museum.
21 Gange, *Dialogues with the Dead*, p. 3.
22 Ibid., p. 64.
23 Bob Brier, *Egyptomania* (New York, 2013), pp. 101–10.
24 Morris Bierbrier, *The Tomb-Builders of the Pharaohs* (Cairo, 1989), p. 135.
25 Tom Hardwick, 'Buying and Selling Tutankhamun', in *Tutankhamun: Discovering the Forgotten Pharaoh*, ed. Simon Connor and Dimitri Laboury (Liège, 2020), pp. 68–71.
26 Lucie Duff Gordon, *Letters from Egypt: 1862–1869* (London, 1902), introduction by her daughter Janet Ross, pp. 1–17, available at www.gutenberg.org.
27 Approximate dates for Mustafa Agha Ayat are based on Dr James Douglas's estimation that he was around fifty when they met in 1861, and Amelia Edwards's remark that he died '12 months since' in an edition (1888) of *A Thousand Miles up the Nile* [London, 1877] (Guernsey, 1989), p. 144.
28 John Romer, *Valley of the Kings* (New York, 1981), p. 130, quoting William Howard Russell's *A Diary in the East* (1869).
29 Edwards, *A Thousand Miles up the Nile*, p. 455, notes Lucie's care for 'little Ahmed' though Lucie's letters do not mention it.
30 Duff Gordon, *Letters from Egypt*, letter to her husband, whom she nicknamed 'Alick', 12 February 1864, p. 118.
31 Ibid., letter to Alick, 25 December–3 January 1865, p. 258.
32 Ibid., letter to her mother, April 1866, p. 279.
33 Ibid., letter to Alick, 19 October 1866, p. 310.
34 Ibid., letter to Alick, 17 March 1866, p. 275.
35 James Douglas Sr, *Photographic Views Taken in Egypt and Nubia, Winter: 1860–1861* (Glenalla, 1862), caption to a photograph of Mustafa Ayat and his family in front of Luxor Temple. Douglas's photo album was published for family and friends, and is reproduced in its entirety in Jennifer Graham, 'Photographic Views Taken in Egypt and Nubia by James Douglas M. D. and James Douglas Jr', master's thesis, Ryerson University, Toronto, 2014, available at www.digital.library.ryerson.ca. Douglas's quotes appear on pp. 111–13.
36 Louisa Blair, 'The Doctor and the Madmen', *The Beaver: Exploring Canada's History* (1 June 2002), available at www.canadahistory.ca.

37 Graham, 'Photographic Views', pp. 111–12.
38 Ibid., p. 13, quoting Douglas's son, James Jr, *Journals and Reminiscences of James Douglas, MD* (New York, 1910).
39 Ibid., pp. 112–13.
40 Ibid., p. 113.
41 Blair, 'The Doctor and the Madmen', p. 7.
42 Graham, 'Photographic Views', p. 113.
43 Barnett's museum moved to another location near the Falls in 1859. According to the museum website Barnett's son, Sydney, acquired Egyptian mummies and artefacts for display before Douglas. See www.niagarafallsmuseums.ca.
44 Barbara Lesko, 'Amelia Blanford Edwards, 1831–1892', available at www.brown.edu.
45 Edwards, *A Thousand Miles up the Nile*, p. 457, from the revised edition of 1888, still in print.
46 Jean Capart, ed., *Travels in Egypt (December 1880 to May 1881): Letters of Charles Edward Wilbour* (New York, 1936), p. 30.
47 Edwards, *A Thousand Miles up the Nile*, p. 135.
48 Bierbrier, *The Tomb-Builders of the Pharaohs*, p. 138.
49 Romer, *Valley of the Kings*, p. 145.
50 Edwards, *A Thousand Miles up the Nile*, p. 410.
51 Ibid., pp. 449–50.
52 Amelia Edwards, 'Lying in State in Cairo', *Harper's New Monthly Magazine* (July 1882), p. 202.
53 Edwards, *A Thousand Miles up the Nile*, p. 449.
54 Ibid., p. 414.
55 Edwards, 'Lying in State in Cairo', p. 200.
56 Ibid., p. 201.
57 Ibid., p. 200.
58 Edwards, *A Thousand Miles up the Nile*, p. 451.
59 The EEF sponsored excavations at high-profile sites later in the 1890s: in 1893, at Deir al-Bahari; Petrie's excavations at Dendera in 1897–8; and several years later at Abydos.
60 Warren R. Dawson, 'Letters from Maspero to Amelia Edwards', *Journal of Egyptian Archaeology*, XXXIII (December 1947), pp. 79, 83–4.
61 Julie Hankey, *A Passion for Egypt: Arthur Weigall, Tutankhamun and the 'Curse of the Pharaohs'* (London, 2007), p. 26.
62 The chair was established in 1892, the year Edwards died. She bequeathed £2,500 to its founding in addition to leaving her collection of Egyptian antiquities to University College.
63 Lesko, 'Amelia Blanford Edwards'.
64 Peter Green, 'Tut-Tut-Tut', *New York Review of Books*, XXVI/15 (11 October 1979).
65 Edward L. Wilson, 'Finding Pharaoh', *Century Magazine*, XXXIV/1 (May 1887), p. 9.

66 Charles S. Robinson, *The Pharaohs of the Bondage and the Exodus* (London, 1887), pp. 24-5, 8, available at www.journals.uchicago.edu.
67 See Part Two.
68 Edwards, 'Lying in State in Cairo', pp. 189-90.
69 Wilson, 'Finding Pharaoh', pp. 3-10.
70 Reeves, *Ancient Egypt*, p. 64.
71 Edwards, *A Thousand Miles up the Nile*, p. 450.
72 Edwards, 'Lying in State in Cairo', p. 186, quoting a letter from Maspero dated 4 August 1881 where he relates his version of the Royal Cache's discovery.
73 Gaston Maspero, *Bulaq Museum Guide* (Cairo, 1883). Author's translation from the French. Maspero also notes that Mariette had purchased two papyri inscribed to Pinudjem I's wife (c. 1070-1044 BC).
74 Capart, *Letters of Charles Edward Wilbour*, p. 48, available at https://opendata.uni-halle.de.
75 Ibid., p. 54.
76 Ibid., p. 63.
77 Maspero, *Bulaq Museum Guide*, p. 316.
78 Ibid.
79 Edwards, 'Lying in State in Cairo', p. 187.
80 Maspero, *Bulaq Museum Guide*, p. 316.
81 Wilson, 'Finding Pharaoh', p. 7. Wilson's 'unique interview' with Brugsch took place several months after the Royal Cache was found. He claimed to recall Brugsch's description of the discovery and emptying of DB320 in great detail, while admitting the quotes were not verbatim. Wilson also visited DB320 with Brugsch, Maspero and Mohamed Abdel Rasul, and photographed them at the mouth of the shaft.
82 Edwards, 'Lying in State in Cairo', p. 187.
83 Wilson, 'Finding Pharaoh', p. 7.
84 Ibid., pp. 6-7.
85 Ibid.
86 Reeves, *Ancient Egypt*, p. 65. The port authorities were probably unaware that Greco-Roman period embalmers were known as 'slitters', a title shared with people who dried and salted fish.
87 Edwards, 'Lying in State in Cairo', pp. 191-8. Edwards cites the Amherst and Abbott Papyri as evidence for the rampant raiding that caused the priests to assemble the Cache.
88 G. E. Smith, *The Royal Mummies* (Cairo, 1912) is available at www.lib.uchicago.edu. For photos and descriptions of the royal mummies, see 'The Theban Royal Mummy Project' online.
89 Nicholas Reeves, 'Studies in the Archaeology of the Valley of the Kings: With Particular Reference to Tomb Robbery and the Caching of the Royal Mummies' (Durham, 1984), available at http://etheses.dur.ac.uk. See also Nicholas Reeves

and Richard H. Wilkinson, *The Complete Valley of the Kings* (London, 1996), pp. 202-7.
90 Reeves, *Ancient Egypt*, p. 81. Jean Vercouttier, *The Search for Ancient Egypt* (Paris, 1986), p. 111, also mentions Mohammed Abdel Rasul's new position. Some of Mohammed's descendants still maintain that he was always a gamekeeper, never a poacher of antiquities.
91 *Baedeker's Guide to Egypt* (1898), p. 227.
92 *Egypt, Handbook for Travellers* (Leipzig, 1898), p. xlv; *Egypt and the Sudan* (Leipzig, 1929), p. l.
93 *Egypt and the Sudan*, pp. xix-xxv.
94 *Egypt, Handbook for Travellers*, p. 227.
95 Charles S. Robinson, *The Pharaohs of the Bondage and the Exodus* (London, 1887), p. 23, available at www.journals.uchicago.edu.
96 Hankey, *A Passion for Egypt*, pp. 47-9.
97 Howard Carter, 'Report on the Robbery of the Tomb of Amenothes II, Biban el Moluk', *Annales du Service des Antiquités de L'Egypte*, III (1902), p. 116.
98 Ibid., pp. 117-18.
99 Ibid., p. 119. Carter refers to the Tomb of Yi-Ma-Dua as 'number 88'.
100 Hankey, *A Passion for Egypt*, p. 77.
101 Ibid., p. 168. Excavators were allowed to take a portion of their finds home until 1983.
102 Arthur E.P.B. Weigall, *The Treasury of Ancient Egypt* (Chicago, IL, 1912), pp. 241-2, available at www.gutenberg.org.
103 Ibid., p. 244.
104 Ibid., p. 251.
105 Ibid., p. 239.
106 Ibid., p. 261.
107 Ibid., p. 239.
108 Ibid., p. 257.
109 Ibid., p. 252.
110 Hankey, *A Passion for Egypt*, p. 78.
111 Weigall, *The Treasury of Ancient Egypt*, p. 248.
112 Ibid., pp. 247-8.
113 Hankey, *A Passion for Egypt*, p. 57.
114 Ibid., p. 58.
115 Weigall, *The Treasury of Ancient Egypt*, p. 248. Rider Haggard was a fan of *The Thousand and One Nights*, and Robert Louis Stevenson's short story collection, *The New Arabian Nights*, appeared in 1882.
116 Hankey, *A Passion for Egypt*, p. 113.
117 Dylan Bickerstaffe, 'The Fury of Amen: The Cursed Play in the Valley of the Queens', *Kmt*, XIX/3 (Autumn 2008), p. 78.
118 Ibid., p. 79.
119 Ibid., p. 80.
120 Ibid.

121 Hankey, *A Passion for Egypt*, p. 361, footnote 34, from Maspero's letter to Legrain dated 27 March 1911.
122 Ibid., p. 60, by Weigall's estimation.
123 Jean-Marcel Humbert, '"King Tut" and the Worldwide *Tut-Mania*', in *Tutankhamun: Discovering the Forgotten Pharaoh*, ed. Simon Connor and Dimitri Laboury (Liège, 2020), pp. 306-7. U.S. ads from the *Detroit News*, 1923; French ones from 1923 and 1926.
124 Hardwick, 'Buying and Selling Tutankhamun', p. 68. Between 1910 and 1930 an estimated 50,000 pieces were sold at auction in London alone. The Egyptian Museum sold small, genuine artefacts in its gift shop until the early 1970s.
125 Paul Brunton, *In Search of Secret Egypt*, 11th edn (London, 1945), pp. 104-5.
126 Ibid., pp. 106-9.
127 'Egyptian Fakir who thrills Paris will come to America', *New York Times* (18 October 1925), www.nytimes.com.
128 Brunton, *In Search of Secret Egypt*, p. 105. Tahra Bey allegedly hypnotized listeners both in and out of the studio during a programme broadcast on Radio France (*TIME*, 6 September 1948). The Egyptian magician was immortalized in *The Adventures of Tintin*, 'The Seven Crystal Balls' (1948).
129 Ibid., p. 274.
130 Ibid., pp. 277, 279-80.
131 Ahmed Fakhry, 'A Report on the Inspectorate of Upper Egypt', *Annales du Service des Antiquités*, XLVI (Cairo, 1947), p. 31. Fakhry completed his report on 17 February 1945.
132 Ibid., p. 36.
133 Ibid., p. 33.
134 Ibid., p. 34.
135 Hassan Fathy, *Architecture for the Poor* (Cairo, 1989), p. 154. Originally published by Egypt's Ministry of Culture, as *Gourna, A Tale of Two Villages* (1969). Fathy's crew included a second foreman from Gurna, 'an enormous man with hands as big as tennis rackets' (p. 157). He noted (p. 15) he'd heard that the solar boat stolen from Amenhotep II's tomb had been sold by a former guard who used the proceeds to buy a large piece of land.
136 Ibid., p. 187.
137 Ibid.
138 Torgny Säve-Söderbergh, ed., *Temples and Tombs of Ancient Nubia: The International Rescue Campaign at Abu Simbel, Philae and Other Sites* (London, 1987), p. 53. The Aswan High Dam was preceded by the granite Aswan Dam (built 1898-1902; raised 1907-12 and 1929-34) which was not able to store water and resulted in billions of cubic metres being emptied into the Mediterranean during the annual flood season.
139 In 1959 Nasser inaugurated Cairo's Nile Hilton, the first of many foreign franchises to gain a foothold in a country whose riverbanks

now groan beneath the weight of sumptuously appointed 20–30-storey hotels.
140 Zahi Hawass, 'From an Archaeologist's Notebook: A Family to be Remembered' (posted 26 April 2001), www.guardians.net.
141 Author's correspondence with Naguib Amin, 24 July 2020.
142 Nevine Aref, 'Secret Tunnels and Ancient Mysteries', *Al-Ahram Weekly* (29 October 2009), available at www.masress.com.
143 Zahi Hawass, 'From an Archeologist's Notebook: The Hidden Chamber of Seti I' (posted 13 June 2001), www.guardians.net.
144 For a full, entertaining account of the Ramses II saga, see Gayle Gibson, 'Ramses I? Names Matter: The Unfinished History of the Niagara Falls Mummies', *Kmt*, XI/4 (Winter 2000–2001), pp. 18–29, and Mark Rose, 'Mystery Mummy: A Royal Body May Be That of Ramses I, but Can We Ever Be Sure?', *Archaeology*, LVI/2 (March/April 2003), available at archive.archaeology.org.
145 'Egypt's "Ramses" Mummy Returned' (26 October 2003), www.bbc.co.uk.
146 Reeves, *Ancient Egypt*, p. 64.
147 Hawass, 'From an Archaeologist's Notebook'.
148 Ibid. Whether or not Sheikh Ali told Hawass the water-boy story, it first appeared in print in Thomas Hoving's *Tutankhamun: The Untold Story* (1978). Hoving, former director of New York's Metropolitan Museum, took the story from an unpublished memoir by Lee Keedick, a New York-based agent who organized Carter's lecture tour of North America in 1924, and claimed Carter had told it to him. See Christina Riggs, 'Water-Boys and Wishful Thinking' (20 June 2020), https://photographing-tutankhamun.com.
149 See 'Qurna History Project', www.qurna.org, a project organized by Caroline Simpson to gather and preserve documentation.
150 Cache Seel, 'It's Settled, Then', *Egypt Today* (February 2007), p. 125. Excavations around Gurna's demolished homesteads yielded several small, relatively insignificant tombs containing a number of mummies, and the tomb of a high priest, empty but decorated. Nevine el-Aref, 'Back to Normal for Antiquities', *Al-Ahram Weekly* (23–9 June 2011).
151 About 60 per cent of Fathy's original construction remains. See WMF site for images and text: www.wmf.org.
152 The remains of a fifth-century Coptic church were unearthed in Luxor and a sandstone Nilometer (used to measure floods) dating to approximately the same period. El-Aref, 'Back to Normal for Antiquities'.
153 Nora Shalaby, 'A Lifeless Museum', *Egypt Independent* (14 December 2009).The 'avenue of the sphinxes' was inaugurated on 25 November 2022, amid much fanfare. See YouTube for clips of an extravaganza reportedly replicating aspects of the ancient Opet festival.

FIVE: A House of Many Stories

1 Barry Kemp, *Ancient Egypt: Anatomy of a Civilization* (London, 1991), p. 183.
2 Emad El-Sayyed, 'Dying for that Ancient Treasure', *Daily News Egypt* (6 June 2008).
3 Whereas over 70 per cent of Egypt's labour force farmed in Nasser's day, in 2010 the agricultural sector employed 20 per cent, and in 2020, 23 per cent.
4 William Kelly Simpson, ed., *The Literature of Ancient Egypt* (Cairo, 2003), p. 191.
5 I met with Salah Awad (pseudonym), his son and friends on 18 June 2009 in Saft al-Laban.
6 'Public Outcry after Salafi Preacher's Fatwa on Antiquities' (10 August 2010), www.almasryalyoum.com.
7 Sidi Abud Bin Abdel Qaddus al-Maghrabi, *A Guide to Some Places of Treasure in Egypt: The Treasures of the Land and Its Hidden Things* (Cairo, c. 2005), pp. 1–2.
8 Ibrahim Abdel A'lim Abdel Barr, *Removing the Veil from Treasure and Antiquities Hunting* (Cairo, 2000), p. 123. I am grateful to Ahmed Shawkat and Humphrey Davies for translating passages from both the quoted books.
9 The reportage aired on satellite TV channel, Mehwar ('the centre'), 11 August 2008.
10 Scam stories collected between 2005 and 2010 from a variety of print and oral sources, in Cairo and Luxor.
11 Ibid.
12 This according to Luxor antiquarian, Francis Amin.
13 For a running count of Egypt's (and other) populations, see www.worldometers.info.
14 For more examples of ancient Egypt's linguistic heritage in the modern Egyptian dialect see Ahmad Abdel-Hamid Youssef, *From Pharaoh's Lips* (Cairo, 2004).
15 Available under the title 'chasing mummies promo', www.youtube.com. '100,000 years of history' is of course a gross exaggeration.
16 'Egypt Ponders Bill to Copyright the Pyramids', *Associated Press* (28 December 2007).
17 Rachel Scheier, 'Egypt Revives Long-Stalled Effort to Renovate Pyramids as Tourism Rebounds', *Los Angeles Times* (27 September 2018).
18 'Pyramid Revamp Fences out Hawkers' (12 August 2008), www.bbc.co.uk.
19 Amelia Edwards, *A Thousand Miles up the Nile* [London, 1877] (Guernsey, 1989), p. 410. As of 2021, state-supervised souvenir production, including replicas of genuine artefacts, was underway to ensure a high standard of craftsmanship.

20 Ramadan al-Sherbini, 'Egypt Continues to Suffer Treasure Hunt Fatalities', *Gulf News* (12 October 2009).
21 Amir is a pseudonym; nearly everyone I spoke to about treasure hunts asked that their names be withheld. All quotes and information regarding Amir and those involved in the Nazlet al-Samman collapse were gathered from meetings in November to December 2010.
22 Arabic online news outlet www.egvip.com (3 October 2009; link no longer active) reported that 'the building owner' (Ragab) confessed to the district attorney that they'd found antiquities, where they were hidden, and the names of his helpers. Other crew members maintained that nothing was found.
23 Conversation with Mahmoud (pseudonym) Nazlet al-Samman, 19 November 2010.
24 Arabic online news outlet www.youm7.com (26 September 2009; link no longer active).
25 Ali Zalat, Samah Abdel Aaty, 'Al-Masry Al-Youm digs up Fayoum Raiders', translated excerpt from the Arabic *Al-Masry Al-Youm* daily newspaper, posted on www.egyptindependent.com (4 December 2010).
26 Conversations with Taha (pseudonym) and his brother, 31 December 2010 to 7 January 2011.
27 Ibid.
28 Ibid.
29 Ibid.
30 Mark-Jan Nederhof, transcrip. and trans., 'The Tale of the Eloquent Peasant', available at https://mjn.host.cs.st-andrews.ac.uk, p. 33.
31 Ibid., pp. 17–19.
32 'Mubarak "An Angel in the Form of a President", the Egyptian Press Celebrates President Mubarak's 20 Years in Office', *Middle East Media Research Institute* (17 January 2002), available at www.memri.org.
33 Ibid.
34 Ibid.
35 Conversation with a Cairo cab driver, 1 September 2005.
36 Beginning around 2017, a large portion of the Cairo Museum's holdings, including nearly all the Tut-related artefacts, was gradually moved to the Grand Egyptian Museum (GEM) located near the Pyramids of Giza. but it remains chock-full of masterpieces.
37 For a round-up of looting reports see Suzie Thomas, 'Egyptian Museum in Cairo: Thefts and Recoveries in 2011' (21 August 2012), www.traffickingculture.org.
38 Nevine el-Aref, '81 Artefacts Missing from Egyptian Museum and Tel El-Faraein' (16 March 2011), www.almasryalyoum.com. The means by which the stolen objects were recovered was not reported.

39 Nevine el-Aref, 'Tomb Raiders', *Al-Ahram Weekly* (12 March 2011); 'Two Pharaonic Statues Stolen near Luxor', *Al-Masry Al-Youm* (19 March 2011).
40 Jeffrey Bartholet, 'Egypt's Saqqara Tombs: A Status Report in Words and Photos', *National Geographic Society Newsroom* (5 February 2011), https://blog.nationalgeographic.org.
41 Ibid.
42 'Egypt Unrest: 846 Killed in Protests – Official Toll' (19 April 2011), www.bbc.co.uk.
43 Kemp, *Ancient Egypt*, p. 319.
44 Maria Golia, 'Wrong about Tamarrod?', *New York Times* (10 July 2013).
45 Simpson, *The Literature of Ancient Egypt*, p. 190.
46 Abu Sir al-Malek was placed on the World Monument Fund Watch List in 2016. See www.wmf.org. See also Betsy Hiel, 'Egyptians No Longer to Tolerate "Cultural Desecration"', *Pittsburgh Tribune-Review* (16 June 2013), www.archive.triblive.com.
47 For satellite images of looted sites, see Tom Mueller, 'How Tomb-Raiders Are Stealing Our History', *National Geographic Magazine* (June 2016), pp. 60–61.
48 Jeffrey Brown, 'Egyptian Scholar Fights Archaeological Looting with Exposure on Social Media' (29 April 2014), video reportage available at www.pbs.org.
49 Mueller, 'How Tomb-Raiders Are Stealing Our History', p. 67.
50 For a video clip of Hanna describing her work see https://about.google/stories/dr-hanna-preserving-egyptian-culture.
51 For a profile of al-Baz and his work, see www.mariagolia.wordpress.com, non-fiction page. Aerial photography was used for finding archaeological sites beginning in the 1920s.
52 See the website of Parchak's tracking project, www.globalxplorer.org, 'about us' page.
53 The Egyptian Antiquities Information System (EAIS), co-financed by the Finnish and Egyptian governments, the first digital mapping project, documented a portion of Egypt's sites over the course of seven years.
54 Mueller, 'How Tomb-Raiders Are Stealing Our History', p. 66.
55 Heather Pringle, 'Space Archeologist Wants Your Help to Fight Looting', *National Geographic Magazine* (17 February 2016). In January 2021, the information GlobalXplorer had reportedly generated nearly 18 million tiles explored by nearly 97,000 volunteers, related exclusively to Machu Pichu, in Peru.
56 Patrick Werr, 'Egypt Cuts Highways Across Pyramids Plateau, Alarming Conservationists', *Reuters* (15 September 2020).
57 Amr al-Azm and Katie A. Paul, 'How Facebook Made It Easier than Ever to Traffic Middle-Eastern Antiquities', *World Politics Review* (14 August 2018), available at www.worldpoliticsreview.com with

screenshots from social media instructing looters. See also al-Azm and Paul, *Facebook's Black Market in Antiquities: Trafficking, Terrorism and War Crimes*, published by the Antiquities Trafficking and Heritage Anthropology Research Project (June 2019), available at www.counteringcrime.org.
58 Triska Hamid, 'The State of Social Media use in the Middle-East' (21 April 2019), www.wamda.com. See also 'Top Fifteen Countries Based on Number of Facebook Users', www.statista.com, accessed January 2021.
59 Al-Azm and Paul, 'How Facebook Made It Easier than Ever'.
60 Emily Sharpe, 'Online Antiquities Smugglers are Taking Advantage of the Coronavirus Crisis', *The Art Newspaper* (29 April 2020), referring to Katie Paul's and Amr al-Azm's Antiquities Trafficking and Heritage Anthropology Research Project (ATHAR), see www.atharproject.org.
61 Amr al-Azm and Katie Paul, 'Facebook's Flawed Plan to End Antiquities Trafficking', *Foreign Affairs* (1 July 2020).
62 CircArt information is available at www.britishmuseum.org.

Epilogue: Wondering

1 Adolf Erman, *Life in Ancient Egypt* (New York, 1971), p. 3.
2 Nicola Davis, 'Talk like an Egyptian', *The Guardian* (23 January 2020).

BIBLIOGRAPHY

Bierbrier, Morris, *The Tomb-Builders of the Pharaohs* (London, 1982)
Braun, Christopher, 'Treasure Hunting and Grave Robbery in Islamic Egypt: Textual Evidence and Social Context', doctoral dissertation, Warburg Institute, University of London (March 2017)
Davies, Humphrey T., trans., *Al-Jawbari: The Book of Charlatans* (New York, 2020)
Dodson, Aidan, and Salima Ikram, *The Tomb in Ancient Egypt* (London, 2008)
El Daly, Okasha, *Egyptology: The Missing Millennium: Ancient Egypt in Medieval Arabic Writings* (London, 2005)
Fathy, Hassan, *Architecture for the Poor* (Cairo, 1989)
Gange, David, *Dialogues with the Dead: Egyptology in British Culture and Religion, 1822–1922* (Oxford, 2013)
Hankey, Julie, *A Passion for Egypt: Arthur Weigall, Tutankhamun and the 'Curse of the Pharaohs'* (London, 2007)
Ikram, Salima, *Death and Burial in Ancient Egypt* (London, 2003)
Irwin, Robert, *The Arabian Nights: A Companion* (London, 1994)
—, *Ibn Khaldun: An Intellectual Biography* (Princeton, NJ, 2018)
Kemp, Barry, *Ancient Egypt: Anatomy of a Civilization* (London, 1991)
Manniche, Lise, *Sexual Life in Ancient Egypt* (London, 1987)
Peet, T. Eric, *The Great Tomb-Robberies of the Twentieth Egyptian Dynasty* [Oxford, 1930] (Eastford, CT, 2005)
Reeves, Nicholas, *Ancient Egypt: The Great Discoveries* (London, 2000)
Riggs, Christina, *Unwrapping Ancient Egypt* (London, 2014)
Romer, John, *Ancient Lives: The Story of the Pharaoh's Tombmakers* (London, 1984)
Savage-Smith, Emilie, ed., *Magic and Divination in Early Islam: The Formation of the Classical Islamic World*, XLII (Aldershot, 2004)
Simpson, William Kelly, ed., *The Literature of Ancient Egypt* (Cairo, 2003)
Spencer, A. J., *Death in Ancient Egypt* (Harmondsworth, 1986)
Vernus, Pascal, *Affairs and Scandals in Ancient Egypt*, trans. David Lorton (Ithaca, NY, 2003)

ACKNOWLEDGEMENTS

I must first thank my Egyptian neighours and interlocutors in Cairo and Luxor, the most instructive and generous of storytellers; and Egyptologist friends Luc Gabolde, Tom Hardwick, Salima Ikram, Ilona Regulski and Vincent Rondot for sharing their remarkable knowledge and excellent company. I am ever grateful to William Lyster for his patience, wit and acuity in vetting my work; to Robert Irwin and Nick Warner for their steady support and expertise; to Ahmed Shawket for his field assistance and translations; and to Aidan Dodson, for his help with images. I am indebted to Christopher Braun for his unparalleled study of medieval Islamic treasure-related texts; to Mark Pettigrew and Bill Jamieson, with whom I corresponded at the outset of this project; to Ray Johnson and Neal Spencer, who kindly assisted my early research; to Barry Kemp, for his illuminating *Anatomy of an Ancient Civilization*; and to Ala'a Awad, whose murals, created in the heat of a civil rights struggle, warmed me to my task. Thanks to Jeff Allen, Francis Amin, Naguib Amin, Dina Bakhoum, Elizabeth Bolman, Jean Colombain, Cecil Czerkinsky, Sherief Elkatsha, Bernard Guillot, Adam Hegazi, Betsy Hiel, Frédéric Illouz, Matjaz Kacicnik, Tania Kamal-Eldin, Adam Lowe, Michael and Vlasta March, Dan Morrison, Lucia Najslova, Ibrahim Rabieh, Mohammed Salem, Olivier Sednaoui, Danae Voormeij, Rupert Wace and my brothers Christopher and David Golia, who each added something only they could add. I must take this opportunity to commemorate lately departed co-inspirators: translator Humphrey T. Davies (1947-2021), whom I consulted frequently while writing this and other books, ever grateful for his friendship, his love of language and of Egypt. Likewise Bernard Guillot (1950-2021), consummate artist and connoisseur of all things Egyptian, and actor/explorer Claudia Boulton (1949-2021) 'conceived in Egypt, born in Rome', alive in the memory of friends around the planet. Finally, I thank my stars for having crossed paths and swords with Stefan Czerkinsky (1951-1985) and Curtis Jones (1941-2009), boon companions, whose outlaw spirits whooshed across my keyboard, now and then, in the decade or so spent producing this book.

PHOTO ACKNOWLEDGEMENTS

The author and publishers wish to express their thanks to the below sources of illustrative material and/or permission to reproduce it. Every effort has been made to contact copyright holders; should there be any we have been unable to reach or to whom inaccurate acknowledgements have been made please contact the publishers, and full adjustments will be made to any subsequent printings. Some locations of artworks are also given below, in the interest of brevity:

Courtesy of Alaa Awad: pp. 103 (*bottom*), 200; Boston Public Library: p. 66; photo Bullenwächter (CC BY-SA 3.0): p. 132; from Richard F. Burton, trans., and Leonard C. Smithers, ed., *The Book of the Thousand Nights and a Night* (London, 1897), photos University of California Libraries: pp. 125 (vol. VIII), 149 (vol. X), 150 (vol. V); from *Century Magazine*, XXXIV/1 (May 1887): pp. 191, 202; photo © Stéphane Compoint: p. 254; David Rumsey Map Collection, David Rumsey Map Center, Stanford Libraries, CA: p. 6; DEZALB/Pixabay: p. 97 (*bottom*); courtesy of Aidan Dodson: pp. 43, 97 (*top*), 100 (photo Martin Davies; *bottom*); from Amelia B. Edwards, *A Thousand Miles up the Nile*, 2nd edn (London and New York, 1888), photo Institute of Fine Arts Library, New York University: pp. 172, 180; from *Forskning & Framsteg*, 3 (Stockholm, 1967): p. 197 (*bottom*); Friedrich-Schiller-Universität, Jena: p. 21; photo © Kyera Giannini/Ancient World Image Bank (AWIB), the Institute for the Study of the Ancient World, New York (CC BY 2.0): p. 59; photos Maria Golia: pp. 12, 50, 63, 198, 199, 245, 262; from *Harper's New Monthly Magazine*, LXV/386 (July 1882): p. 186; courtesy of Salima Ikram: pp. 62, 101 (photo © Francis Dzikowski; *bottom*); © Institut français d'archéologie orientale (IFAO), Cairo: p. 103 (*top right*); photo Matjaz Kacicnik, all rights reserved: p. 104 (*bottom*); Library of Congress, Prints and Photographs Division, Washington, DC: pp. 106, 215; courtesy of Adam Lowe, © Theban Necropolis Preservation Initiative and Factum Foundation for the Ministry of Antiquities in Egypt: pp. 100–101 (*top*); from G. Maspero, *History of*

Egypt, Chaldea, Syria, Babylonia, and Assyria, vol. II (London, 1901), photo Robarts Library, University of Toronto: p. 181; from Albert Mayer, ed., *The Book of the Dead* (London, 1925): p. 33; The Metropolitan Museum of Art, New York: pp. 28, 87, 98 (*bottom*), 99 (*top*), 195; Minneapolis Institute of Art, MN: p. 185; photos © Musée du Louvre, Paris, Dist. RMN-Grand Palais: pp. 98 (photo Christian Décamps; *top*), 196 (photo Georges Poncet); Museo Egizio, Turin: p. 37; Museum of Fine Arts, Boston: p. 104 (*top*); photo © Manna Nader, Gabana Studios Cairo: p. 17; © Paul Strand Archive/Aperture Foundation, New York, photo courtesy of Yale University Art Gallery, New Haven, CT (gift of Lisa Rosenblum, B.A. 1975, 1988.98.1): p. 222; private collection: pp. 115, 162, 197 (*top*); photo Janusz Recław (CC BY-SA 3.0): p. 51; Rijksmuseum, Amsterdam: pp. 107, 135; courtesy of Nathalie Sergent, © Archives Théâtre des Champs-Elysées, Paris: p. 217; courtesy of the Theban Mapping Project, the American University in Cairo: p. 44; TopFoto: p. 219; © The Trustees of the British Museum: pp. 102, 193 (*bottom*); Paul Vinten/iStock.com: p. 103 (*top left*); The Walters Art Museum, Baltimore, MD: p. 99 (*bottom*); courtesy of Nick Warner: p. 168; from Arthur Weigall, *Burning Sands* (New York, 1921): p. 213; Wellcome Collection, London (CC BY 4.0): pp. 25, 26 (photo Carole Reeves), 122, 194.

INDEX

Page numbers in *italics* refer to illustrations

Abbasid 111–14, 134
Abdel Rasul, family 170–71, 176, 179, 182, 186, 188, 190, 209, 218, 223–5, 265
   Ahmed 178, 179, 187, 189
   Abdel Rahman 207
   Hussein 189
   Mohammed 190, *191*, 203
   Musa 204
   Sheikh Ali 221, *222*, 223
Abu Simbel 122, *197*, 220
Abu Sir 246–8
Admonitions of an Egyptian Sage 47, 257
Akhenaton (Amenhotep IV) 80, 183, 210, 212
alchemy 114, 121–2, 131, 139, 154–5
   see also occult sciences
algebra 114
Al-Azhar Mosque 113, *115*, 233
Amenhotep I 28, 58, 80, 94, 183
Amenhotep II 36
Amenhotep III 29, 51, 210
amulets
   ancient 31, 38, 67, 86, 93, 99
   medieval 123, 126, 140
   modern 166, 170
Anubis 12, 19, 32, 170, 212, 238
Arab Conquest 105–9, 111–12
astrology 113, 116, 126–7, 140, 145, 234
Aswan High Dam 10, 219–20

automation/automatons 127–9, 146–8
Ayat, Mustafa Agha 171–8, 188–9, 223

Baghdad 111, 116, 134, 136, 232–3
al-Baghdadi 136–8, 143, 163, 165
beauty, ancient concept of 23
Bible 10, 49, 161, 167, 169, 180, 182, 209
black market
   ancient 83, 88
   modern 260, 214
Bonaparte, Napoleon 161, 164
Book of Charlatans 141, 153
Book of Hidden Pearls 153–60, 209
Book of Knowledge of Ingenious Devices 128–9, 145
Books of the Dead 14, 31–3, *33*, 148
Browne, William G. 163
Brugsch, Émile 190, *191*, 192, 224
Brunton, Paul 215–16
bureaucracy 16, 32, 39, 54, 55, 66, 228, 264

Cairo
   markets 140, 143, 153
   medieval 113, 118–19, 134, 136, *137*
   modern 183, 203, 229–30
Carter, Howard 205–9, *206*, 224
Černý, Jaroslav 59–60, 84

301

Champollion, Jean-François 166, 182, 263
chaos 16, 30, 39, 69, 82
Copts (Egyptian Orthodox Christians) 105, 114
  Easter 237
  language 238
  monks 122-3, 237
corruption 48, 65-6, 68, 78, 82, 93-5, 256, 264

death, ancient concept of 17, 18, 34-5
De Morgan, Jacques 41
Deir al-Medina (tomb-builders' village) 58, 59, 60, 80, 84, 96
demons 68
Denon, Vivant 164
Dickens, Charles 169
Diodorus 230
Douglas, Dr James 173-6, 223
Duff Gordon, Lucie 171-3

Edwards, Amelia Blanford 176-82, 184, 187, 190, 192, 201
Egyptology 167-9, 177, 182, 263-6
Egyptomania 161, 170
El-Baz, Farouk 258

Fakhry, Ahmed 216-18
famine 82
  'year of the hyenas' 93, 119, 133
farmers (*fellahin*) 163, 204, 218, 220-21
farming
  ancient 15, 18, 27, 29, 38, 51, 53
  modern 163, 203, 219-21
Fantasia 171, 177
Fathy, Hassan 218, 225
Fatimid 113-14, 118-19
Flaubert, Gustave 109
food offerings 24-6, 26, 27, 56
  for feasts 57
  as payment 33, 63-4
Free Officers' Revolution 10, 218, 221, 230
Fustat 107, 111, 118-19, 133-4, 155

gambling 152
geomancy 126, 146, 193
gold
  ancient 27, 28, 30-32, 41, 52, 56-7, 79, 82-3, 86, 87-8, 87, 91-2, 94, 98, 99, 104
  medieval 108, 110-12, 114, 118, 121-2, 128, 142, 147-8, 155-6
  modern 170, 173, 191, 201, 209, 239, 241, 260
Gurna 163-4, 166-7, 172, 188-9, 198, 199, 203-4, 207, 209-10, 214, 216-17
  New Gurna 218, 219, 225

al-Hakim 116-17
Hanna, Monica 258-9
Hawass, Zahi 221, 225, 238-40, 255
Herodotus 19, 20, 72
hieroglyphs 110, 122, 189
Horus 31, 69, 250
House of Wisdom (*dar al-hikma*) 114, 116, 119, 128
huruf (letter magic) 126

Ibn Battuta 136
Ibn Khaldun 137-40, 143-4, 153-4, 165
Ibn Tulun, Ahmed 112
al-Idrisi 120, 122, 153
imperialism
  ancient 68
  modern 162, 204, 252
Irwin, Robert 145, 151
Isis (goddess) 19, 31, 71, 104, 186
Isis (queen) 87-8
Islam 107-8, 113-14, 126, 137-8, 152

jinn 123-4, 209, 210, 212, 233, 235, 236-7, 244

Kamal, Ahmed Bey 159-60, 190, 192, 202, 224
Karnak 50, 51-3, 51, 57, 213-14, 226

Index

Kemp, Barry 7, 11, 54, 227, 256
Khedive Isma'il 162, 203
Khusraw, Nasir 118-19

Lane, Edward William 164
Lighthouse of Alexandria 106, 107
Luxor 178, 214
   renovations 225-6
   Temple 51, 57, 82, 163, 171, 172
   Winter Palace 215

maat 14, 16, 18, 32, 48, 96, 249-50
magic
   ancient 9, 14, 17, 26-7, 29-31
   medieval 105, 120, 124, 126-7, 137, 139-41, 153-4
   modern 159, 165-6, 215, 229, 233-4, 236, 261
Mamluks 112, 134, 135-8, *135*, 143, 240
al-Maqrizi 138, 143
Mariette, Auguste 40, 166-7, 172, 181, 252
Maspero, Gaston 160, 181-3, *181*, 187-90, *191*, 201, 210, 214
mastaba 18, 97
al-Masudi 111, 121, 145
Medinet Habu Temple 50, 52, 163, 262, 265
Medjay (necropolis police) 47, 79, 82, 88, 258
Memphis 8, 49, 50, 56, 166
Merenptah 61, 68, 71, 96, 205
mirabilia 110, 128, 146
Mohammed Ali 10, 165, 219, 229
Mubarak, Hosni 229-30, 250-51, 255
   Gamal 229, 230, 251
mummia 130-31, 143
mummification 19-22, 61, 105, 130, 184

Nasser, Gamal Abdel 219-20, 230, 237
Nazlet al-Samman 240-43

Nile River 10, 14-16, 49, 82, *104*
   drought 117-18, 133
   last flood 221
   Nubian Campaign 220

occult sciences 105, 116, 119-20, 124-9, 139, 145, 153
The One Thousand and One Nights
   medieval context 105, 117, 125, 144-6, 148, 149, 150, 151
   modern context 176, 212, 232-3
oracles 80-82, 93-5
order, ancient concept of 16, 32, 39, 48, 69, 70, 76, 82, 93
Osiris 19, 27, 31, 35, 71, 95, 186, 247

Paneb 68-75, *103*
patriarchy 228
Peet, T. Eric 83-4
Petrie, Flinders 41, 182, 205, 209
pharaoh, role and title of 54-6
plague 136-8, 143, 163, 165
priesthood, ancient 53, 81, 89-90, 93-6
propaganda 39, 220-21, 251
punishment 36, 85, 91, 118, 137, 143, 189, 200, 229, 249, 261
pyramids 106
   medieval context 110, 120-21, 148
   modern context 183, 221
   wall 239-40, 245

Qenhirkhopeshef (scribe) 64-9
Qur'an 110, 114, 126, 244, 247

Ra 19, 50-52, 56-7, 69, 80, 90
Ramesseum 52-3, 92, 178, 265
Ramses I 95, 201
   mummy of 223-4
Ramses II 21, 22, 47, 52, 56, 61, 68, 75-6, 95, 183, 201
Ramses III 50, 53, 76, 78-9, 183
Ramses IV 22, 79, 205
Ramses V 79, 205
Ramses VI 79, 205
Ramses IX 82, 85, 169

Ramses XI 83, 84, 89, 90, 93, 94
rebellion
　ancient 37–40, 75–6, 89
　modern 165, 203, 252–6
Red Mercury 235–6
religious festivals, ancient 57–8
Royal Cache 10, 96, 182–5, 186–8, *186*, 190, 191–2, *191*, 201, 202, 203–5, 218, 223–4

Saft al-Laban 231–2
Saladin 119
satellite imagery 258
satire 77, *103*, *62*
scribes 61, 64–6, *66*
Seekers (guild) 112, 118–19, 122–4, 127, 134
Sekhmet 68, 99, *103*, 213
Seth 19, 39, 69–77, *102*
Seti I 47, 51, 95, 101, 183, 185, 201, 222–3
Seti II 66, 71, 74
sex 72–5, 236, 247
silver
　ancient 28, 83, 85–6, 88, 90–93
　medieval 108, 118, 121, 147–8, 155–6
Sphinx 8, 57, 109, 121, 148, 170, 194, 240
St John, Bayle 164–6
storytellers 144, 151, 261
strikes 77–8, 230
Suez Canal 161, 178, 189, 203–4, 219, 229, 240
sycophancy 249–51

Tahra Bey 215–17, *217*
Tale of the Eloquent Peasant 249–50
Tales of the Marvellous and News of the Strange 146–8
taxation 33, 100, 139, 165, 172
temple robberies (20th Dynasty) 92–3
temples 16, 53–4, 97, 194

Thebes (ancient Luxor) 49–54, 78–9, 89, 96
Thoth 32, 36, 65, 124, 148
Thutmosis IV 8
tomb builders 42, 59–64, 71, 91, 101
tomb robberies, ancient
　attitudes towards 39, 48
　court prosecutions 85–92
　early 20th century 205, 207–8
　economic impact 48, 83, 89
　to refinance the state 93–5
　Second World War 216–17
tomb security 42–9, 60
tomb of Yuya and Tuya 40, 210–11, *211*
tourism 167, 168, 214, 220, 226, 257
treasure-hunting
　attitudes towards: medieval 130, 139; modern 229, 231, 235, 248–9, 253
　dangers of 45, 123
　as entertainment: medieval 117, 152, 158–9; modern 178–9, 193, 238
　housing collapses resulting from 199, 229, 231, 235, 241
　Internet use for 152, 227, 234, 236, 257, 259–60
　manuals: medieval 122–3, 153–9; modern 209, 233–4
　scams: medieval 140–43; modern 236, 265
Tutankhamun 20, 25, 27, 31, 45, 183, 205, 214–15, 225, 252–3

Valleys of the Kings and Queens 46, 104, 208, 212

Weigall, Arthur 40–41, 205, 208–14
Whitman, Walt 169
wigs 23, 25, 58, 184, 213
Wilbour, Edwin 188
women
　ancient 23, 46, 53, 56, 63, 72
　modern 75, 163, 203, 237–8